Economic growth and distribution in China

Economic growth and distribution in China

NICHOLAS R. LARDY

Assistant Professor of Economics

Yale University

CAMBRIDGE UNIVERSITY PRESS

Cambridge

London   New York   Melbourne

Published by the Syndics of the Cambridge University Press
The Pitt Building, Trumpington Street, Cambridge CB2 1RP
Bentley House, 200 Euston Road, London NW1 2DB
32 East 57th Street, New York, NY 10022, USA
296 Beaconsfield Parade, Middle Park, Melbourne 3206, Australia

First published 1978

Printed in the United States of America
Typeset by Huron Valley Graphics, Ann Arbor, Michigan
Printed and bound by Vail-Ballou Press, Inc., Binghamton, New York

Library of Congress Cataloging in Publication Data
Lardy, Nicholas R
Economic growth and distribution in China.
Bibliography: p.
Includes index.
1. China – Economic conditions – 1949-
2. China – Economic policy – 1949-   I. Title.
HC427.9.L36   330.9'51'05   77-27508
ISBN 0 521 21904 3

Contents

0842149

Tables

Preface

This book is an attempt to extend our knowledge of the character of the resource allocation system in the People's Republic of China. Over the past few years, economists outside of China have been able to reach a considerable degree of consensus concerning quantitative measures of China's aggregate economic performance. While further research will certainly lead to a more refined understanding of the pattern of structural change of the Chinese economy, the broad picture of growth of agriculture, industry, and gross national product has now been fairly well established. Much less is known, however, about the structure and operation of the system of resource allocation and, in particular, how this system has influenced the distributive characteristics of China's economic development.

While economists have studied intensively the interrelationships between economic growth and income distribution in market economies, little attention has been given to examining these relations in the context of planned economic systems. Beyond the reduction or elimination of property income in the modern sector, there is no a priori expectation that planned systems will necessarily mitigate the unfavorable trade-offs between economic growth and income distribution that frequently have been found in the early stages of economic development in market-oriented systems. This study seeks to explain how the complex evolution of China's bureaucratic, administrative system of resource allocation since 1949 has been constrained by distributive and equity goals held by the leadership. Moreover, through the use of provincial level data that previously have not been used systematically, I attempt to quantify, if only in a rather crude fashion, the relationship between the system of resource allocation and the ability of the central government to achieve distributive goals. Throughout the book, dashes appearing in tables indicate that data are not available.

This study could not have been completed without the support of many people. My greatest debt is to Alexander Eckstein who encouraged and guided my research from its inception and continued to provide insightful criticisms of various drafts of the manuscript right up to the time of his death a year ago. Robert Dernberger, John Michael Montias, Michel Oksenberg, Dwight Perkins, Thomas G. Rawski, and Lloyd G. Reynolds all read the manuscript and made many substantive suggestions which contributed to improving the final version.

David Denny, John Philip Emerson, Robert Michael Field, and Gregory Sukharchuk were all extremely helpful in facilitating the collection of provincial and municipal fiscal reports and other Chinese materials that provide the empirical basis for much of the analysis in Chapters 2 and 3. In addition, I received sustained assistance from the staff of both the University of Michigan Asia Library, particularly Wei-ying Wan, and the East Asian Collection of the Yale University Library, particularly Anthony Marr. Edwin G. Beal facilitated my research at the Library of Congress during several stays there. Finally I wish to acknowledge the generous financial support I have received from the Social Science Research Council and the Yale Concilium on International and Area Studies.

N. R. L.

New Haven, Connecticut
December 1977

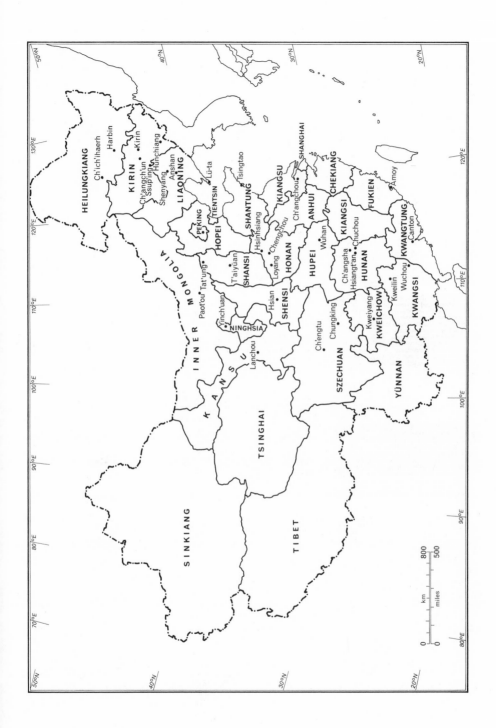

HEILUNGKIANG

KIRIN
Ch'ich'ihaerh
Harbin
Kirin
Ch'angch'un
Ssup'ing Hunchiang
Shenyang Anshan
LIAONING
Lü-ta

INNER MONGOLIA

PEKING
TIENTSIN
HOPEI
SHANTUNG
Tsingtao
Taiyüan
SHANSI
Hsinhsiang
Loyang Chengchou
HONAN
Paot'ou Tat'ung
Yinch'uan
NINGHSIA
Hsian
SHENSI
Lanchou
KANSU

SINKIANG

TSINGHAI

TIBET

Chengtu
Chungking
SZECHUAN

KIANGSU
Ch'angchou
SHANGHAI
ANHUI
CHEKIANG
Wuhan
HUPEI
KIANGSI
Chuchou
FUKIEN
Amoy
Ch'angsha
Hsiangt'an
HUNAN
Kweiyang
KWEICHOW
Kweilin
Wuchou
KWANGTUNG
Canton
KWANGSI
YÜNNAN

50°N
40°N
30°N
20°N

130°E
120°E
110°E
100°E
90°E
80°E
70°E

120°E
110°E
100°E
90°E
80°E

km 800
500
miles
0
0

1

Economic growth and equity in a dualistic economy

The degree of central control of resource allocation is one of the most important aspects of our understanding of China's experience. In recent years, there has been increasing agreement that the rate of growth of gross domestic product since 1949 in the People's Republic has been impressive, not only in comparison with other large densely populated less-developed countries, but particularly compared with China's pre-1949 growth experience.[1] Performance in the industrial sector has been especially strong. It is, however, more difficult to judge the extent to which the character of Chinese economic growth and social development has been influenced by the central government's control of the resource-allocation process. In particular, little is known about whether China's relatively favorable growth performance has been accompanied by comparable achievements of welfare and distributional goals and, if so, to what extent centralized economic policy is an important explanatory variable.

A growing body of evidence suggests that the initial stages of modern economic growth have frequently or even usually been accompanied by increasing inequality in the distribution of personal income. Although data on the distribution of income in developing countries are particularly weak, it appears that the benefits of rapid economic growth have not been broadly distributed, but in many cases have accrued primarily to the upper 40 percent of the population.[2] In countries such as India, where aggregate economic growth has been less impressive, development has probably resulted in an absolute as well as relative decline in the average income of the very poor (Mellor, 76). This pessimistic assessment is not altered by consideration of the distribution of public services. These have also tended to benefit disproportionately upper-income groups (Bardhan).

Although the causal linkages between economic growth and increasing inequality are not fully understood, there is a growing con-

1

sensus that deliberate economic policies can mitigate the adverse distributive consequences of economic modernization. These include policies to alleviate structural factors, such as maldistribution of land, differential access to education and other social services, and increasing intersectoral disparities in output per worker. Land redistribution is usually viewed as one of the most promising policies for improving the overall distribution of income, particularly because of the concentration of lower-income households in the agricultural sector. Empirical and simulation studies by William Cline and others tend to cast serious doubt on the traditional view that redistribution would have adverse consequences for either agricultural production, because of losses of economies of scale, or for savings and investment, because of the presumed higher savings rates of upper-income groups (Cline, 378–83; World Bank, 21–2). Irma Adelman and Cynthia Morris, Albert Fishlow, and others stress the efficacy of human-resource development strategies, particularly improved access to education for poorer income groups (Adelman and Morris; Fishlow). Other recommendations include reducing factor price distortions (Cline, 387–90), alleviating inequality in the interregional distribution of output (Fishlow, 397), and subsidizing food and other wage goods.

Actual implementation of most of these recommendations depends critically on both the availability of suitable economic policy instruments and a political leadership committed to a more equitable growth path. Many authors concerned with alleviating income inequality in less-developed countries make passing reference to the need for altering leadership attitudes. Few, however, come to grips with the question of what policy instruments for redistribution exist in a mixed economic system in the absence of a fundamental transformation of the underlying political and economic structure. The policymaking process in many less-developed countries is more suited to protecting the special interests of the wealthy minority than to insuring a broad distribution of the benefits of economic growth. Fiscal systems are, for example, notoriously weak as a redistributive policy instrument. The tax structure is frequently unusually regressive, whereas expenditures are only rarely for the benefit of the poorest elements of society. Even correction of factor price distortions, which might allow the market mechanism to achieve a more equitable distribution of the benefits of growth, meets serious opposition from vested interest groups.

Presumably, centrally planned economies have a range of policy instruments not available in mixed economies that could be used to achieve distributive goals. It is not clear, however, that equity considerations rank high in the preference functions of the leaders of most centrally planned economies. In some cases policies leading to increased intersectoral, interregional, as well as interpersonal inequality have been adopted as a means of achieving more rapid economic growth. The most well known case is the decline in the average living standard and increased inequality that accompanied the first and second five-year plans in the Soviet Union (1928–37).

This study examines the degree of central control of resource allocation in the People's Republic of China since 1949 and relates this pattern of control to the character of Chinese economic growth, particularly to the ability of the central government to achieve distributive and equity goals. Since the formation of the People's Republic the leadership has grappled continuously with the trade-off between central control and economic efficiency. A high degree of central control has been desired both to increase greatly the rate of saving and investment; as a means of rapidly accelerating the rate of economic growth; and also to allocate a substantial portion of these resources to the producer-goods sector, as a means of fundamentally transforming the structure of the economy. To achieve these goals, in the early 1950s the leadership systematically adopted a highly centralized system of economic planning and management based largely on the Soviet model. This model is characterized by its centralized, vertical lines of planning and administration and a high degree of reliance on bureaucratic, administrative (as opposed to market) means of resource allocation. The adoption of this model in China was reflected in the evolution of the crucial role of central planning agencies and industrial ministries in economic management during the First Five-Year Plan (1953–7).

This highly centralized system was relatively successful in increasing the rate of investment and accelerating the rate of overall economic growth. However, it was also a source of considerable economic inefficiency. The concentration of economic decision-making power in Peking not only undermined local initiative and enthusiasm, but led to bureaucratic delays that reduced output. In response to these considerations, in the latter years of the first Five-Year Plan the Chinese began to modify the traditional Soviet approach to eco-

nomic planning by introducing a substantial degree of decentralization in economic planning and management.

The willingness of the central government leadership to relinquish
its control of the economy as a means of achieving increased economic efficiency appears, however, to have been constrained by its
commitment to distributional and equity goals. That is, the Chinese
economy of the 1950s was marked by extreme dualism along several
dimensions. Most important, there was a large and growing gap in
the level of output per worker in the agricultural and industrial sectors of the economy. The magnitude of this gap, which will be explored in greater detail in the following section of this chapter, appears to be greater than that found in most contemporary less-developed countries. To a large degree, of course, this simply reflected the
high population density in the rural sector of the economy and the
very early stage of economic development in China. In addition to
these large sectoral disparities in output per worker, China was also
marked by extreme interregional economic inequality. These interregional disparities appear to be of the same order of magnitude as
those found in countries that the economic development literature
treats as classic cases of North–South dualism (Lardy 1977, 14–16).

In this highly dualistic economic environment the Chinese government depended on highly centralized economic policy instruments to
prevent growing inequality in the distribution of income. Most important, the center's control of the structure of wages in the industrial
sector partially mitigated income differentials that could have arisen
from interindustry and interregional differentials in product per
worker. Equally important, the central government controlled the regional distribution of investment funds as well as expenditures for
social services, particularly health and education. As will be shown
below, these centrally administered policy instruments were used to
achieve a significant reduction of disparities in per capita output
among different regions. However, because of the extremely high
costs of achieving growth in these less-advanced areas, this diminution of interregional inequality was achieved only with considerable
sacrifice in terms of aggregate economic growth foregone.

Because of this complex balancing of growth and equity considerations, the economic reforms that were introduced in the 1950s represented a careful compromise between centralization and decentralization. That is, the leadership thought decentralization was necessary to improve economic efficiency, but that excessive decentraliza-

tion would undermine basic economic control and, eventually, perhaps political control as well. The leadership was particularly concerned that economic decentralization would lead to increasing inequality in the regional and personal distribution of income. This,
the economic reforms introduced in the 1950s were aimed at decentralizing economic administration while retaining relatively centralized control over those policy instruments most necessary to maintain a high rate of investment and to prevent increasing inequality in
the distribution of income.

The scope of this study

This study explores the origins of the economic reforms that were
introduced in the latter years of the First Five-Year Plan and traces
their evolution through the Fourth Five-Year Plan (1971–5). The
focus throughout is on the mechanisms that have been used to pursue the somewhat contradictory goals of decentralizing economic administration and coordination while retaining a relatively high degree of central control of economic planning and resource allocation.
Although not primarily comparative in nature, this study also relates
Chinese economic reforms both to theoretical models of decentralized decision making under socialism and to economic reform in the
Soviet Union and Eastern Europe. In addition, the potential redistributive capabilities of policy instruments in China are compared
with those available in other less-developed countries where a more
equitable distribution of income is increasingly recognized as a goal
of development policy.

   This study is limited in several ways. First, the study is largely
empirical. The goal has been to formulate hypotheses concerning
changes in the degree of central control that can be empirically tested.
In most cases these hypotheses have evolved from my conceptualization of centralization and decentralization within the framework of a
highly dualistic economy. Because I believe it can be shown that
unfavorable distributive consequences would accompany most forms
of decentralization of resource-allocation power in China, my hypotheses are tested with data sets that reflect distributive outcomes. This
conceptualization and my empirical approach focus the analysis on
actual outcomes of the resource-allocation process. Institutional
analysis is provided primarily as a means of understanding specific
empirical findings and thus is far from exhaustive.

Secondly, this study is limited in its sectoral focus. It emphasizes those sectors of the economy where the degree of central government control appears to have been most influenced by the economic reforms introduced in the late 1950s. The degree of central control of agriculture in the First Five-Year Plan period was substantially less than in other sectors of the economy. For example, Peking relied more on indirect means such as price setting than on direct planning to determine agricultural production (Perkins 1966, 21–98). Although the formation of communes in the late 1950s changed agricultural organization at the local level, it did not radically alter the degree of central control. Thus the study focuses largely on nonagricultural sectors of the economy, particularly industry and government services.

Finally, although this study attempts to understand economic planning in China in broad terms, much of the analysis focuses on the fiscal system. That is, although in a centrally planned economy it is primarily the economic plan that determines the allocation of resources among alternative uses, for reasons explored below the degree of central control and particularly the commitment of the central government leadership to the attainment of distributive as well as other economic goals can best be measured through the fiscal system. Thus, this study not only compares the overall role of the budgetary process in the allocation of resources in China and other less-developed countries, but in particular focuses on the distributive aspects of the fiscal and budgetary process.

Before analyzing the specific forces that have influenced the adoption of centralized or decentralized forms of economic management and decision making in China, I begin with a brief review of selected theoretical models of decentralized decision making within the context of socialist institutions. The remainder of this introductory chapter outlines the specific features and Western interpretations of the decentralization of the late 1950s and explains the methodology used to examine the degree of central government control of the resource-allocation process.

Resource allocation under socialism

Centralized economic planning and public ownership of the means of production are the hallmarks of socialism. Although centrally planned systems frequently achieve high rates of growth, critics have long challenged the ability of such systems to allocate resources efficiently among alternative uses. The classic argument was made by Ludwig von Mises. He believed that the absence of private ownership of the means of production and market-determined prices precluded a rational allocation of resources. Because prices determined outside the market would not reflect scarcity relationships, socialist economic planners would be unable to achieve an optimal allocation of resources.

On the basis of works by Pareto and Barone, others subsequently argued that market-determined prices were not necessary for the attainment of an optimal allocation of resources, but could be replaced by a system of planners' preferences. With knowledge of resource availability and their own preferences, planners could theoretically solve a set of simultaneous equations to determine rational prices that could be used in planning production. However, von Hayek charged that in practice central planners would not be able to gather all the information necessary to arrive at an efficient allocation of resources (Hayek, 201–43). Planners would require complete information not only on the availability of physical resources, but also on all potential production techniques. Even if this information could be gathered successfully, von Hayek argued that the actual compilation of a rational plan would take years.

In response to this critique of the theoretical ability of socialism to allocate resources efficiently, Oscar Lange advanced his now famous model of decentralized economic decision make under socialism (Lange). The essence of his model was simple. Central planners, instead of allocating all inputs and planning all outputs in physical terms, would set accounting prices for primary and intermediate goods through a tâtonnement-like process and would establish behavioral rules for enterprise managers. Managers, constrained only to minimize the average cost of production, to produce at a level of output where marginal cost equals price, and to take the accounting prices as fixed, would be free to select among all methods of production and factor combinations. Markets would determine the prices of consumer goods and workers' wages. Planners could still determine the rate of savings and investment and modify the distribution of income resulting from the market-determined wage rates. By trial-and-error determination of the prices for primary and intermediate products, planners could achieve the desired output mix.

Under the Lange solution, the burden of information collection and processing borne by central planners would be substantially reduced. The central planners would be relieved of the task of collecting detailed information on the availability of primary resources and on the technical production coefficients of each firm. The level and composition of output of each firm would be determined within the enterprise rather than by the central planning authority. Lange argued that this procedure would be more efficient because it avoided the high costs of transferring dispersed information to a single planning agency. Further economies would be gained because the center would no longer have to supply detailed input and output targets to each firm but would simply communicate a single price vector that would guide the production decisions of all firms. Thus even in an economy marked by a growing number of commodities and increasingly complex interfirm and intersectoral relations, planners would be able to attain an efficient allocation of scarce economic resources.

Lange's model of economic decentralization transfers the locus of decision-making authority from the central government all the way down to enterprise managers. Industry managers are retained in Lange's scheme, but their sole function is to regulate the entry and exit of firms. Furthermore, his model relies heavily on markets for the distribution of commodities, even though prices are set parametrically by the central planning board.

Alternatively, one could envisage a type of decentralization in which the locus of decision-making authority was transferred to intermediate levels of government administration without increased reliance on the use of markets to allocate resources. Peter Wiles describes this type of decentralization as "decentralized command" (Wiles, 131–46). Typically, decentralized command enhances the authority of local state organs in economic planning and management. Not surprisingly, in contrast to market decentralization, decentralized command tends to reduce the independence of enterprises. Lines of administration are shortened and as a result, local governments are in a position to control enterprises more closely than when they are under the management of a distant ministry.

The informational characteristics of decentralized models of resource allocation have been analyzed more rigorously in the models developed by Leonid Hurwicz and Thomas Marschak. Hurwicz in particular regards the structure of information, rather than the locus of decision-making authority, as the most important variable in measuring the degree of centralization or decentralization of resource-allocation systems. Centralization is characterized by the flow, to a single participant, of information regarding the technologies and preferences of all other units in the economic system. Decentralized systems, on the other hand, are characterized by information flows that are operational and anonymous. The flows are operational in the sense that they transmit proposals horizontally to other firms as opposed to simply reporting information to superiors. They are anonymous in the sense that the origin of the information does not influence the response of the recipients. Similarly, systems are described as informationally more efficient if they require less information for their operation.

By now it has been shown that the class of informationally decentralized systems capable of achieving static optimality in classical economic environments (those with convex production sets and without indivisibilities and externalities) is far broader than the perfectly competitive market mechanism.[3] These include systems in which the center sends out messages concerning quantities; processes combining price- and quantity-guided elements; and price-guided processes, of which Lange's model is an example. Some informationally decentralized models produce an efficient allocation of resources even in the presence of increasing returns to scale or indivisibilities – conditions that cause the competitive market mechanism to fail.

Thus, despite von Hayek's objections, most writers agree that theoretical models of market socialism, including Lange's, can achieve an allocation of resources that has all the efficiency characteristics of the competitive free-market system. However, actual socialist as well as market systems deviate widely from their respective pure models. Furthermore, some models do not provide incentives adequate to insure that the participants follow the rules postulated by the models. Consequently, the theoretical issues raised by von Mises and von Hayek, particularly the costs of information gathering and processing, remain central to an understanding of the efficiency characteristics of centrally planned economic systems.

Growth, equity, and central control

The decision of the Chinese government to adopt the Soviet model of centralized economic planning was motivated by a series of reinforcing considerations. Foremost was the full commitment of the new leadership to the development of China as a major industrial and military power. They recognized that a rapid acceleration in the rate of growth could be attained only through a substantial increase in the rate of investment. The new leadership perceived the Soviet pattern of development as the only means to achieve the required increase in the rate of investment and the desired allocation of an unusually large portion of investment for heavy industry, particularly those sectors required for the creation of a modern defense industry.

However, the adoption of the relatively centralized Soviet model of economic planning was also partially deteimined by important distributional and equity goals held by the Chinese leadership. Some of these goals have been enunciated in numerous public speeches of high Party officials, most notably Mao Tse-tung, and have received explicit and formal endorsement in important Party documents as well. Others are implicit in the policy actions taken since 1949. The first of these was the desire to begin to realign the geographic distribution of industry. The leadership considered the inherited pattern of industrial development, in which industrial output capacity was concentrated in the Northeast (Manchuria) and a few major coastal enclaves, to be the result of decades of foreign domination of the domestic economy (Mao Tse-tung 1977, 12). They were determined to moderate this pattern of industrial concentration not only because of strategic military considerations, but also because, in the long run, growth leading to increasing regional disparities in the level of development ran counter to their goal of creating a politically unified and economically integrated nation-state. Their sensitivity to growing interregional inequality reflecting the increasing economic domination of a few large cities was particularly acute (Mao Tse-tung 1969, 377–8; Li Fu-ch'un, 21).

Secondly, the leadership wanted to insure a more equitable distribution of services. In 1949 large areas of the country lacked adequate health care, education, and other social services. Even within the more-developed regions of the country there were substantial geographical inequities in the provision of these services.

Finally, the new leadership wanted a centralized system of planning and administration that would allow them to control the level and structure of wages in the industrial sector. The pattern of economic growth foreseen by the leadership would substantially increase what were already quite sizable intersectoral disparities in output per worker. The First Five-Year Plan envisaged substantially more rapid growth of industry than of agriculture and only a modest increase in the industrial labor force. Furthermore, most of the output growth was to be concentrated in the producer-goods sector. The central government was interested in assuring that these growing inter- and intrasectoral disparities in value added per worker were primarily channeled via the budget to increased capital formation rather than contributing to rising levels of consumption and to greater disparities in the incomes of urban and rural residents.

The existence of substantial interprovincial and intersectoral disparities in the level of economic development meant that the attainment of these distributional and equity goals would require a relatively centralized system of economic planning. The size of the disparities among different regions is shown in Table 1.1, which gives provincial per capita output in industry and agriculture in 1952, the eve of the First Five-Year Plan.

The distribution of industrial output was particularly uneven – per capita industrial output in the highly industrialized Northeast and coastal cities of Peking, Tientsin, and Shanghai ranged from 1.6 to 18 times the national average. By contrast, in all regions except the Northeast there was at least one province where the level of per capita industrial output was less than 40 percent of the national average. In Kweichow and Yünnan industrial output was less than one-third of the national average.

On the other hand, the pattern of agricultural output was much more evenly balanced, reflecting the long-time settlement and cultivation of most of China's arable land. Only in Heilungkiang, Inner Mongolia, Tsinghai, and Sinkiang was per capita output substantially above the national average.[4] Similarly, with the exception of the municipalities where cultivated land was limited, there was only one province, Yünnan, where per capita output was as low as three-fourths of the national average.

However, on the whole the degree of interregional inequality that had been produced by China's pre-1949 market-oriented economic system was quite marked. Furthermore, as is suggested by the data in Tables 1.2 and 1.3, these substantial differences in output across provinces were a product of both extreme intersectoral inequality and considerable variation across provinces in industrial output per worker. Overall, the degree of inequality of intersectoral output per worker in China appears to substantially exceed that of other countries at comparable levels of development.[5] Given this large intersec-

Table 1.1. *Provincial per capita output, 1952 (national average = 100)*

Province	Industry and agriculture	Industry	Agriculture
Northeast			
Liaoning	165	377	105
Kirin	155	166	151
Heilungkiang	221	277	215
North			
Hopei	98	60	116
Shantung	92	73	104
Honan	71	33	82
Shansi	78	76	83
Inner Mongolia	148	45	187
Peking	—	483	—
Tientsin	—	1,244	—
East			
Kiangsu	85	108	83
Anhui	59	35	67
Chekiang	97	81	102
Shanghai	444	1,864	13
Central			
Hupei	109	58	124
Hunan	83	40	101
Kiangsi	98	58	116
South			
Kwangtung	85	80	91
Kwangsi	76	33	94
Fukien	74	53	85
Southwest			
Szechuan	68	43	80
Kweichow	73	30	91
Yünnan	63	32	75
Northwest			
Shensi	82	42	101
Kansu	83	35	102
Tsinghai	129	38	156
Sinkiang	121	62	148
Ninghsia	—	10	—

Sources: Appendix Tables A.1 and A.2; official provincial population data.

Table 1.2. *Net output per worker, by sector, 1952 (yuan)*

Industry	871
Modern	1,594
Handicraft	354
Agriculture	159

Sources: Output data: Ishikawa, 56, 64. Employment data: industry: Emerson, 134; agriculture: Schran 1969, 64.

Table 1.3. *Industrial output per worker by province, 1952 (national average = 100)*

Shanghai	178
Kwangtung	96
Kiangsi	82
Hunan	58

Sources: Output data: Field, Lardy, and Emerson. Employment data: National: Emerson, 134; Shanghai: Liu Chih-ch'eng, 60; Kwangtung: *Nan-fang jih-pao* (Southern Daily), 10 August 1957; Kiangsi: *Nan-ch'ang kung-jen pao* (Nan-ch'ang Worker's Daily), 17 September 1957; Hunan: *Hsin Hu-nan pao* (New Hunan Daily), 28 December 1958.

toral disparity, one might postulate that most of the variation in total output per capita across provinces was due to interprovincial variation in the structure of the labor force. However, as the data in table 1.3 make clear, part of the variation in provincial output levels arises because of differences in output per industrial worker among provinces. For example, per capita industrial output in Shanghai was 18 times the national average, not only because an unusually high portion of the population was employed in the industrial sector, but also because output per worker in the industrial sector was about 1.8 times the national average. Similarly Hunan's industrial output was less than 40 percent of the national average, not simply because the industrial labor force made up a smaller portion of its population but also because labor productivity was only about 60 percent of the national average.

The juxtaposition of these interregional, intersectoral, and intrasectoral per worker differentials and the commitment of the leadership to develop industry in backward areas, improve the distribution of social services, and mitigate interpersonal income differentials had important implications for economic planning. The central government required a system of distributing economic resources that would assure that the provision of social services was not dependent on local resources. Similarly, they were well aware that the resource costs of achieving comparatively rapid rates of growth in backward regions were quite high (Kuo Tzu-ch'eng, 31). Thus they required the means for altering the geographic distribution of investment that was contributing to comparatively rapid growth in more developed areas. Finally, they required a system in which enormous intersectoral and interregional differentials in worker productivity would not be fully reflected in wage differentials and in which growing value added per worker would be available for financing government expenditures rather than wage increases.

Adoption of the Soviet model of planning

In response to these considerations and with the advice and support of the Soviet Union the new government sought a highly centralized, Soviet-style planning system. This would provide the mechanisms for redistributing resources to meet their goals of rapid economic growth, balance between inland and coastal industry, and improved distribution of social services. The Soviet model could not, however, be transferred to China forthwith. The Chinese economy was suffering from rampant inflation, depressed levels of industrial production, and general disruption from more than two decades of war and civil war. In addition, large parts of the economy were still in private hands and government lacked the data and trained personnel required to initiate large-scale planning.

Nonetheless, the Chinese did systematically adopt elements of Soviet central planning as rapidly as possible. This extension of central control proceeded according to key functional areas and later by key sectors. Almost immediately upon its inception the new government took control of the banking and fiscal system, thereby securing the means to stem the inflation and also to control indirectly the remaining private sector. During the initial period the government also extended state ownership over an ever-growing portion of the economy. By the end of the recovery period (1949–52), the government had begun to establish a state statistical system that served the needs of state economic planners. Direct physical planning by the state had begun only in a few key heavy industries. However, the central government effectively used its financial powers to control indirectly a wide spectrum of economic activity.

The more formal economic planning that began during the First Five-Year Plan period increased central control. The central government established overall goals, which in turn were broken down into specific physical production targets for each sector and branch of the economy. Planners also controlled the evolving structure of the economy by allocating investment resources among alternative uses. The role of the central government in planning was not limited to industry and closely related sectors such as transportation and communication, but also extended to social and educational programs where physical targets specified increases in school enrollments, the number of new hospital beds, etc.

The mechanisms by which physical output targets were achieved are familiar to students of the Soviet and Chinese economies. The most important element is the system of material supply planning. Important raw materials and major producer goods, such as coal, timber, cement, steel products, metal-cutting lathes, etc., were directly allocated by the central government. Based on estimates of technical coefficients, the central authorities allocated to each major enterprise the inputs necessary to meet the output targets specified in the enterprise plan. The number of raw materials and major intermediate goods subject to this system of direct central government distribution increased steadily throughout the First Five-Year Plan period, from only 28 in 1952, rising to 96 in 1953, 134 in 1954, 163 in 1955, and then to 235 by 1956 (TCKT Data Section 1957b, 29).

The second crucial mechanism of central government control was the fiscal and banking system. Under the unified fiscal system adopted in the early 1950s, the state budget became the repository for virtually all enterprise profits as well as tax revenues. All major investment projects were included in the annual national economic plan and financed from the state budget. The State Bank monitored the expenditure of these funds to assure that they were utilized according to the state plan. Thus, enterprises could not finance investment from their own earnings but depended on state investment grants financed through the budget. Even enterprise working capital was controlled by the center through the budgetary and the state banking system.

Finally, the center controlled most prices, wages, and foreign trade. The prices of industrial and most agricultural products were determined administratively rather than through the market. This price-setting authority was used to manipulate directly the terms of trade between agriculture and industry. The structure of wages on an industry by industry basis and also in most branches of the service sector was also controlled from the center. The central government also exercised a monopoly position in foreign trade, establishing export plans for each industry and using foreign-exchange earnings to finance the imports of capital goods needed in high-priority sectors. Only in the agricultural sector did the central government rely primarily on indirect means, such as prices, to guide production (Perkins 1966, 21–98).

The role of local governments in planning

The mechanisms of central government planning discussed briefly above, are well understood. The degree of centralization inherent in these arrangements is, however, elucidated by examining the role of provincial and local governments in the planning process.[6] This examination will not only highlight the powers of the central government, but will also provide background information for evaluating the economic reforms implemented in the latter half of the 1950s.

Economic planning in China is a complex process that proceeds simultaneously in two partially overlapping hierarchical systems. The national economic plan is essentially an aggregation of two fundamentally different types of economic plans–those that are compiled according to vertical, sectoral lines of administration and those that are compiled on horizontal, territorial lines of administration. The sectoral plans are nationwide and cover all enterprises under the management of a single ministerial system, regardless of location. Horizontal plans, on the other hand, are compiled on a provincial basis and thus are multisectoral. However, they include only enterprises and institutions that are managed by local governments. The balance between these two fundamentally different approaches to planning and administration has varied considerably over time and the changing emphasis has been at the heart of the centralization–decentralization debate in China.

The First Five-Year Plan period was marked by the growing domination of the vertically organized system of planning and administration directed by the central government. This was true not only in industry and closely related activities such as trade unions (Harper,123–6), but also to a lesser degree in education as well. On the eve of the First Five-Year Plan, 68.2 percent of China's industrial output nominally was included within the scope of the horizontal economic plans of local governments. However, most of this output was produced by low-priority sectors, primarily handicrafts or privately owned firms. These sectors generally were not incorporated in provincial economic plans unless they had contracts for supplying or processing goods for the state sector. Local governments actually controlled only one-fourth of state-managed industry.[7]

Almost all large-scale modern industrial enterprises were controlled directly by the central government ministries. These ministries and other central agencies – not local governments – were responsible for planning the level of employment, output, and investment, as well as the distribution of the products of these plants. This emphasis on the vertical ties between enterprises and their controlling ministries in Peking meant that provincial governments had no means of systematically coordinating economic activities within their boundaries.

The relative priority of the central and local government sectors of the economy is starkly reflected in the distribution of investment funds during the First Five-Year Plan period. These data are available for the years 1955–7. During this period, over 80 percent of all budgetary investment was controlled directly and channeled to the central-state sector.[8] This was simply a reflection of the priorities in force during this period. Agriculture, municipal public utilities, local industry, and local transporation – all under the management of local governments – were low-priority sectors. Modern industry, modern transportation and communications (particularly railroads) – almost all under the management of the center – were high-priority sectors and received the bulk of investment funds.

This pattern of investment allocation led to relatively more rapid growth of centrally managed industry. Measured in constant prices its share of total national industrial output grew from less than a third in 1952 to almost one-half by the end of the First Five-Year Plan period (Hai Ch'ü-niao).

Even in education, an area that traditionally falls within the purview of local governments, the central government reserved for itself a considerable direct administrative role. Many of the most important institutions of higher education, including all of China's comprehensive universities, were administered directly by the Ministry of Higher Education rather than by provincial governments. These institutions included not only such well-known universities as Peking, Nankai, Tsinghua, Futan, and Chungshan, but also a large number of lesser-known universities such as Amoy, Anhui, Chengchow, Inner Mongolia, and Nanking. In addition, the major provincial agricultural colleges were administered by the Ministry of Agriculture rather than by the provincial governments. The plans for these educational institutions were included in the plans of central government ministries, particularly Higher Education, rather than in the provincial education plans.

Another, more fundamental factor limited the role of provincial governments in the planning process: the predominance of the central planning organizations and ministries in determining the targets in each province's plan. In 1951 the center initiated a policy of unified leadership and multilevel administration (*t'ung-i ling-tao, fen-chi kuan-li*) in economic policy. Under this arrangement, local governments compiled economic plans for enterprises and other activities that they managed. This was recognized explicitly as a means of dealing with very large numbers of medium- and small-scale plants that utilized widely differing levels of technology to produce similar products. Local authorities were recognized to have superior information that would enable them to draw up local plans that would take these unique local factors into account (Government of the PRC 1956a, 213–14).

Although local governments were able to exercise some of their planning authority in the early part of the First Five-Year Plan period, their powers were eroded steadily by the increasing role of the central government. Particularly after the elimination of the private ownership of industry in the so-called socialist transformation of the mid-1950s, numerous sources report that the center controlled virtually all major provincial plan targets (Chang Hsüan-san; Ch'en Hsüeh; Hsü Fei-ch'ing 1957, 3; Jung Tzu-ho 1958, 1; Ko Chih-ta 1956a; Liao Chi-li 1958a). That is, central government control was not limited to enterprises and institutions under its direct management, but extended to include most programs that were nominally under local management. This central control was exercised by two important means – direct determination of the output, investment, and distribution plans of many enterprises managed by local governments; and indirect fiscal control of a broad range of other provincial programs.

Central government ministries sent production requirements and other plan targets directly to a broad range of enterprises that nominally were managed locally. For example, if the products of a provincially managed enterprise were distributed through the state's material-supply planning system, the enterprise's output targets and distribution plans would be controlled by the center. This limited the ability of the provincial governments to utilize these outputs within the province. Beyond this, local governments had difficulty in obtaining inputs for the manufacture of products that were not subject to state distribution. Local planners were advised that "if it becomes difficult to obtain raw materials for the production of such goods, then while striving to economize such raw material is as are available, possible steps should be taken to discover new sources of raw materials so that the output of these goods can be suitably increased" (Government of the PRC 1956a, 219).

Secondly, as will be discussed in Chapter 2, the central government also developed an elaborate system of fiscal controls through which it indirectly controlled many provincial programs. Thus, the central government's determination of provincial plan targets was not limited to the industrial sector, but included provincial programs for social services and government administration. These controls did not merely stipulate the total outlay in a few categories, but included highly disaggregated expenditure targets. In 1958 Jung Tzu-ho, the vice-minister of finance, conceded that virtually all these expenditure targets, including those for purely local programs, were centrally determined (Jung Tzu-ho 1958, 1).

In summary, provincial plans were limited in scope–the output targets of most modern industrial enterprises and the great bulk of investment were planned and administered directly from Peking without local participation. Secondly, the central government played a dominant role in planning the limited activities that nominally fell within the scope of horizontally compiled provincial plans. Only the lowest-priority programs were effectively administered by local management and, in general, they were starved for sufficient resource inputs.

The 1950s decentralization discussion

This highly centralized system of economic planning, particularly fiscal management, was the subject of a far-reaching debate in the mid-1950s. This debate over the appropriate balance between centralization and decentralization could not, however, be resolved merely by weighing the complex trade-off between central control and efficiency. As has already been suggested, the existence of a second closely related trade-off between efficiency and equity played an important constraining role. The salience of this constraint was enhanced by the highly dualistic structure of the economy, which made the attainment of many distributive and equity goals dependent on centralized economic policy instruments. In the paragraphs below I attempt to convey the nature of the complex debate concerning these two sets of trade-offs. Fortunately, like similar discussions in the Soviet Union and Eastern Europe, much of this debate entered into the public record. Although a few crucial speeches have never been released,[9] the economic journals of the 1950s contain a vigorous and spirited debate on the merits of alternative approaches to economic planning. The journal of the State Planning Commission, *Chi-hua ching-chi* (Economic Planning), is a particularly rich source of information.

From these materials it is clear that the central issue in this debate was the appropriate balance of economic decision-making power between the central planning agencies and industrial ministries on the one hand, and the provinces and local governments on the other. In other words, the debate concerned the appropriate balance of vertical, functional lines of planning and administration on the one hand, and horizontal, territorial lines on the other. In Chinese terms, the former was termed advocating the primacy of vertical (*t'iao-t'iao*) relations, whereas the latter approach was termed emphasizing horizontal (*k'uai-k'uai*) relations. Central government officials and planning agencies, since at least the beginning of the First Five-Year Plan, had expanded their control over the economy by developing and extending their functional, vertical lines of control and management over an increasingly wide scope. However, the efficiency of vertical administration was inherently limited by the combination of China's vast geographic size, limited transportation and communications capacity, and the great economic heterogeneity of the inherited industrial plant.

Although the planning capabilities of the center were increasing rapidly during the 1950s, the size of the state sector was also growing. The socialist transformation of private enterprises in the mid-1950s substantially increased the number of state enterprises and also, because of their relatively small size and limited capital, increased the range of technology employed by plants that were controlled by each industrial ministry. At the same time, the scope of commodities subject to central-state distribution also was expanding rapidly. Not only did the number of raw materials and producer goods subject to unified distribution increase from less than 30 in 1952 to well over 200 by 1956, but the portion of total output of these products entering state distribution channels also rose. Prior to 1956 the burden on the state's unified distribution system was mitigated by allowing a significant portion of materials subject to state distribution to be allocated through free markets. The market mechanism was used to allocate significant quantities of such products as pig iron, nonferrous metals, diesel engines, and machine tools to final users, particularly to relatively low-priority firms managed by provincial and local governments. In 1956 however, there was an abrupt increase in state investment, increasing the state-sector demand for materials relative to aggregate supplies. Consequently, the quantity of materials distributed through market channels was sharply reduced; virtually the entire output of these commodities now was allocated through the state's distribution system.[10] Provincial and locally managed firms thus became more dependent on the central government's material distribution system for the supply of crucial raw materials and producer goods. This created tensions in economic planning and management that contributed to an intensification of the decentralization debate that began toward the end of the First Five-Year Plan.

Concomitantly, the very extension of centralized, vertical control increasingly provoked criticism by local government leaders. In a retrospective article published in 1958, local officials were said to have begun complaining of excessively rigid centralized control of the economy as early as 1953 (Lin Yün, 37). It was not until after Mao's April 1956 speech, "On the Ten Major Relationships," however, that explicit discussion of these issues began to appear in Chinese newspapers and periodicals. Mao's speech pointedly urged a reduction of the central government planning bureaucracy and greater autonomy for local economic administrators. In short, he was siding with those who emphasized the horizontal (*k'uai-k'uai*) rather than the vertical (*t'iao-t'iao*). Mao specifically charged that the proliferation of central adminstrative agencies managing local programs and enterprises had undercut local initiative and responsiveness to local conditions and needs.

The various ministries don't think it proper to issue them [orders] to the Party committees and the people's councils at the provincial level, they establish direct contact with the relevant departments and bureaus in the provinces and municipalities and give them orders every day. . . . The central authorities should take care to give scope to the initiative of the provinces and municipalities, and in their turn the latter should do the same for the prefectures, counties, districts, and townships, in neither case should the lower levels be put in a straight-jacket [Mao Tse-tung 1977, 16–17].

Mao's speech was followed by almost two years of discussions concerning shortcomings in the existing system of planning and the appropriate degree of centralized economic control. This debate culminated in the decentralization measures enunciated in late 1957.

These discussions specifically linked a number of sources of economic inefficiency to the limited role of local governments in economic management and planning. Most obvious, highly centralized economic controls did not allow local officials to act on information available to them so as to improve economic management and production efficiency. Because of the relatively limited capability of the center to collect and process information, centralized decisions were inevitably made on the basis of less complete and more highly aggregated information than was available locally. Not surprisingly, the plan targets and norms determined on the basis of this information were frequently inappropriate to specific local conditions. Local leaders were required to seek special permission to alter these targets during plan implementation, leading to unnecessary delays and reduced output.

Because of the extreme emphasis on vertical links in economic planning and management, local governments had no means of coordinating economic development in their regions. The lack of coordination was particularly apparent in investment planning, commodity allocation, and labor planning. This frequently led to waste and inefficiency. For example, it was common for both a central ministry and a local government to construct factories in the same area that were to utilize local raw materials (Ma Yin-ch'u, 41; Hai Ch'ü-niao). In the absence of effective coordination, these projects competed for the same raw materials. Similarly, central government enterprises built their own machinery repair shops even when local shops could have handled the work (Ch'en Ta-lun, 34; Ma Yin-ch'u, 41). Comparable problems arose in labor planning. Local labor bureaus, nominally charged with the responsibility of drawing up local labor balances, were unable to control effectively the hiring or retirement of staff and workers, largely because they were unable to incorporate the wage and labor plans of centrally managed enterprises in their overall plan (Howe, 115).

There was a similar lack of horizontal coordination in material supply planning (She I-san; Ch'en Ta-lun, 34). During the First Five-Year Plan, provinces, autonomous regions, and directly administered municipalities established a network of horizontally administered supply agencies. At the same time, central government ministries established partially overlapping vertically organized supply networks with their own warehouses and commodity reserves. The defects of this system became particularly apparent in 1956, when the rate of investment increased sharply. The growing emphasis on distributing raw materials and intermediate goods through vertical channels led to widespread hoarding and severe shortages (Men Tso-min, 10–11). In short, commodity distribution within a single region was fragmented and unnecessarily inefficient. Local governments were unable to coordinate material supplies, because a large part of the system was administered through direct vertical lines from Peking.

In short, the Chinese experience of industrial planning and management during the First Plan appears to support the hypothesis that economic efficiency within hierarchical organizations declines as the number of levels of administrative control that lie between two interdependent activities and their nearest common superior increases (Koopmans and Montias, 71–5). Economic activities, particularly investment decisions and the physical allocation of labor and raw materials within a geographic region, are highly interdependent and in a planned economic system demand close coordination. But the formal common superior linking a locally managed firm supplying an important input to a nearby ministerial plant would be the Materials Allocation Bureau – many levels up the administrative chain at the apex of the entire structure of economic planning. Given the high costs of attaining and processing the timely, detailed, and accurate information necessary for the efficient coordination of supplies by the bureau, supply decisions were inevitably based on highly aggregated and incomplete information.

In addition to these problems of coordinating the vertically and horizontally organized hierarchies, the system of highly developed expenditure controls undercut local incentives. Under the center's system of revenue sharing and expenditure controls, there was no relation between local revenue collections and local expenditures.

Furthermore, localities that overfilled revenue plans were unable to keep any additional revenues for their own use. This clearly affected the enthusiasm of local leaders for raising state revenues. Because, as will be discussed in Chapter 2, local governments were important revenue-collecting agents for the state, this affected the overall national budget and economic plan. It also indirectly affected the enthusiasm of local planners for the development of locally managed industry. Although rapid growth of local industry increased revenues, it did not necessarily lead directly to a proportionate increase in local expenditures. Local expenditures were centrally controlled and increases in local revenues could be simply offset by reductions in other revenues that were shared between the center and the locality. The absence of a link between local revenues and expenditures concerned some local officials, one of whom said, "When our income each year is so big, why is the amount used locally so small?" (Yü Wei-hsin, 14).

The need for introducing some decentralization in the system of economic management was also linked specifically to the evolving strategy of economic development (Chou En-lai, 1956b; Po I-po; Chinese Communist Party 1956; State Planning Commission). Toward the end of the First Five-Year Plan, economic planners and political leaders were increasingly aware that the Soviet model of economic development, which had been adopted in the early 1950s, was not well suited to Chinese economic conditions, particularly its relatively early stage of development and quite different factor endowment. Most importantly, in China emphasis on the development of industry at the expense of agriculture could not be sustained as long as in the Soviet Union. Increasingly, the relatively slow growth of the agricultural sector was seen as a bottleneck slowing the rate of overall economic growth.[11] As a result, early discussions of the Second Five-Year Plan indicated that more state funds and modern industrial inputs would be allocated to the agricultural sector.

In addition to assigning a higher priority to agriculture, central planners decided to place less emphasis on large-scale capital intensive projects. There were several reasons for this. First, the large-scale capital intensive projects were heavily dependent on Soviet financial and technical assistance. By 1955 the Soviets were refusing to extend additional new economic credits. Thus preference for greater selfreliance in industrial development was at least partially externally imposed. Secondly, the leadership was increasingly aware of the long gestation period of large-scale Soviet-aided projects. Although these projects absorbed almost half the government's planned industrial investment during the First Five-Year Plan (Government of the PRC 1956a, 39), previously existing plants were the source of about two-thirds of the growth of industrial output during this period (Yeh Kung-chia, 528). A decision was made to put more of China's limited investment resources into medium-and small scale plants that could be completed more rapidly. Finally, the economic planners were confronted by increasing urban unemployment. Although this was to be solved eventually by mass transfers of people to the countryside, the leaders initially hoped that adopting less capital-intensive means of production would increase labor absorption in the industrial sector.

This evolving development strategy naturally led to a greater role for local governments in economic planning and administration. The role of the center in direct agricultural planning was minimal, so an increased priority for this sector automatically increased the role of local planners, as did increasing the number of medium and small-scale industrial projects. Control by the center was most effective when resources were concentrated on a few very large projects. It was explicitly recognized that local governments could more efficiently manage small projects. Jung Tzu-ho specifically linked the financial reform of 1958 to local governments' requirements for more resources to finance these programs (Jung Tzu-ho 1958, 1).

Thus by the end of the First Five-Year Plan period, several coalescing forces led the Chinese leadership to reexamine seriously the premises on which economic planning had been based. The reevaluation of the appropriate degree of central control in economic planning and management was particularly stimulated by the increasing size of the central-state sector, local dissatisfaction with the predominant role of the center, and Mao's own personal interest in stimulating local initiative and reducing the role of the central government bureaucracy. Furthermore, the changing sectoral and technological priorities envisaged for the Second Five-Year Plan also independently suggested the need for some decentralization of economic planning and management.

As has been suggested above, however, the Chinese faced a fundamental choice – whether to decentralize by expanding the role of the market in allocating resources or by transferring administrative powers to intermediate levels of government administration. Decentralization through the market would tend to place greater economic power in the hands of production units themselves and reduce the role of both higher-level planning agencies and intermediate administrative levels. Administrative decentralization or decentralized command, on the other hand, would have quite different consequences. It would enhance the role of intermediate levels of administration and simultaneously reduce the scope of authority of production units.

Discussion of economic reform in China focused almost exclusively on administrative forms of decentralization rather than decentralization through the market. Mao's own speech leaves little doubt that the key issue was the appropriate degree of administrative decentralization. He did not suggest that substantial resource-allocation powers be devolved to production units, either through the introduction of market forces or through an expansion of the role of workers in factory management. Mao's goal was apparently to reduce central interference in areas where provincial authority had been eroded and to expand local decision-making power. He viewed this as instrumental in increasing local enthusiasm and stimulating initiative.

In addition to Mao's influence on the character of the decentralization discussion, it also seems clear that in China there was no unified set of forces that might have led to serious consideration of market decentralization. In the Soviet Union and in several countries in Eastern Europe, the perceived need for economic decentralization is a response to the growing complexity of their economies and increasing labor shortages in the industrial sector. Although highly centralized economic planning is relatively effective in bringing about a structural transformation in the early stages of economic growth, as development proceeds the number of products grows and intersectoral relations multiply. Consequently, direct administrative planning becomes less and less efficient as a means of resource allocation.

Similarly, labor shortages and increasing complexity of production tasks give rise to the need for greater reliance on material incentives as a means of increasing labor productivity. In the Soviet Union, the early decades of industrial growth after 1928 were dependent on the transfer of prodigious quantities of manpower from the agricultural to the industrial sector. Because the possibility of continuing this intersectoral labor transfer was limited by low productivity in the agricultural sector itself, it became apparent during the 1950s that increased industrial output would become increasingly dependent on improvements in labor productivity, rather than simply expanding employment. Similarly, after 1928, increasing complexity of production required greater division of labor and more reliance on wage differentials, rather than normative appeals as a source of incentives. Increased labor productivity and greater use of material incentives, in turn, depended on the ability of the consumer-goods sector of the economy to provide higher-quality products that would satisfy the demands of industrial workers. By the 1950s, some Soviet economists had begun to articulate the view that this could best be accomplished by enhancing the role of the market in determining the output mix and the allocation of fixed investment.

Finally, the introduction of market forces, particularly in several Eastern European countries, was specifically linked to the important role of the foreign trade sector. Hungarian economic planners in particular wanted to increase the share of their exports going to Western countries. Introduction of market forces and the linking of enterprise success in expanding exports with enterprise profitability was seen as a means of increasing the competitiveness of domestic producers in the international economy (Balassa, 1, 13–15).

In summary, political leaders in centralized economic systems are reluctant to place substantial reliance on market forces because this directly reduces their own power. However, the cost of highly centralized, bureaucratic decision making is increasing inefficiency. Central collection and processing of the flow of information required to sustain administrative planning become increasingly cumbersome. Inevitably, it is argued, some form of decentralized economic decision making must be introduced to sustain the rapid rates of economic growth that are so highly prized. The peculiar nature of the sources of inefficiency leads to consideration of various forms of market decentralization.

None of these forces, however, appear to have contributed substantially to the Chinese decentralization debate. The Chinese economy was at a considerably less-advanced stage of development than either the Soviet Union or the countries of Eastern Europe that introduced economic reforms in the 1950s and 1960s. Per capita gross domestic product in China may have been only about one-tenth that in the Soviet Union in the 1950s and an even smaller fraction of per capita income in the more advanced Eastern European countries that began to discuss reform seriously in the mid-1960s.[12] In spite of rapid economic growth from 1949 to 1957, the intersectoral relationships in the Chinese economy were still relatively simple (Perkins

1968, 602–4). Furthermore, far from suffering a shortage of labor in the industrial sector that might have suggested the need to introduce market forces, the Chinese faced a serious problem of industrial unemployment (Howe, 39). Finally, the foreign trade sector of the Chinese economy was very small and oriented primarily toward other planned economies rather than the West.

The lack of a sustained discussion of price reform in China would also suggest that market-oriented decentralization measures were not considered seriously. The focus on more market-oriented decentralization in the Soviet Union and some countries in Eastern Europe naturally led to a serious discussion of price reforms. That is, it was widely recognized that the improvement in economic efficiency envisaged as a result of the decentralization of economic planning and management was dependent on a thorough overhaul of existing administered prices and the introduction of considerable price flexibility. In contrast, although in the 1950s in China there was some critical examination of problems in the existing price structure, there was little recognition of the potential role of markets and flexible prices as an alternative to the more centralized, bureaucratic methods of resource allocation that were then in use.[13]

Thus the Chinese search for a model for economic reform focused almost exclusively on administrative forms of decentralization. Local leaders, a major force pressing for reform, clearly preferred a decentralization of administrative powers that would enhance their own role rather than a market decentralization that would tend to reduce their control over production units. Furthermore, many of the factors that had led to serious consideration of market decentralization in the Soviet Union and Eastern Europe were not particularly relevant in China.

In spite of this relatively narrow range of acceptable solutions, it was almost two years before a satisfactory decentralization formula could be found. The major dilemma confronting the leadership was to formulate a more decentralized structure of planning and control that would enhance the coordinating role of local governments as a means of improving economic efficiency, while at the same time retaining centralized control of the economic policy instruments most crucial for the attainment of structural and equity goals.

Regional leaders, emboldened by the Chairman's April 1956 speech, were quick to press for greater independence in economic planning and management. However, their goals clearly exceeded those publicly enunciated by Mao. Mao's call for "a further extension of the power of the region" was actually quite circumscribed. The regions, he suggested, should be "allowed to run more projects" but only "under the unified plan of the center." This formulation was much like the slogan introduced in 1951 of "unified planning, multi-level administration," under which local economic powers had continuously eroded. In practice, local governments had become responsible for implementing plans drawn up at the center.

Local leaders wanted more than simply an increase in the number of projects they managed under unified central plans. Rather, they sought authority to initiate programs independent of overall central government control. They wished, in short, not only to be free of excessive central government interference in areas already nominally within their sphere of authority but also to be able to mobilize resources to develop entirely new programs.

Local leaders pressed for reform in several forums. Beginning in May, the State Council convened a series of meetings to consider modifications of the system of planning and administration. Local officials also pressed their claims for reform directly with Chou En-lai and other national political leaders and economic planners. In a thirteen-day plenary session of the Third Session of the First National People's Congress in June 1956, provincial deputies put forward a number of "serious criticisms" of the work of the central government. Although the full text of Chou's speech in response to these criticisms has never been published, a New China News Agency summary of his address reported that he had conceded that the division of power between the central and local authorities required further delineation and that excessive concentration of power in the hands of the central government had impaired efficiency and local initiative. Although offering no details, Chou did state that a draft decentralization program had already been formulated and referred to local governments for study and discussion. He said that the details of the plan would be finished in the latter half of 1956 and that the reform would be implemented in 1957 (Chou En-lai, 1956a).

Despite this optimistic timetable, discussions over the appropriate form of decentralization continued. At several party and government meetings convened in the ensuing year, central government leaders readily admitted that overcentralization of planning and management had impaired economic efficiency. Central leaders, however, were considerably less forthcoming in committing themselves to specific

0842149

solutions. For example, hints contained in Liu Shao-ch'i's report to the Eighth Party Congress in the fall of 1956 regarding the nature of the solution that was being developed could hardly have encouraged local officials (Liu Shao-ch'i, 77–8). Liu suggested that the central government only enunciate general principles to guide local governments in the areas of agriculture, small and medium-size industry, local transportation and commerce, local health and education, and finance. But local authorities at the provincial, municipal, county, and township levels were to be given expanded authority to make specific arrangements for the implementation of these programs in a way that would be most suited to local conditions. This really amounted to little more than a reiteration of powers that were nominally already vested in local governments.

Chou En-lai also discussed economic reform in his speech to the Congress (Chou En-lai 1956b, 310–12). He advocated a clearer delineation of local economic authority, a transfer of many enterprises to local management, and an end to central government departments bypassing the State Council in issuing plan targets to local governments. These reforms would be significant because the scope of authority of local governments would be strengthened and expanded and, more importantly, they would be insulated from direct interference by central ministries.

Discussion over the precise form that the decentralization should take continued after the Eighth Party Congress. This discussion, however, was not simply a confrontation of central versus local interests. Because no simple division of interest existed between the center and the provinces on the issue of centralization versus decentralization, the dividing lines among contending groups probably were more complex. Provincial leaders may have been relatively united in their desire for more autonomy in managing enterprises and for increased flexibility in arranging their budgets. They certainly must have been sharply divided, however, on the issue of substantially reducing the resource-allocation powers of the center.

As will be shown in Chapter 2, the less-developed provinces were the major beneficiaries of centralized economic planning. In effect, the center, through its control of the budgetary and planning process, carried out a systematic redistribution of income and wealth in favor of many less-developed areas. Because weakening of central control would reduce or eliminate this transfer, these less-developed provinces probably opposed a substantial devolution of resource-allocation powers to provincial governments. In short, although there may have been a rough convergence of provincial interests on the trade-off between control and efficiency, it is quite likely that provincial positions on the trade-off between efficiency and equity diverged significantly.

Unfortunately, there is only indirect evidence to support this interpretation. Unlike the decentralization debate in Yugoslavia that occurred in the mid-1960s, no open split occurred in China between economists from more and less-developed regions. In the Yugoslav case, economists from poorer regions argued vigorously against economic decentralization on the grounds that it would undermine the ability of the center to continue redistributing investment funds in their favor. They argued that this redistribution should be continued as a matter of national policy, irrespective of the low rate of return associated with investment in less-developed regions. These low rates of return, they argued, were due to historic factors that had left them with inadequate social overhead capital. Economists from more-developed regions argued that decentralization of investment would improve overall resource allocation by ending what they regarded as the wasteful subsidy of investment in backward republics. In short, they believed that the rate of economic growth could be significantly accelerated by allocating investment resources according to traditional rate-of-return criteria. They did not deny the existence of a trade-off between the goals of aggregate growth and regional balance, but argued simply that the attainment of improved regional balance carried too high a price in terms of growth foregone (Milenkovitch, 178–86).

To recapitulate, the Chinese decentralization appears to have been motivated by a complex mix of both economic and political factors. On the one hand, there was apparently a broad consensus that the system of economic planning and management that had evolved during the First Five-Year Plan period was too highly centralized. It was a source of increasing inefficiency, both directly because of the inherent limits on the efficiency of centralized planning in a country of China's size and economic heterogeneity and also indirectly through its effect on incentives and local enthusiasm.

There is also evidence of an evolving consensus that economic development in the Second Five-Year Plan would be based less on large-scale capital-intensive investment and would place more emphasis on the development of small-scale plants and the agricultural sector. Because local governments had a larger role in these functional areas, this naturally would place more authority in their hands.

Finally, the discussion was heavily influenced by political factors. Mao clearly favored a pattern of economic planning and management that was less dependent on a large centralized economic bureaucracy for daily economic decision making. Provincial leaders, particularly those from more-developed areas, must have been particularly receptive to this view. A substantial decentralization of resource-allocation authority would increase the volume of resources at their disposal. Authorities from many less-developed provinces as well as central planners, however, probably actively opposed a wholesale downward transfer of economic authority.

The interplay of these contending forces probably had much to do with the delay in the announcement of the reform. Furthermore, the lack of serious consideration of decentralization through an expansion of the role of markets as a means of resource allocation was to have a profound effect on the overall character of the reforms.

The 1958 decentralization

The major outlines of the decentralization were publicly unveiled in late 1957, when the State Council promulgated the decentralization decrees that had been approved by the Third Plenum (Chinese Communist Party 1958). Reforms of industrial, commercial, and financial management were announced in November and scheduled for implementation beginning in 1958 (State Council 1957a, b, c). During 1958, the initial trio of directives was supplemented by more detailed reforms of taxation, price control, grain management, planning, and materials distribution (State Council 1958c–f, h). In each of these areas, new authority was transferred from the central government to provinces, autonomous regions, and provincial-level municipalities.

Reform provisions

The reforms contained many important concessions to provincial interests. They not only expanded the sphere of activities subject to provincial management, but equally important, gave provincial governments the mechanisms to improve horizontal coordination of all economic activities regardless of whether they were centrally or locally managed.

The most important expansion of the sphere of provincial management was the transfer of large numbers of industrial and almost all commercial enterprises to local management. Only a few key heavy industrial enterprises remained under the direct management of the central government ministries. Provincial authority, particularly in the areas of price control, taxation, and fiscal management, was also enhanced by the reform. Provinces were given the authority to set prices for all products, except for agricultural commodities subject to planned or unified purchase and industrial products subject to unified state distribution. Provincial tax authority was expanded by setting forth a number of cases in which provinces could adjust tax rates and change the coverage of certain taxes. Decentralization of financial management expanded the scope of revenues and expenditures of local governments and in addition gave provincial governments more control over the composition of their expenditures. Extrabudgetary revenues of local governments also were expanded and local governments were given increased authority over the use of budgetary surpluses.

Several measures strengthened horizontal lines of economic planning and management, particularly in commodity distribution and labor-supply planning. Provincial governments, for the first time, were given a role in determining the distribution of materials subject to unified distribution. They were allowed to adjust the timing and quantities of materials supplied to central government enterprises in their areas. Also for the first time, they obtained authority to distribute freely part of the output of provincial enterprises producing products subject to unified state distribution. Provinces also received the prerogative of adjusting amounts of planned purchase and planned supply of grain that were set by the central government. More significant, provincial quotas for grain delivery to the central government were fixed for five years and provinces were given the authority to control future increases in purchased grain. Finally, local governments were given the authority to reassign the managerial and technical personnel in central government enterprises.

All these powers were, in effect, consolidated in September 1958, when provincial governments were given the authority to compile comprehensive regional plans that would include all enterprises regardless of their level of managerial control. Thus regional plans were no longer to include only locally controlled enterprises but also were to include enterprises that remained directly under the central government ministries (Wang Kuei-wu, 13; Liao Chi-li 1958b, 19). In theory, vertically organized planning was abolished and the national plan was to become an aggregation of these comprehensive regional plans. Furthermore, the system of unified commodity distribution was substantially decentralized. The number of commodities subject to unified distribution was reduced by about two-thirds, and local government responsibility for the distribution of commodities was enhanced (She I-san; State Council 1958f). Central government enterprises were no longer to obtain their material inputs from a centrally administered system of vertically organized supply agencies, but were to apply to a locally administered, horizontally organized system for their required material inputs. Finally, the scope of the local labor plan was broadened to include all enterprises in the area, not simply those that were locally managed. Although the central government retained the power to set many of the targets contained in each province's plan, the reform substantially strengthened local control by lessening the importance of vertical lines of planning and administration.

The character of the reforms

The thrust of the reforms was to expand the powers of local governments. Indeed, in the short space of ten months the central government had announced that it was, in effect, giving up a portion of the most important instruments at its disposal for planning and managing the economy. The reform, however, primarily transferred the center's administrative decision-making power to local governments, rather than enlarging the scope of economic activities controlled through market allocation. Equally important, the reform carefully preserved relatively centralized control over certain crucial types of economic decisions. As will become clear below, I believe that this aspect of the reform has been largely ignored and that, in turn, this has led to major misinterpretations of the character of Chinese growth and development over the last two decades.

The Chinese reform was clearly not a step in the direction of decentralized decision making of the type conceptualized by Lange. That is, Lange's model of economic decentralization places primary emphasis on the role of enterprise managers and markets in the resource-allocation process. Enterprise managers have full responsibility for determining the bill of goods to be produced. Industry managers only determine the level of total output by regulating entry and exit of firms in the industry. They have no authority to intervene in decision making within the enterprise. Thus, the Lange scheme provides no role for intermediate levels of government and only a minor role for industrial ministries. Enterprise managers are essentially autonomous units buying their inputs and selling their outputs on open markets at prices determined by the central planning board.

The Chinese reform, by contrast, envisaged only a minor increase in the role of markets and the autonomy of enterprises. Although the number of mandatory targets in the enterprise plan was reduced (State Council 1957a), most power was transferred to intermediate levels of government administration. Most important, the reform did not call upon enterprises to determine their own production targets in response to prices set by a central planning board. Although the reform reduced the quantity of information flowing to the center, it did not change the character of this flow. Many enterprises continued to send detailed information to the central ministries concerning their production capacities, inventories, labor force, etc., rather than sending operational messages horizontally to other firms. Of course, many more firms now reported this information to their superordinate local government and the information transmitted onward to the center was presumably more aggregated than prior to 1958. Either the center or the province in turn continued to send specific production targets to each firm rather than a single price vector that would apply to all firms. Thus the Chinese reform also differed fundamentally from the type of decentralized decision-making models advanced by Hurwicz and others.

The Chinese reform was also substantially different from that adopted by the Soviet Union in 1957. The Soviet reform abolished the central government ministerial apparatus in the industrial sector and replaced it with a system of about 100 regional economic councils called *sovnarkhozy*. By establishing *sovnarkhozy* that cut across previously existing lines of industrial administration and abolishing the ministries, the government hoped to break the extreme vertical rigidity and ministerial autarky that had developed in the system of economic planning and administration. The Chinese reform, by contrast, preserved the ministerial system. As will be further developed in Chapter 3, the continuing role of the ministries is crucial to understanding the Chinese reform.

Finally, the texts of the decentralization directives as well as articles published by those intimately involved in national economic planning clearly explained that crucial decisions were not to be decentralized. In particular, they stated that the center would continue to control the level of investment expenditures within each province, the transfer of local revenues between the province and the center, and the interprovincial transfers of major capital goods. In addition, the center was to continue to control the output targets for most important industrial and agricultural products, the enrollment plans of most institutions of higher education, the structure of wages and the total wage bill of workers in the nonagricultural sectors of the economy, and several other important targets (State Council 1958c).

Western interpretations of the decentralization

The effect of the decentralization has been one of the most widely discussed questions among students of contemporary China (Schurmann, 196; Oksenberg, 108). Studies by both economists and political scientists, although differing in emphasis and details, have frequently advanced the view that the decentralization led to a fundamental realignment in the balance of economic powers between the provinces and the central government (Schurmann,195–210; Donnithorne 1966, 1972a, 1972b, 1974b; Etienne, 137–9; Durand, 223). The transfer of broad economic powers from the center to the provincial governments is viewed as having substantially reduced the ability of the central government to control the allocation of the nation's economic resources.

This fundamental realignment is, in turn, viewed as having far-reaching implications for a broad range of important issues related to our understanding of China's development experience. Most importantly, it is widely believed that this decentralization drastically changed the character of Chinese economic planning. The national economic plan no longer reflected primarily allocation decisions of the central leadership but rather became simply an aggregation of provincial plans that were compiled on the basis of narrowly defined regional interests rather than on the basis of broad national goals.

In short, in this view provincial control of most investment decisions has given rise to increasing provincial self-sufficiency and autarky. It is widely believed that provincial political leaders have reinvested their own resources in industrial and social programs that more directly benefit their own economic development rather than allow them to be used by the central government for the attainment of national goals.

Advocates of this view predict that the shift in the locus of resource-allocation power from the center to the provinces has had two important results. First, because of their increased capability to resist transferring their resources to the center, the more-developed provinces would gain a long-run comparative growth advantage as compared with poorer provinces (Donnithorne 1972b, 613; Etienne, 139). It was expected that this would be reflected in a modified pattern of provincial growth after the decentralization. Secondly, it was thought that, because most planning would now be on a provincial basis, the transfer of resources among provinces would be sharply reduced (Li Chohming, 24–5). In effect, integrated national planning, controlled from the center, was thought to have largely ended. In summary, those holding this view, which I label the "autarky hypothesis," assert that since 1958 Chinese economic development has been characterized by increased local economic self-sufficiency and increased provincial independence from central economic control.

What evidence has been advanced in support of this view, particularly considering the continuing central government role in basic resource-allocation functions indicated in the reform directives themselves? First, as discussed above, many specific features of the decentralization seemed to indicate a transfer of substantial resource-allocation powers to provincial governments. Furthermore, observed events supported the view that many of these provisions were actually being implemented. It is clear, for example, that enterprises were being transferred to local governments as early as the fall of 1957 (Vogel 1969, 224). By June 1958 80 percent of the center's enterprises had been transferred (New China News Agency). As a result, the share of industrial output produced by local enterprises increased from 54 percent in 1957 to an estimated 73 percent in 1958 (Editorial 1958a).

As shown in Table 1.4, the enhanced role of provincial governments in financial management appeared to be even more dramatic. Central government spending in 1958 declined by 14 percent, while that of provincial governments increased by almost 150 percent to comprise over one-half of total government spending. By contrast,

Table 1.4. *Division of government spending, 1951–60*

Year	Central government expenditures		Local government expenditures	
	million yuan	% of total	million yuan	% of total
1951[a]	8,890	74.7	3,020	25.3
1952[a]	11,930	71.1	4,860	28.9
1953[a]	16,300	75.8	5,190	24.2
1954[a]	18,590	75.5	6,040	24.5
1955[a]	22,910	78.1	6,420	21.9
1956[b]	21,720	71.5	8,850	28.9
1957[c]	21,610	70.7	8,990	29.3
1958[d]	18,680	45.6	22,274	54.4
1959[e]	25,118	47.6	27,651	52.4
1960[f]	33,890	48.4	36,130	51.6

Note: The division for 1951–9 is based on final accounts; 1960 is based on budgeted expenditures.
Sources: [a]Ko Chih-ta 1957b, 37. [b]Li Hsien-nien 1957, 23. [c]Li Hsien-nien 1958, 9. [d]Chin Ming, 31. [e]Obolenskiy 1961b, 2. [f]Li Hsien-nien 1960, 60.

prior to 1958 the local proportion of total government spending had never reached 30 percent. There was a comparable increase in the role of local governments in revenue collection. After the decentralization revenues collected directly by the center declined from about 40 to 20 percent of total government revenues (Ch'en Hsüeh, 11; Hsü Fei-ch'ing 1959, 13; Ko Ling, 20).

In addition to this empirical evidence, there is no doubt that the analysis of Western observers has also been heavily influenced by Chinese rhetoric supporting the principles of self-reliance and local self-sufficiency. For more than a decade Chinese media have given disproportionate attention to enterprises that are able to pull themselves up by their own bootstraps. Output-increasing innovations that do not require outside resources are praised as successful examples of mass cooperation and innovation. Similarly, although less frequently, local governments that are able to accelerate their rates of growth with minimal central government assistance are praised for tapping the potential of existing enterprises. These statements clearly have reinforced the belief that the contemporary Chinese economy is most insightfully analyzed and understood as a series of relatively independent economic systems, in which interprovincial resource flows are sharply curtailed and in which provinces rely on internally raised resources.

A major objective of this study is to investigate the validity of the hypothesis of increased provincial autarky summarized above. This investigation is based not only on an analysis of qualitative materials, such as official regulations and descriptive articles published in Chinese economic journals, but also on the systematic use of provincial economic data. Several kinds of data will be employed to shed light on the complex of growth-versus-distribution issues. Of these data, the most analytically useful are derived from the operations of the fiscal system, particularly from the fiscal relations between the central government and the provinces. Whereas the fiscal system and the nature of central-provincial fiscal relations are explored in some detail in Chapter 2 and specific empirical tests based on the data are advanced in Chapter 3, the remainder of this introductory chapter explains the nature of this data base and considers why fiscal data provide a particularly useful basis for approaching the issue of the degree of central control of resource allocation.

The fiscal decentralization as a case study – methodology

Although economic decentralization in China has encompassed a broad spectrum of economic functions, this study focuses on fiscal management, both because of the availability of fiscal data and, more important, because of the close relationship between physical planning and the budgetary process in China. In addition, focusing on the fiscal system facilitates comparative analysis of the allocative power of economic planning in China since 1949 and other developing countries with mixed rather than centrally planned economic systems. Furthermore, this approach highlights the vast increase in the resource-allocation power of the Chinese central government since 1949 compared with the prerevolutionary period.

Physical planning and fiscal management

Fiscal management and national economic planning are intimately interrelated, because planning is carried out in both physical and monetary terms. That is, although economic plans are drawn up primarily in physical terms, the state budget provides almost all the funds necessary for the implementation of the plan. Thus the real intersectoral and interregional resource flows provided for in the physical plan are accompanied by intersectoral and interregional fiscal flows. A complete system of financial control in effect supports physical planning and the physical allocation of resources (Perkins 1968, 619–21).

The complementary nature of the planning and budgetary process is most evident in the industrial sector. Nonreturnable state budgetary grants finance most investment and provide the bulk of the working capital to finance current production. For example, if an enterprise requires additional capital goods (such as machine tools) or intermediate products (such as steel or nonferrous metals) to fulfill its plan, these will be allocated physically through the system of unified distribution of producer goods. Simultaneously, the state fiscal plan provides the enterprise with a budgetary grant to pay for the required machine tools or materials.

The intimate relationship between the state economic plan and the budget is not confined to the industrial sphere. The budget provides the salaries and other funds necessary to meet the targets for increases in school enrollments, expansion of health services, and other social programs that are specified in the plan in physical terms. Government administration and defense expenditures are also entirely financed from budgetary grants.

Because of this close relationship between the planning and budgetary process, the share of national output allocated through the budget provides a most useful summary measure of the ability of the central government to control the distribution of resources among alternative uses. Although the portion of resources allocated through the budget is typically relatively large in advanced industrialized societies, less-developed countries are usually characterized by considerably weaker fiscal mechanisms. The share of gross domestic product allocated through the government budget in a number of less-developed countries with per capita incomes of under 100 dollars in the 1950s is shown in Table 1.5. The shares for countries other than China range from a low of 5 percent in Afghanistan and Ethiopia to 19 percent in Burma. In no other country does the share of gross domestic product allocated through the budget even approach that in China – 30 percent.

This large share represents a distinct increase in the potential role of the state in support of industrial development compared to the prerevolutionary period, when a lack of revenues effectively constrained government-sponsored modernization programs. At the end of the nineteenth century, the revenues of the central government

Table 1.5. *Government revenue shares in less-developed countries, 1957–60*

Country	Revenues as a % of gross national product
Afghanistan	5
Burma	19
Cambodia	12
China	30
Ethiopia	5
India	10
Indonesia	13
Liberia	16
Nigeria	11
Pakistan	10
Sudan	12
Thailand	12

Sources: Harley Hinrichs, "Determinants of Government Revenue Shares Among Less Developed Countries," *Economic Journal,* vol. 75, no. 299: 552, for all countries except China. Data for China are for 1957. Gross domestic product from Liu Ta-chung and Yeh Kung-chia, 66; revenue data from State Statistical Bureau 1960, 21.

were only 1 to 2 percent of China's gross domestic product. (Perkins 1967, 487). Under the somewhat more vigorous fiscal program of the Nationalist government after 1928, central government revenues were only about 3 percent of domestic product. Even when provincial and local revenues are included, the total government revenue share of domestic product was less than 5 percent (Rawski 1975c, 6). In short, prior to 1949 the potential direct role of the government in fostering economic development was far more limited than in most of the developing countries shown in Table 1.5.

The role of the budget in resource allocation in China since 1949 has been significantly greater than in either most other less-developed countries or pre-1949 China for several reasons. Most obviously, because the modern industrial sector is entirely state owned, the scope of economic planning in China is much broader than in most less-developed countries. The role of the budget is further enhanced because investment in the state sector is financed almost entirely through budgetary grants rather than by direct enterprise reinvestment of their own profits. Finally, the unitary nature of the

Chinese budget enhances its role in the resource-allocation process in a way that is not captured by the data in Table 1.5. These data include the revenues of all levels of government administration, but in China the revenues of provincial and subprovincial governments are actually subject to considerable degree of central government control.

By way of contrast, the Indian federal government controls only a portion of total government budgetary revenues. State governments determine both the basic tax rates and the allocation of the proceeds of several important revenue sources, and the federal government policy instruments for influencing the allocation of these revenues are very weak (Eapen).

Fiscal management and resource redistribution

As discussed earlier in this chapter, the attainment of the central government's economic goals necessitated substantial intersectoral and interregional resource redistribution. Rapid development of heavy industry required a transfer of the large profits of light industry into investment in the producer-goods sector. Achievement of a geographically more balanced pattern of industrial development required the transfer of the profits and taxes of coastal industry to backward inland areas. A more equitable distribution of social services depended on a similar transfer of fiscal revenues to subsidize expenditures of local governments in less-developed areas. Thus, a primary indicator of the degree of centralization in Chinese economic management and planning is the degree to which the central government is able to carry out these interregional and intersectoral resource transfers.

In theory the pattern of interregional resource transfers could be measured by studying interregional trade flows. If comprehensive data on interprovincial transfers of steel, coal, machine tools, grain, and other commodities were available, one could identify those provinces that have enjoyed an import surplus and those that have suffered a long-term net resource outflow. Similarly, the intersectoral flows of resources could be measured by studying the physical transfer of resources between sectors. In practice published reports do not begin to provide the data necessary for such an undertaking. For example, although national economic plans specify the geographic location of many investment projects, they cannot be used to mea-

sure interregional resource transfer because these plans fail to specify the geographic sources of the physical inputs required for these
projects. In practice even Chinese planners do not have sufficient
data to calculate the interregional flow of resources by directly measuring all commodity flows (Fang Ping-chu, 6).

However, the intimate relationship between the plan and the budget makes it possible to use provincial fiscal data to estimate the
interregional resource flows inherent in the plan. If interprovincial
flows of real resources were balanced in value terms, there would be
no net revenue flows between provinces. Each province's programs
would be limited to those that could be financed from its own income. Some of the necessary inputs would come from outside the
province, but in the absence of capital markets the overall trade
flows between regions would be balanced and, as a result, each province's revenues and expenditures would be balanced. However, if a
provincial plan calls for labor and material inputs in excess of those
that can be financed locally, the central government must supply the
inputs by unilaterally transferring them from other provinces. Thus
the province would benefit from a net inward transfer of materials or
an import surplus. This balance-of-trade deficit is financed by capital
inflows provided by the Ministry of Finance. These capital inflows,
which provide financial subsidies equal to the value of the net import surplus, primarily take the form of nonreturnable central budgetary grants. In short, the value of budgetary subsidies received by a
province provides a measure of the net inflow of materials; in provinces that are net suppliers of materials to other regions, the outflow
can be measured by the flow of revenues remitted to the central
government. As will be explained in detail in Chapter 2, provincial
financial reports can be used to measure the size of these unilateral
physical transfers. National fiscal reports give comparable data on the
intersectoral transfer of resources. In addition to these transfers
through the budgetary system, resources are also transferred through
the bank credit system and through relative price changes. These
mechanisms are discussed more fully below.

Changes in the degree of unilateral resource redistribution

There is little direct evidence available that bears on the ability of
provincial governments to exercise their increased authority to set
commodity prices, alter tax rates, control the distribution of grain

and industrial commodities, or formulate comprehensive provincial economic plans. However, if provincial governments were increasingly able to mobilize resources for their own use and resist transferring them to the central government, one would expect to observe a substantial change in the resource-allocation pattern after the decentralization.

Because provinces would still benefit by exporting goods in which they enjoyed a comparative advantage, there would be no a priori reason to expect a decline in the balanced trade flows between provinces. Unilateral transfers, however, would be dramatically decreased as more-developed provinces increased the portion of their resources used locally and successfully resisted centrally planned net resource outflows. Provinces that had previously depended on central government transfers would be in a weaker position after decentralization because of the reduced redistributive powers of the center. Because interregional resource transfers are financed primarily through corresponding fiscal transfers, changes in central–provincial fiscal flows can be used to analyze intertemporal changes in the capability of the government to carry out net resource transfers among provinces. Thus, changing central–provincial fiscal flows provide a broad measure of the extent to which the locus of resource-allocation powers has shifted over time.

These fiscal flows still provide only a partial measure of the degree to which the center transfers resources interregionally: Transfers can also be financed through short-term credits provided by the State Bank, and in the long run there can also be so-called invisible transfers arising from changes in relative prices. For any given year the subsidy of a less-developed region would include not only the budgetary subsidy but also any net credits allocated to the provincial branch bank by the People's Bank (Fang Ping-chu, 2–3; Wang Hu-sheng, 25). Thus the net inflow of commodities to a province measured in current prices (its import surplus) is simply the sum of its net budgetary subsidy and the net funds allocated by higher-level banks to finance local loans. These latter two items may be thought of as the long- term and short-term capital inflows financing the region's balance-of-trade deficit (import surplus).[14]

In general it would appear that bank loans are of secondary importance as a redistributive policy instrument. Chinese sources state that the redistribution of resources financed through bank credits was only temporary (Wang Hu-sheng, 25) whereas the budgetary subsidies, which were never repaid, financed permanent transfers. The hypothesis that bank credits were far less important than the budget is also supported by data on the volume of bank loans outstanding at any one time. For example, total bank credit outstanding at the end of the First Five-Year Plan was only about 20 percent of cumulative budgetary expenditures during the period (Hsiao, 125–6; Li Hsien-nien 1958, 5). Except for 1956, when the share of loans allocated to the agricultural sector surged from its usual level of about 10 percent to about one-half, the distribution of bank credits must have been roughly proportional to the growth of industrial output, because loans were used primarily for financing temporary working capital in the manufacturing and commercial sectors. So-called permanent or retained working capital, which in 1957 for example was almost half of all working capital of firms in the state sector (Hsiao, 125), was financed with nonrepayable budgetary grants. Because bank credits were thus tied primarily to current levels of production rather than being used to finance fixed investment or permanent working capital, it would appear that they were not used primarily as a deliberate redistributive policy instrument. A definitive test of the hypothesis that credits were a secondary redistributive policy instrument must, however, await a detailed examination of the relationships between the People's Bank and its provincial branches.

Finally, changes in relative prices can influence the distribution of real resources over time. As will be discussed in some detail in Chapter 5, the central government has deliberately manipulated relative prices to reallocate resources between the industrial and agricultural sectors. However, the degree to which industrial product prices have been changed over time to benefit some regions at the expense of others is somewhat less clear. For example, little is known about the relative prices of minerals and other industrial raw materials. Increases in these prices relative to those of manufactured goods, for example, would constitute an invisible transfer in favor of regions specializing in mining and other raw materials production. Similarly, by absorbing the transport costs when supplying producer goods to more remote regions at uniform national prices, the state indirectly subsidizes less-developed regions. Little is known about the magnitude of this subsidy and measuring its change over time will require more detailed studies of China's price policies than are currently available.

Fiscal control

In addition to revealing the extent of net interprovincial resource transfers, a study of the budgetary system sheds light on central financial control of local government programs. Although important sectors of the economy are controlled primarily through physical plans, a wide range of activities are controlled by the center primarily through the financial system. Although the usual characterization of financial plans in Soviet-type systems as "passive" is largely correct in China's industrial sector, in other spheres financial controls are clearly more "active" or directly controlling. In China's industrial sector for example, physical planning predominates and financial planning occupies a distinctly secondary role. Output plans and input plans for enterprises are the most obvious examples of this type. Other activities such as government administration and numerous social programs where the major input is wage payments rather than intermediate goods are, however, less amenable to direct physical control. For example, although national and provincial plans specify future annual increases in enrollment at various levels of education, the real control of education and other social programs was financial. Each province's expenditures for a variety of subcategories of educational programs were determined by the central government on the basis of desired increases in enrollments, student–teacher ratios, and nationally determined salary schedules. Examining the degree of disaggregation in the expenditure categories provides an additional perspective on the degree to which the central government is able to regulate economic and social programs that were nominally under the management of provincial governments.

Availability and reliability of fiscal data

There is a large body of fiscal data for the 1950s from several levels of government administration that can be used to analyze various issues outlined in this introductory chapter. Fiscal reports from almost all provinces, autonomous regions, provincial-level municipalities, and for a large number of municipalities are available, usually for several years in the mid-to late 1950s. These fiscal reports, which are compiled on the basis of a uniform system of accounts, contain detailed information on the structure of local expenditures and revenues and also on intergovernmental revenue flows. Although provincial expenditure data have not been available since 1960, an increasing number of provinces have released information on central–provincial revenue flows that is qualitatively comparable to that for the 1950s.

Interpretation and analysis of provincial and municipal fiscal reports, particularly of central–provincial fiscal relations in the 1950s, is greatly facilitated by several important publications of the Ministry of Finance. These include the annual or semi-annual *Chung-yang ts'ai-cheng fa-kuei hui-pien* (Compendium of central government fiscal laws and regulations), which was published during the 1955–9 period. The Research Institute of Public Finance published an important two-volume collection of fiscal directives from the Ministry of Finance and articles on financial administration written by national and provincial finance officials, *Shih-nien lai ts'ai-cheng tzu-liao hui-pien* (Collection of materials on finance during the last ten years). Another important commemorative volume *Chung-hua jen-min kung-ho-kuo shih-nien ts'ai-cheng ti wei-ta ch'eng-chiu* (Ten great years of financial accomplishments of the People's Republic of China), collected a number of important articles, several of which were not available in the West in their original sources. Finally, periodicals of the Ministry of Finance, especially *Ts'ai-cheng* (Finance), deal primarily with issues in fiscal administration and are indispensable for understanding the evolution of financial administration. These and other sources provide valuable information for understanding and interpreting fiscal reports of local governments.

Chinese fiscal data, in addition to their relative availability and utility in analyzing the degree of central control, are also highly reliable. This gives them an advantage over other types of data, particularly for the years 1958–9.

The reliability of budgetary data on revenue and expenditure data arises primarily from the State Bank's control of budgetary funds. In early 1950 the People's Bank of China was designated as the government treasury. Since that time it has served both as the government depository and has also exercised significant control over expenditures. Because the government imposed restrictions on the use of cash in the early 1950s, all major transactions in China are carried out through bank transfers. This applies to interenterprise transactions, most tax payments, and fiscal transfers between different levels of government administration. The most important uses of cash are for the payment of wages in industry and in the retail sector.

The pervasive role of the State Bank substantially reduces the possibility of inaccurate fiscal data. Unlike some types of physical production, local governments could not exaggerate claims for revenues collected. Local tax accounts in the state Bank were subject to audit, so an exaggeration of revenues was easily detected. Furthermore, there was no incentive to overreport revenue collections. Because most revenues were shared with the central government, overreporting would have automatically increased the payments the local government had to make to the center and reduced the funds available locally. Similarly, there was little capability to underreport tax revenues. The actual collection of most taxes was through bank transfers. Because the State Bank remained highly centralized even after 1957, local government officials have few means of concealing revenues.

Dwight Perkins' study of the reliability of fiscal data presents empirical evidence that supports this analysis. He argues that although production data were exaggerated during the period 1958–61, revenue data remained basically reliable. He used reported production data and information on tax rates to estimate industrial and commercial tax collections. Perkins found that his estimates of tax revenues in 1950–7 were quite close to those actually reported in annual government fiscal reports. However, reported revenues in 1958 and 1959 lagged substantially behind his estimates. This led him to conclude that industrial production data had been relatively reliable through 1957 but subject to substantial falsification in 1958 and 1959. This view is, of course, consistent with numerous studies of industrial output growth during this period. Although this test does not eliminate the possibility of upward bias in tax revenues, Perkins concluded that "it appears more likely that the revenue reported was actually collected" (Perkins 1966, 244).

2

Centralization of economic and financial planning, 1949–1957

How did the planning and budgetary system evolve in the years prior to the decentralization that was introduced in late 1957? What was the nature of the budgetary and planning process, particularly the mechanisms of central government control? More important, how did the evolution of fiscal relations between the center and the provinces reflect the complex trade-offs between central control and efficiency and between efficiency and equity?

The desire of the center to use the budgetary and planning process to exert a growing influence over the allocation of resources is reflected in the broad scope of the budget, the unitary nature of the budgetary process, the vast intersectoral and interregional transfers of resources carried out during this period, and the rising rate of capital formation. Although this far-reaching degree of central control was relatively effective in achieving certain structural and equity goals, it was also a source of increasing friction between the center and the provinces. In an effort to reduce this friction and in particular to provide greater economic incentives for local growth and development, the central government undertook a number of adjustments of the fiscal system even prior to the major decentralization introduced at the end of the First Five-Year Plan.

Each of the adjustments of the fiscal system in the 1950s was an attempt to resolve the basic centralization–decentralization dilemma. This dilemma was created by the desire to insure centralized fiscal control while allowing enough decentralization to stimulate local economic growth. Centralized control was required to assure more equitable provision of public goods and to mobilize resources to promote rapid overall economic growth and structural change. However, highly centralized control tended to reduce flexibility and stifle local initiative, undercutting the incentives for mobilizing local resources.

49

The first section of this chapter explores the scope of the Chinese budget, whereas the subsequent three sections examine in some detail the degree of central control inherent in the budgetary and planning process. The latter sections also explore the efforts of the central government to mitigate the friction and inefficiencies inherent in this highly centralized planning process and relate these efforts to the development of subprovincial budgetary and planning organizations.

The national budget

The Chinese national budget is a unified budget–that is, it is a consolidated budget that includes the revenues and expenditures of all levels of budgetary administration. Unification is carried out at each level. The national budget includes the budgets of the central government and the budgets of the provinces, autonomous regions, and independent municipalities.[1] Provincial budgets include not only the expenditures undertaken directly by the provincial government itself but also those of its subordinate *hsien* (county), *shih* (municipality) and, after 1953, *hsiang* (township) levels of government[2] (Government Administrative Council 1952). The budgets of independent municipalities include those of their subordinate *ch'ü*(district). *Hsien* budgets include those of their subordinate *hsiang*.

The scope of the budget

The scope of the Chinese budget is quite broad, not only in comparison with other less-developed countries, but even compared with some other planned economies. During the first two five-year plans in the Soviet Union, retained profits and the portion of retained depreciation allowances used for investment purposes financed a substantial portion of total investment. Initially, 40 percent of investment in industry was financed from retained profits (Davies, 103). The growth of budgetary allocations reduced this share in the later years of the First Plan, but between 1932 and 1940 the portion of industrial investment financed from nonbudgetary sources rose from 11 to 30 percent (Davies, 256, 279). By contrast, during the First Five-Year Plan the Chinese systematically reduced the portion of investment financed from nonbudgetary sources by collecting virtually all enterprise profits and depreciation funds through the state budget. In addition, in China other sources of expenditure not under budgetary control are relatively limited.

The Chinese departed from the Soviet practice of the 1930s of financing industrial investment partially from retained profits and depreciation funds for several reasons. First, because the Chinese followed a pricing policy quite different from that of the Soviets, enterprise profits in China were far more important fiscally than in the Soviet union. Rather than relying primarily on turnover taxes, the Chinese preferred to set industrial prices relatively high and rely more on profit remissions to finance state expenditures. As a result, after 1954, enterprise profits were the single most important source of state revenue. Peking maximized its control by requiring that virtually all enterprise profits be remitted as budgetary revenue.

Secondly, allowing enterprises to retain a substantial portion of their profits would have significantly reduced the ability of the central government to redistribute resources both intersectorally and geographically. This would have led to further concentration of industry in the several major coastal centers that had been the initial sources of most industrial output and enterprise profits. This naturally would have further increased the differential in the level of economic development between the coastal and inland areas, an outcome that the leadership firmly opposed. Equally important, profit retentions by enterprises would have reduced the ability of the central government to allocate very large proportions of investment resources to the heavy industrial sector. Profit rates generally were higher in light industry than in other sectors, and their contribution to the state budget, in relation to their output levels, far exceeded that of heavy industry (Sun Yeh-fang, 12; Rawski 1975b, 10–15). Most of these profits were reinvested in heavy industry.[3]

Finally, the leadership felt that planning skills at the enterprise level were inadequate to allow enterprises to control substantial investment funds (Ko Chih-ta 1957b, 76). Consequently, the Chinese chose to channel a substantially higher proportion of enterprise profits through the state budget than was the case in the Soviet Union during the 1930s.

Several sources of funds, however, were not allocated by the budgetary mechanism. These included funds controlled by enterprises, agricultural surtaxes and other miscellaneous fees controlled by local governments, labor insurance funds administered by trade unions,

and investment funds of enterprises administered jointly by the state
and private interests.

Enterprise funds. State enterprises administered three types of
funds outside the budgetary mechanism – major repair funds, bonus
funds, and retained profits. All large enterprises established major
repair funds to finance the maintenance and repair of their existing
equipment. Major repair funds, which were administered through
the People's Bank, were financed by a small portion of each enterprise's depreciation. Bonus funds were used, beginning in 1952, to
pay premiums to workers and technical personnel for outstanding
individual performance. In general, these funds were limited to 10 to
12 percent of the enterprise's total wage bill or to 1 to 3.5 percent of
total profits (T'ao Sheng-yü 1956, 10; Ko Chih-ta 1957b, 98). They
were awarded to the enterprise conditionally, on the fulfillment of
profit and output plans.

In 1954, the bonus system was expanded to permit retention of a
portion of above-plan profits (Ministry of Finance 1955a; Ko Chih-ta
1957b, 80). These retentions supplemented bonus funds but were
managed differently and used for different purposes. Initially set at
40 percent of above-plan profits, they were used to finance limited
investments or to supplement enterprise working capital. With State
Council approval, retained profits could also be used for certain
other purposes. These funds, however, were controlled by industrial
departments rather than by individual enterprises. These departments could redistribute the funds among their subordinate enterprises to finance projects beyond the capability of a single enterprise.

In addition to these funds of state-managed enterprises, prior to
1957 public–private jointly operated enterprises were not financed
through the state budget. These enterprises did not operate under
the system of economic accounting. Instead of remitting all their
profits and receiving a budgetary appropriation for their expenditures, they were allowed to use the system of "offsetting revenues
with expenditures" (*i-shou ti-chih*). Under this arrangement, only the
difference between their revenues and expenditures was remitted to
the state budget. Beginning in 1957 the jointly operated enterprises
were required to adopt economic accounting practices similar to
state enterprises. Thus this source of extrabudgetary funds was eliminated (State Council 1956c; Wang I-lun 1957; Ch'en Shu-t'ung 1957;
Chi Chin-chang 1957; Chang Yu-yü 1957).

Funds of local governments. In addition to extrabudgetary funds of enterprises, local governments also managed funds outside budgetary channels. In the early years of the People's Republic, these funds were relatively large because subprovincial budgetary administration had not yet been fully established.[4] However, even after the state budgetary system was more fully developed the center allowed local governments to collect an agricultural surtax that was not incorporated into the national budget (Ko Chih-ta 1957b, 35). These surtax revenues were used by local governments to finance rural wired-broadcasting systems and to repair local water conservancy systems, roads, bridges, government buildings, and schools. Because these projects could be implemented primarily with local materials, they were not entered in the state economic plan and funds for them were not included in the state budget (Ko Chih-ta 1957b, 38).

Trade union funds. The social insurance fund of the All-China Federation of Trade Unions was also administered outside the budget. First established in 1951, it was funded by enterprise contributions of 3 percent of their total wage bill (Government of the PRC 1956b, 33–4). One-third of this was contributed to the national organization to finance its retirement homes, orphanages, and homes for the disabled. The remaining portion was retained by the enterprise's trade union to finance retirement, death, maternity, disability, injury, and health benefits. The number of workers covered by these social-insurance programs increased substantially during the 1950s. In 1952, only 3.3 million workers, about 10 percent of the nonagricultural labor force, was covered by labor insurance. By 1957, the number had risen to 11.5 million (State Statistical Bureau 1960, 218).

The Chinese planned eventually to include insurance expenditures in the state budget but this did not occur during the first plan (Ko Chih-ta 1957b, 145; Li Hsien-nien 1956, 5). The unions' insurance funds were relatively small. The amounts shown in Table 2.1, for example, are equal to about 3 percent of state budgetary expenditures on social, education, and health programs. However, these funds were probably concentrated in health and pension programs and were nearly 10 percent of outlays in these categories.

Summary. Table 2.1 summarizes official Chinese data, estimates by other Western authors, or new tentative estimates of the volume of funds in each of the extrabudgetary categories discussed above. Al-

Table 2.1. *Extrabudgetary funds, 1953–7 (millions of yuan)*

	1953	1954	1955	1956	1957
Enterprises					
Major repair funds[a]	380	460	560	660	800
Bonus funds[b]	160	210	240	290	400
Above-plan profits[c]	–	–	504	603	639
Public–private joint[d]	43	186	345	780	–
Local governments					
Agricultural surtax[e]	250	180	150	320	400
Labor unions					
Insurance funds[f]	92	120	127	165	256
Total	925	1,156	1,926	2,818	2,495
Budgetary revenues[g]	21,760	26,230	27,200	28,740	31,020
Extrabudgetary revenues as a percent of budgetary revenues	4.2	4.4	7.1	9.8	8.0

Note: This table covers only the major sources of extrabudgetary revenue in the nonagricultural state sector of the economy. In addition, agricultural producer cooperatives and agricultural supply and marketing cooperatives also managed funds outside the budget. Private firms, prior to the socialist transformation in 1955–6, also controlled extrabudgetary funds not reflected in this table.

Sources and methods of estimation:

[a] Yeh Kung-chia, 541.

[b] T'ao Sheng-yü (p. 9) reported that total bonus funds for the years 1952 through 1956 were approximately one billion (American billion) *yuan.* I have distributed this amount over these years in proportion to total enterprise profits in each year. Lo Keng-mo (p. 17) estimated that bonus funds were 2.8 percent of enterprise profits in 1957. Officially reported data on enterprise profits (Li Hsien-nien 1958, 3) were used to calculate that bonus funds were about 400 million *yuan* in 1957.

[c] Lo Keng-mo (p. 17) estimated that in 1957 retained above-plan profits of central government enterprises were 4.5 percent of enterprise profits. I assumed the same percent applied in enterprises under local government administration and used total reported profits (Li Hsien-nien 1958, 3) to calculate above-plan profits in 1957. I assumed the same percent of total enterprise profits was retained in 1955 and 1956 and again used official data on total enterprise profits (Li Hsien-nien 1956, 1; Li Hsien-nien 1957, 17). Because locally managed firms were generally less advanced and because there is some indication that the system of profit retentions was expanded during these years, both these assumptions probably lead to a slightly upward-biased estimate of above-plan profit retentions. No profits were retained prior to 1955 (see discussion in text).

[d] The sum of these expenditures in Shensi, Kiangsu, and Chekiang in 1956 was 78 million *yuan* (Chao Po-p'ing; Ch'en Shu-t'ung 1957; Jen I-li). The share of national industrial output originating in these three provinces was about 10 percent. I assumed that 78 million *yuan* was 10 percent of these enterprise expenditures in 1956. This represented 5 percent of state budgetary expenditures on economic construction. The estimate for 1953–5 was constructed by assuming that the 1956 ratio between the share of output produced by public–private enterprises and their expenditures (expressed as a percent of all economic construction expenditures) also applied in 1953–5.

though hard data for several of the components are limited, the general magnitude of these funds can be estimated with some confidence. Funds expended annually outside the budgetary control mechanism by enterprises, local governments, and trade unions are estimated to be less than 10 percent of total budgetary expenditures. The relatively comprehensive scope of the national budget contributed significantly to the effectiveness of central fiscal control. On the other hand, the existence of funds managed outside the budgetary control mechanism provided incentives for local initiative and substantially increased the flexibility of the overall budgetary process. The extrabudgetary funds managed by local governments were particularly important in satisfying special local needs that could not be adequately met through the state budget.

The centralization of the budgetary process

The broad scope of the budget, considered in a comparative context in Chapter 1 and in more detail in the preceding section, only begins to convey the potential resource-allocation power of the budgetary and planning process in China. The unified fiscal system involves far more than including revenues and expenditures of lower governmental units within a consolidated state budget and limiting the scope of extrabudgetary expenditures. Far more important is the center's ability to control both the revenues and expenditures of provincial-level governments through the economic planning and budgetary process.

The central characteristic of this process is the absence of a functional link between the level of revenues and the level of expenditures at any level below the consolidated state budget. That is, al-

Table 2.1. *(cont.)*

===

[e]The value of the agricultural surtax can be calculated from data in Li Ch'eng-jui (1959, 192–3). These data, however, are compiled on a crop-year basis. To convert these to a fiscal-year (calendar) basis, I have assumed that the fiscal yield of the agricultural surtax is the sum of two-thirds of the previous year's and one-third of the current year's surtax. This is done because most of the surtax is collected in the fall, following the autumn harvest, but is not reflected in fiscal accounts until the following year.

Labor union funds for 1953 and 1954 were reported by the State Statistical Bureau (1956, 43). Because there is little evidence of a liberalization of the benefits financed by trade unions after 1954, I simply assumed these funds increased in proportion to the number of workers and other employees covered by labor insurance plans as reported by the State Statistical Bureau (State Statistical Bureau 1960, 218).

State Statistical Bureau 1960, 21.

though the principle of balancing budgetary revenues and expenditures is the most important tenet of budgeting at the national level, at the provincial and the subprovincial levels, there is no relationship between revenues collected and expenditures (Lin Yün, 38; Ko Chih-ta 1957a; Ko Chih-ta 1957b, 48–9; Fang Ping-chu, 1–2; Wang Hu-sheng, 24). The level of spending at each level is determined in the first instance by that level's economic plan. This plan in turn is subject to the approval of the next highest level of government administration. Thus county plans must be approved by the province, and provincial plans must all be approved by the central government.

Thus expenditures at each level are determined on the basis of the outlays necessary to finance the planned programs for economic development, social services, and government administration. Fiscal control of the latter programs is particularly important because they are less amenable to direct physical management by higher levels of government administration. Although there has been considerable variation over time in the ability of local governments to influence the composition of their approved level of expenditures, the ability of the central government to set the level of these expenditures in each province does not appear to have ever been fundamentally undermined. As will be documented below, this control has been used to carry out a substantial redistribution of resources from rich to poor regions within China.

The origins of centralization

The origins of this system of control must be traced to severe economic difficulties confronting the leadership in the immediate post–Civil War period. Immediately after coming to power, the new leadership took a number of significant steps toward establishing a unified fiscal system. Facing rampant inflation and lacking any effective budgetary mechanism, the leaders were unable to balance the government budget–the key point of their antiinflation program. They sought remedies to this unfavorable situation in several important national tax and fiscal meetings. These meetings led to the announcement of a new fiscal program in 1950 (Government Administrative Council 1950a–f).

The most important measures were announced in March 1950, less than six months after the formation of the new government. These measures established central features of the fiscal system that have endured up to the present. Most important, they established both the unitary nature of the tax system and the principle of central control of the level of local expenditures. The legislation gave Peking the power to determine the general types of taxes, their coverage, and the specific rates and collection procedures for all taxes regardless of whether they were actually collected directly by the central government or through subordinate levels of government administration (Ministry of Finance 1952). The central government established tax bureaus and offices extending to the sub-*hsien* level to assure that these regulations were observed (Ministry of Finance 1950a).

The decrees initiating this system of "unified management" (*t'ung-i ling-tao*) in fiscal affairs actually established the central government as the only level of independent budgetary administration. All receipts from the agriculture tax, various industrial and commercial taxes, commodity taxes, the sales tax, and customs revenues were to be uniformly allocated and spent by the central government. Because these taxes composed over 90 percent of all government revenues, this measure immediately established the primacy of the center in the resource-allocation process.

Several less-important revenues were assigned to large administrative regions (Government Administrative Council 1950b). These included the tax on interest income; stamp, business, slaughter, property, house, and animal taxes; special luxury-goods taxes and license fees for boats and vehicles. In addition, local governments were allowed to retain a fixed share of revenues collected over and above centrally determined targets. These local retentions included 80 percent and 70 percent of above-quota collections of the agriculture tax and industrial and commercial taxes, respectively (Government Administrative Council 1950b, 37). Because local revenues and these above-quota retentions of central revenues were far from sufficient to finance even relatively limited local outlays, the central government provided block grants to cover most local expenditures (Lin Yün, 36).

This highly centralized system of revenue and expenditure controls was, however, essentially a short-term expedient used to deal with the unusual financial problems of reconstruction and to provide a period to establish a more formalized system of revenue sharing and expenditure controls. As will become clear, however, the center was never willing to abandon its fundamental control of both the revenues and expenditures of provincial governments.

A separate measure, also announced in March 1950, which designated the People's Bank of China as the government's treasury, was designed to eliminate imbalance in revenues and expenditures of the government (Government Administrative Council, 1950f). Although local governments' tax collections in the first few months of 1950 were almost equal to the planned levels, remission of these revenues to the central government occurred with a considerable lag (Wang Wen-ching, 22). Partly because of this, the central government financed part of its own expenditures by note issue, thus contributing further to the price inflation of the early 1950s. The new regulations required all levels of government to deposit tax receipts in the national treasury within a short time limit. Provincial and local governments were thus prohibited from temporarily using budgetary receipts as working capital, and the inflationary note issue by the People's Bank was reduced.

Additional measures to strengthen the central government's control were introduced. To make budgetary control through the bank more effective, the banking network was expanded and cash transactions were severely limited (Government Administrative Council, 1950e; Ministry of Trade). The number of branch banks increased from 700 in early 1950 to over 5,000 by the end of 1951 (Hsiao, 34). Regulations promulgated in March and December 1950 required all enterprises to clear all transactions through the State Bank. The use of cash in transactions between enterprises was prohibited, and other types of cash payments were severely limited. Enterprises were required to make daily deposits of cash received and could not retain more than three days of currency needs at any one time. Through these and coordinated measures controlling the issuance of bank credit, the central government increased its financial supervisory powers over all expenditures.

The center's powers were further enhanced by the promulgation of a system of uniform revenue and expenditure categories to which all lower levels of government administration adhere in the compilation of their own budgets and final accounts (Ministry of Finance 1950b). The center's direct control of most expenditures limited the immediate significance of this regulation. However, in later years, as the expenditures of provincial and local governments grew in importance, this evolving system of accounts facilitated central government budgetary control and the compilation of the national budget from its components.

The 1951 reform

In 1951, the first decentralization of the fiscal system was undertaken (Government Administrative Council 1951b,c). Instead of all major expenditures being undertaken directly by the central government under unified management, a policy of "centralized leadership and multilevel responsibility" (*t'ung-i ling-tao, fen-chi fu-tse*) was begun. This reform, which was undertaken primarily to facilitate a doubling in the level of total government expenditures, established a more formal three-level system of budgetary administration, introduced the principle of revenue sharing, and provided increased incentives for local government collection of central government revenues (Government Administrative Council 1951b; Editorial 1951b).

The new policy established three levels of independent budgetary administration – the central government, large administrative regions, and the provinces. Designation of a level of government as a level of budgetary administration was marked by several features. Most important, it was usually followed by the creation of a local planning organization that was responsible for compiling the local economic plan. In terms of budgetary administration, it meant that the lower level of government was no longer primarily an agent of revenue collection. Rather than turning over its revenues to the next highest level, and having its programs financed entirely by appropriations from above, the subordinate level retained some of these revenues to finance its local economic-plan activities. If retained revenues were insufficient, additional subsidies were provided to finance expenditures at the lower level.

Independent levels of budgetary administration also established their own budgetary reserves to meet unanticipated expenditures or shortfalls of revenues. Prior to the establishment of these funds, unanticipated expenditure needs could only be financed by appealing to higher levels for additional funds. Although the size of budgetary reserves was controlled from above, these reserves gave local governments some additional flexibility in fulfilling their plan and budgetary targets.

After 1954, independent budgetary units also established their own "circulating funds" (*chou-chuan chin*) (Government Administrative Council 1953). These were specially earmarked funds retained to compensate for the lag between revenues and required expenditures. Circulating funds used to finance the shortfalls in the early part of the year were replenished toward the end of the year, when agricultural taxes and other important enterprise revenues became available.

The establishment of successively lower levels of government as units of budgetary and economic planning was closely linked to reforms in the tax system. Extension of budgetary administration was accompanied by a substantial reduction in the number and size of locally collected surtaxes. The incorporation of these surtaxes into the regular tax structure reduced extrabudgetary funds. Because the center administered regular taxes more closely than surtaxes, these tax reforms further enhanced Peking's fiscal powers. When locally collected extrabudgetary surcharges were eliminated, regular revenue sources were assigned to finance the expenditures of these lower levels of government administration.

In addition to the establishment of large administrative regions and provinces as levels of budgetary administration, in 1951 the budgetary system at the municipal level was also strengthened (Government Administrative Council 1951a; Editorial 1951a). Thirteen large municipalities directly administered by either the center or large administrative areas were established as independent budgetary units (Shabad, 24–6). Instead of having all their expenditures financed by direct appropriations from above, they were assigned revenues that had previously gone to higher levels. These included property, deed, and slaughter taxes, and revenues from municipally managed enterprises. Coincident with the assignment of these municipal revenues, other important surtaxes (such as those on slaughter, business, and entertainment taxes) were incorporated into the basic tax structure (Li Cha, 259). Thus budgetary revenues were increased and revenues outside the control of the budget were reduced.

At this time, counties (*hsien*) were not yet a level of budgetary or economic planning. *Hsien* expenditures for government administration, public security, education, cadre training, and other programs were financed directly from provincial budgets. The expenditures of special districts (*ch'uan-ch'ü*), the administrative level between the province and the county, were also financed directly from provincial budgets. This county and special-district financing took the form of special provincial appropriations rather than the assignment of specific revenue sources.

To finance these expanded provincial-level expenditures, in 1951 Peking also introduced a system of revenue sharing. That is, rather

Table 2.2. *Sources of budgetary revenue (percent)*

	1950	1953	1954	1957	1959
Agricultural tax	29	12	12	10	6
Industrial and commercial taxes[a]	35	38	34	36	29
Enterprise profits	13	35	38	46	62

[a] Includes the industrial–commercial business tax, the industrial–commercial income tax,
the commodity tax, and beginning in 1953 the commodity circulation tax.
Source: Ecklund, 20.

than enlarging the scope of purely local revenues, the center supplemented the system of block grants with a system of central–provincial revenue sharing. An understanding of this system of revenue sharing is facilitated by a familiarity with the sources of government revenue.

There are two major sources of government revenues: taxes and enterprise profits. Major taxes include agricultural, industrial and commercial, and commodity taxes. In addition, there are a number of less-important revenues, such as the salt tax, customs taxes, and miscellaneous local taxes (Government Administrative Council 1950b). The other major source of government revenues is enterprise profits. Although they are usually referred to simply as "profits," they actually include depreciation funds, revenues from the sale of fixed assets, and returns to the state of excess working capital, as well as profits (Ko Chih-ta 1957b, 75; Feng Li-t'ien, 32). The government also receives income from the sale of domestic bonds (during the 1950s) and from domestic insurance operations. Finally, proceeds from foreign loans and credits are treated as current government revenue.

The relative importance of various revenue sources has changed substantially since 1950. Initially, agricultural taxes were the single most important revenue source, financing nearly 30 percent of the state budget. As the industrial sector of the economy recovered from war damage and new industrial capacity was added, the share of revenues from industrial and commercial taxes and enterprise profits increased dramatically. Table 2.2 reflects these changes. Although industrial and commercial tax revenues grew rapidly, by 1954 enterprise profits were more important. Profits have remained the single most important revenue source since that time.

Under the system of revenue sharing introduced in 1951, provin-

cial governments received revenue from the center via two mechanisms. First, they shared in the proceeds of agricultural and industrial and commercial taxes in the form of "income shared by adjustment," (*t'iao-chi fen-ch'eng shou-ju*). The central government annually allocated a share of these revenues to each province to cover a
part of the shortfall between the province's expenditures and its local
income. Secondly, direct subsidies from the center continued to be
granted to cover the remaining shortfall.

The system of budgetary administration introduced in 1951 was a
substantial improvement over the earlier system, in which almost all
expenditures had been undertaken directly by the central government. It facilitated a substantial expansion of government expenditures and initiated a system of revenue sharing that provided substantially enhanced incentives for local revenue-collection efforts.
Under the old system of block grants, there had been little direct
incentive to fulfill targets for revenues that were transferred in their
entirety to the central government treasury. These incentives were
particularly important because the agricultural and industrial and
commercial taxes were the source of almost two-thirds of government
revenue at this time.

However, there remained a number of shortcomings in the system.
Most important from the point of view of the center, the redistributive powers of the fiscal system did not extend below the *hsien* level.
That is, although the 1951 reform led to the incorporation of county
and special-district revenues and expenditures within the state budget, *hsiang* (township) revenues and expenditures remained outside
the scope of the national budget. *Hsiang* services included rural primary school education, cultural and health programs, and limited
construction and repair projects. These activities were financed entirely from surcharges and special fees that were closely tied to the
level of local agricultural output.[5] Because *hsiang* expenditures were
not incorporated into the *hsien* budget, there was no mechanism for
redistributing resources below the *hsien* level.

Secondly, provincial governments objected to several features of
the new system. For example, surpluses arising from underfulfill-
ment of expenditure targets or overfulfillment of revenue targets had
to be remitted to the central government at the end of the year. This
system of remission was called "in one slice at the end of the year"
(*nien-chung i-tao k'an*) (Li Min-li, 43; Ko Chih-ta 1957a, 38). Provincial governments wanted to have unrestricted use of their surpluses

to finance increased expenditures in the following fiscal year (Hsü Fei-ch'ing 1957, 3).

For the central government, the issue was more complex (Jung Tzu-ho 1957). It was interested not only in controlling the volume and composition of local expenditures but also in providing maximum incentives for economies in local expenditures. Furthermore, following standard Soviet practice, the banking system's provision of credit relied partly on the mobilization of surplus budgetary funds from all levels of government (Hsiao, 138–43). In the early 1950s, the People's Bank was allowed to utilize the government budgetary surplus as a source of credit funds. Because revenues exceeded government expenditures during this period, the bank used the surplus that accumulated during the year to implement its credit plan. At the end of the year, although the government budget listed a surplus, these funds had in fact already been loaned through the bank. Although this surplus was listed as a source of budgetary revenue for the following fiscal year, expenditure plans did not require the utilization of these funds(Ko Chih-ta 1957b, 144; Feng Li-t'ien, 32). The cumulative surplus from the 1950–4 period was largely immobilized in 1955 as part of a general alignment of the budget and the State Bank (Hsiao, 146).

Beginning in 1955, a more formal mechanism for coordination of the budget and the bank was instituted – the credit fund. Each year's budget included a specific appropriation to the State Bank as a credit fund. This source of funds was then formally supplemented at the end of the year with the addition of the realized budgetary surpluses of the central government and, initially, the provinces as well (Hsiao, 147–50).

Thus, allowing provincial governments to retain their surpluses and spend them for their own purposes would have reduced the deposits of the budget in the State Bank. The State Bank would then have had to expand the money supply further, either through the creation of new deposits or the issuance of more currency. As a part of its antiinflationary program, the central government minimized these additions to the money supply by mobilizing the surplus revenues of all local governments.

However, the policy of remission encouraged year-end fiscal extravagance (Ko Chih-ta 1957b, 154–5). Because provincial governments had to remit surpluses, invariably there was a year-end rush to spend funds that had been authorized but not yet actually spent.

This situation could arise, for example, if temporary physical short-ages due to materials-distribution problems caused construction projects to fall behind schedule. Although these projects would be given additional funding in the next fiscal year, local leaders felt that a large carry-over of unfinished projects would reduce their allocation for new projects. As a result, they always attempted to complete planned projects and exhaust authorized funds. This sys-tem not only failed to provide incentives for local governments to reduce costs but, in addition, the rush to complete projects invaria-bly had an unfavorable effect on the quality of work completed (Hu Tzu-ming).

Beyond this incentive problem, the provinces felt that the reve-nue-sharing provisions of the new system were inadequate. First, provincial governments objected to Peking's annual determination of income shared by adjustment and subsidies. Provincial govern-ments wanted to reduce their dependence on these subsidies by receiving a sufficiently large, fixed share of important revenues. Secondly, although the First Five-Year Plan concentrated most pro-jects under the direct management of the central government, it also called for increased expenditures on local industry, transporta-tion, commerce, and education and social programs (Government of the PRC 1956a, 215–32). Beginning in 1953, provincial-level plan-ning commissions were established to compile the plans covering these local activities. These considerations suggested the need to introduce a further degree of decentralization of economic and fiscal planning, particularly to provide increased revenues to finance local programs. A series of additional reforms were thus undertaken in 1953 and 1954.

Establishment of hsien budgetary and planning administration

In 1953, the scope of the national budget was substantially broad-ened when the *hsien* was established as a level of budgetary and economic planning (Government Administrative Council 1952; Ko Chih-ta 1957b, 35; Chou Chung-fu, 19). The three-tiered hierarchy of center, large adminstrative region, and province was, in effect, re-placed by center, province, and county. Following this reform, most *hsiang* expenditures were incorporated into *hsien* budgets. That is, although the sub-*hsien* level was not established as a unit of inde-pendent budgetary administration, all regular *hsiang* expenditures became part of the *hsien* budget. These included administrative expenditures, cadre living allowances, teachers' salaries, and other *hsiang* school expenses.

To finance its own expenditures and those of its subordinate *hsiang*, *hsien* revenues were expanded to encompass sources previously assigned to the provincial and municipal levels. These included business, slaughter, property, and deed taxes; special consumption and etiquette fees; license fees; and revenues of *hsien*-managed enterprises. If these revenues were insufficient to finance *hsien* expenditures, provinces assigned shares of the industrial and commercial business taxes as *hsien* revenue.

This change meant that for the first time the central government had the means to effect redistribution as low as the *hsiang* level. Expenditures for local education, government administration, and other programs were no longer financed from sources that were entirely a function of the level of development in each *hsiang*. Instead, they were underwritten by the budget of the *hsien* and, in turn, *hsien* revenues were broadened to finance these new expenditures. Provinces were expected to distribute revenues among *hsien* to enable them, in turn, to redistribute revenues among their subordinate *hsiang* (Government Administrative Council 1952).

In addition to regular *hsiang* expenditures, which were underwritten by the state budget, *hsiang* continued to collect agricultural surtaxes to finance additional extrabudgetary expenditures (Government Administrative Council 1952; Ko Chih-ta 1957b, 35). These programs, which were not included within the scope of the *hsien* economic plan, included public works such as small-scale water conservation projects and the repair of roads, public schools, and government buildings. Although these expenditures had to be approved by the *hsien*, the surtax gave *hsiang* governments flexibility in arranging expenditures for purely local purposes. The *hsiang*-level agricultural surtax was, however, reduced from its previous rate of 15 percent to a maximum of 7 percent.

Just as in 1951, when large municipalities were established as a level of budgetary administration, the development of *hsien* financial management was accompanied by a reduction of extrabudgetary revenue sources. Most important was the reduction in the *hsiang* agricultural surtax. Locally collected surcharges on industrial and commercial taxes and the property tax were also reduced. They were partly merged into the regular tax structure by upward adjustment of the basic rates. Thus the volume of revenues collected was not reduced, but the proportion entering the budget was increased.

This adjustment of subprovincial finance had an important expansionary effect on national revenues. The extension of budgetary administration to the *hsien* level and the accompanying modifications of the tax structure contributed to an increase in government revenues that was not matched again in the First Five-Year Plan period.[6]

In addition to these changes in subprovincial fiscal administration, in 1953 large administrative regions lost the independent budgetary administrative status they had enjoyed during 1951–2 (Government Administrative Council 1952). Beginning in 1953, large administrative regions were treated as a component of the central government budget, a position held by other central government units such as industrial ministries. This loss of status meant that the regions no longer had any regular revenues but were financed entirely by regular appropriations from the center's budget. Revenues previously shared between regions and provinces were now assigned entirely to the latter.

Peking achieved' several major objectives through the development of municipal and subsequently county-level fiscal and plan administration. Most important, the establishment of budgetary administration as low as the *hsien* level and the incorporation of *hsiang* expenditures into the *hsien* budget gave the center the power to effect substantial redistribution at the lowest level of government administration. Secondly, the downward extension of budgetary control was accompanied by the merger of many local surcharges into the regular tax structure. This expanded the revenues under the control of state budgetary administration. Finally, the establishment of *hsien*-level budgetary and planning administration facilitated the expansion of the role of local governments in the planning process that was envisaged in the First Five-Year Plan.

The 1954 reform

The establishment of provincial planning commissions in 1953 and the gradual organization of county-level planning commissions in 1953 and 1954 gave rise to substantially increased local-expenditure requirements. In order to finance these expenditures, Peking initiated another major fiscal reform in 1954 (Government Administrative Council 1953; Lin Yün, 40). The most important change was the introduction of a broader system of revenue sharing between the central and provincial governments. All revenue sources were divided into four categories: "local fixed income" (*ti-fang ku-ting shou-ju*); "central government fixed income" (*chung-yang ku-ting shou-ju*); "income shared at a fixed rate" (*ku-ting pi-li fen-ch'eng shou-ju*); and "central government income shared by adjustment" (*chung-yang t'iao-chi fen-ch'eng shou-ju*).

Under the new system, provinces where expenditures regularly exceeded local fixed income were given fixed shares of the agricultural and industrial and commercial taxes – the two revenue sources in the new category of income shared at a fixed rate. These revenues were to be shared at this fixed rate for a period of several years. The commodity tax and the new commodity circulation tax replaced the agricultural and industrial and commercial taxes in the category of adjustment revenue. As in the past, the rates at which these latter revenues were shared were determined annually. As a result of these changes, the revenues that provinces had potential access to, either through sharing at a fixed rate or by adjustment, increased to about 50 percent of total government revenues.[7]

In addition to the expansion of provincial revenue sources, the 1954 reform contained several other important concessions to provincial interests. Most important, provincial governments were allowed to retain their surpluses for use in the following fiscal year. This was to placate local objections to the annual remission of surpluses to the center. The 1954 reform also introduced special concessions in autonomous areas. These regions received all revenues in both the adjustment and shared categories as local fixed income. They were also to receive additional direct subsidies to cover any remaining shortfall between approved expenditures and local revenues.

Although these reforms facilitated the expansion of the role of local economic and budgetary planning, the center maintained a relatively high degree of control by continuing to limit provincial financial authority. For example, although the reform introduced the concept of permanent revenue sharing, revenues actually shared on a permanent basis were limited. Further, the rates of sharing were set so that shared and adjustment revenues together would only cover 60 to 80 percent of total provincial expenditures (Government Administrative Council 1953, 82). Consequently, even though these revenue categories included a substantial portion of total national revenues, provinces continued to depend on central government subsidies to finance a significant portion of their outlays. The center, through its control of these subsidies and the sharing rates for other revenues, still determined the overall level and rate of expenditure increase in each province.

The phrase "local fixed income" seemed to imply that provincial governments would have full discretionary control over these funds. But total provincial expenditures continued to be controlled by the center; when these amounts were less than local fixed income, provincial governments were compelled to remit a portion of these nominally "local fixed income" sources. For example, Shanghai, unlike most other provincial-level governments, was not allowed to retain any of the funds in either the adjustment or shared categories (Sung Chi-wen). All the income from industrial and commercial, agricultural, and commodity taxes was remitted to the central government. Of the remaining revenue sources, all of which were nominally "local fixed income," Shanghai still had to remit 5 percent.

Furthermore, because surpluses had to be used to finance uncompleted projects or as part of budgetary reserves in the following year, the 1954 reform did not allow provinces to increase their expenditures beyond those approved by the central government. The use of surpluses was limited to programs that the center previously had included in approved provincial expenditures and financed from shared revenues. By allowing provinces to finance some of these expenditures from their surpluses, the center reduced shared revenues and used these as a source of funds for increased bank credits.

Because of these restrictions, it was not long before provincial officials began to complain again about overcentralization of the fiscal system (Ch'en Hsüeh, 12; Heng K'ai, 8). In particular, provincial officials renewed their objections to the center's treatment of their surpluses. One source reports that, after the 1954 reform, "the local comrades aptly remarked 'they [surpluses] can be looked at but cannot be enjoyed; in the end they will go to the central government' " (Lin Yün, 37). The name of the new method for dealing with surpluses, "limited use, periodic use, and inclusion in the [provincial] budget in place of an appropriation" (*hsien-chi shih-yung, fenchi shih-yung, lieh-ju yü -suan ti-ch'ung po-k'uan*), reflected the true nature of the reformed system (Ko Chih-ta 1957a; Li Min-li, 43).

Summary

The evolution of the structure of economic planning and budgetary administration during the first two to three years of the First Five-

Table 2.3. *County and municipal expenditures (as a percent of provincial expenditures)*

Province	Year	Percent
Heilungkiang[a]	1957	47
Kirin[b]	1956	52
Hopei[c]	1957	44
Kiangsi[d]	1957	62
Kwangsi[e]	1957	58
Kwangtung[f]	1954	70
Kweichow[g]	1956	46
	1957	51
Szechuan[h]	1957	72

Note: Percentages, except for Kwangtung and Kweichow (1956), are calculated on the basis of planned expenditures.
Sources: [a]Yang I-ch'en. [b]Wang Huan-ju 1956. [c]Hu K'ai-ming 1957. [d]Hsü Kuang-yüan 1957. [e]Tung Ching-chai. [f]Chi Chin-chang 1955. [g]Hsü Chien-sheng 1957. [h]Chang Hu-ch'en 1957.

Year Plan led to a substantial decentralization of economic planning authority. Following the formation of provincial economic commissions in 1953, the volume of provincial expenditures grew rapidly, almost doubling between 1952 and 1957. By 1955 over 1,400 counties had established economic planning commissions that were taking an increasing role in local plan coordination (Chou Chung-fu, 19). This increased role was reflected most clearly in the growing importance of county-level expenditures. As shown in Table 2.3, by the end of the First Five-Year Plan period municipal- and county-level expenditures usually accounted for more than half of all expenditures in the consolidated provincial budget.

Although provincial- and subprovincial-level expenditures were increasing rapidly, this growth was both constrained within a relatively narrow scope and subject to considerable central influence. Most important, the evolution of the system of economic and financial planning had still not provided a mechanism for coordinating all economic activities within each region. That is, the scope of local planning and the level of expenditures had grown to accommodate the increased emphasis on the provision of social services and a modest growth of local industry, but there was still no mechanism to coordinate the vertical and horizontal components of the plan at the local level. Indeed, in some ways the expansion of the importance of the vertical hierarchical dimension of the planning process had caused increased economic inefficiency. These constraints on local economic planning are most easily understood by examining the distribution of expenditures among levels of government and the system of central control of the composition of local expenditures.

Expenditures

Like government revenues, expenditures at all levels are arranged in a unified structure of accounts. The major expenditure categories are economic construction; culture, education, public health, and welfare; national defense; and government administration (Liu Hsi-shu 1952, 14; Ko Chih-ta 1957b, 91). Economic construction expenditures include funds for fixed investment and for increases in working capital in industry and construction, agriculture, forestry and water conservancy, transport and communications, and urban public utilities. Social expenditures include a broad range of programs. The most important are education, public health, and culture, but this category also encompasses expenditures for government and military pensions, welfare, publishing and broadcasting, cadre training, and scientific research.

National defense expenditures include both operational expenditures for the three branches of the People's Liberation Army and defense construction outlays (Ko Chih-ta 1957b, 129). Some important defense-related expenditures do not fall into the defense expenditure category. Investment in plants producing military equipment appears to be included in economic construction expenditures. Military pensions and scientific research expenditures of nonmilitary research institutes whose work focuses on defense-related projects are also excluded from the defense expenditure category. In addition, expenditures associated with the militia and military conscription are financed from government administration expenditures or the category "other expenditures" (Ministry of Finance 1955b, 44, 67). Expenditures for military demobilization are included with social expenditures (Ko Chih-ta 1957b, 46). Expenditures for military recreational facilities and military athletic activities are carried in the national budget in the physical culture subcategory of social expenditures (Ministry of Finance 1955b, 61). Expenditures for medical treatment of active duty and retired military personnel are probably included in the budget under health expenditures, and relief for

Table 2.4. *Distribution of state budgetary expenditures, 1950 through mid-1956 (percent)*

Category	Central	Local
Economic construction	83.8	16.2
Culture, education, and health	28.2	71.8
National defense	100	0
Administration	20.1	79.9
Credits and loan repayments	100	0
Other	76.7	23.3

Note: Data are based on final accounts.
Source: Ko Chih-ta 1957b, 38.

retired military personnel and their dependents is incorporated into social relief expenditures (Ko Chih-ta 1957b, 120).

Government administrative expenditures include salaries and administrative costs of government organs, including public-security, judicial, and prosecutorial organs, as well as subsidies to People's Democratic Parties and other people's organizations. Expenditures of the Chinese Communist Party are also financed under this category (Ko Chih-ta 1957b, 126).

Distribution of expenditures: central –provincial level
The principle governing the division of these expenditures among different governmental levels is that programs generally are both managed and financed from the same level (Wang Ching-chi, 28). Thus expenditures of enterprises and educational institutions managed by central ministries are included in the central government's economic plan and are incorporated into the budget of the central government. Similarly, programs incorporated into provincial economic plans are financed through provincial budgets. Thus, the composition of expenditures at each governmental level reflects the character of the programs administered at that level. Some expenditures, such as national defense and the repayment of foreign loans and credits, fall entirely in the central government budget. Economic construction expenditures are financed primarily from the center, whereas social programs and government administration are primarily locally financed.

These differences are reflected in Table 2.4. This table shows the distribution of aggregate national expenditures in various categories and by level of government during the period January 1950 through

Table 2.5. *Distribution of state budgetary expenditures, 1955, 1956, and 1957 (percent)*

Category	1955[a]		1956[b]		1957[c]	
	Central	Local	Central	Local	Central	Local
Economic construction	87.3	12.7	79.3	20.7	78.2	21.8
Culture, education, and health	25.8	74.2	30.4	69.6	26.7	73.3
National defense	100	0	100	0	100	0
Administration	16.4	83.6	15.4	84.6	11.7	88.3
Credits and loan repayments	100	0	100	0	100	0
Other			30.3	69.7	34.2	65.8

Note: All percentages are calculated on the basis of final accounts.
Sources: [a]Li Hsien-nien 1956, 1, 3. [b]Li Hsien-nien 1957, 17, 23–4. [c]Li Hsien-nien 1958, 6–7, 9.

Table 2.6. *Distribution of state budgetary capital construction investment, 1955, 1956, and 1957 (percent)*

Year	Central	Local
1955 (actual)[a]	83	17
1956 (planned)[a]	81	19
1957 (actual)[b]	79	21

Sources: [a]Li Hsien-nien 1956, 7. [b]Li Hsien-nien 1958, 9.

June 1956. The table shows that the central government dominated expenditures for economic construction, defense, and credit and loan repayments, while local governments dominated expenditures for social programs and government administration.

The increasing importance of economic planning at the provincial and local level is, however, reflected in an annual breakdown of the distribution of expenditures. This trend is shown in Table 2.5, which highlights in particular the increased local share of expenditures for economic construction in the last two years of the First Five-Year Plan period.

In spite of this increased local share of expenditures for economic construction, Peking's direct control of most capital investment meant that the center continued to dominate economic construction expenditures. Because investment expenditure was concentrated in industry, construction, and transportation and communications, all of which are encompassed in economic construction, the central government's share of these expenditures was usually 80 to 85 percent. Table 2.6, showing the division of capital investment expenditures between the central and provincial governments for the years 1955 through 1957, reveals that despite a slight rise in the local share, the center continued to manage directly over three-fourths of capital investment.

Not only was the volume of local investment small, other local economic construction expenditures were also limited. They were concentrated primarily in small-scale local industry, municipal construction, agriculture, water conservancy, and forestry. Because these programs were assigned a relatively low priority in the First Five-Year Plan, local spending on economic construction was small as a percent of total economic construction expenditure. On the other hand, central financing of almost all expenditures for enterprises of the Ministries of Metallurgy, Chemicals, Machine Building, Fuels, Electric Power, Oil, Geology, etc., assured central government domination of economic construction (Ministry of Finance 1955b, 46–7).

In contrast with economic construction, the scope of central government social and education activities was narrower. It was limited primarily to financing outlays for the National Academy of Sciences and its associated research institutes, centrally administered universities and national minority academies, international student exchange programs, the New China News Agency, the People's Publishing House, and the like (Ko Chih-ta 1957b, 46). The vast majority of social expenditures were for education and health. Because these services were provided primarily at local levels, 70 to 75 percent of social expenditures were financed from subnational budgets. Similarly, because most of the bureaucracy was concentrated at subnational levels, 80 to 85 percent of government administrative expenditures were financed through provincial and subprovincial budgets.

Consequently, the structure of expenditures at different levels varied widely. Table 2.7 shows the composition of national, central government, and aggregate provincial expenditures for 1956 and 1957. This table demonstrates the degree to which central government expenditures were dominated by economic construction and national defense. On the other hand, the proportion of social and administrative expenditures at the provincial level was far greater than at the central government level.

Distribution of expenditures: intraprovincial level
Data on the functional distribution of intraprovincial expenditures are quite limited. Although provincial fiscal reports sometimes give

Table 2.7. *The structure of government spending by level, 1956 and 1957 (percent)*

Category	Total 1956[a]	Total 1957[b]	Central 1956[a]	Central 1957[b]	Provincial 1956[a]	Provincial 1957[b]
Economic construction	52	49	58	54	37	36
Culture, education, and health	15	16	6	6	36	39
National defense	20	18	28	26	0	0
Administration	9	8	2	1	25	23
Credit and loan repayments	2	4	3	6	0	0
Foreign aid	1		2		0	
Appropriations for increase in bank credit	0	5	0	7	0	0
Other	1	1	0	0	1	1

Note: Columns may not add to 100 because of rounding. All percentages are calculated on the basis of final accounts.
Sources: [a]Li Hsien-nien 1957, 17, 23–4. [b]Li Hsien-nien 1958, 6–7, 9.

Table 2.8a. *The structure of provincial expenditures, Kiangsi, 1957 (percent)*

Category	Total	Provincial government only	Subprovincial
Economic construction	35	67	14
Culture, education, and health	40	23	50
Administration	25	9	35
Other	1	1	1
Total	100	100	100
Percent of total spending at each level	100	38	62

Source: Hsü Kuang-yüan 1957.

Table 2.8b. *The structure of provincial expenditures, Kwangsi, 1957 (percent)*

Category	Total	Provincial government only	Subprovincial
Economic construction	34	51	21
Culture, education, and health	42	28	52
Administration	22	16	27
Other	1	1	0
Total	100	100	100
Percent of total spending at each level	100	42	58

Source: Tung Ching-chai.

the distribution of total expenditures between the provincial government itself and subprovincial governments, this is usually done on an aggregate rather than a functional basis. Exceptions are Kiangsi and Kwangsi, where it is possible to distinguish the structure of provincial from subprovincial expenditures for 1957. Tables 2.8a and 2.8b show the composition of aggregate provincial expenditures, provincial government expenditures alone, and aggregate subprovincial expenditures for these two provinces.

Tables 2.8a and 2.8b reveal two interesting points. First, expenditures of subprovincial governments sometimes surpass those of provincial governments. This is true not only in Kiangsi and Kwangsi, but, as was shown in Table 2.3, in other provinces as well. Furthermore, this concentration of spending at the subprovincial level is not limited to the end of the First Five-Year Plan period – the year shown in the table. As early as 1954, for example, *hsien* and *hsien*-level municipalities accounted for 70 percent of Kwangtung's total expenditures (Chi Chin-chang 1955).

Secondly, provincial spending was concentrated on economic construction whereas subprovincial expenditures were primarily for social programs and government administration. In other words, aggregate provincial expenditures are heavily weighted toward administrative and social expenditures because these expenditures predominate at subprovincial levels of government.

Central government expenditure controls

The differing structure of central and provincial expenditures, shown in Table 2.7, reflects differences in the scope of economic planning at different levels rather than the expenditure preferences of different levels of government. The degree of central control of local expenditures is evident both in the structure of central–provincial revenue-sharing rates and in the center's system for controlling the composition of local expenditures.

Control of aggregate provincial expenditures

As stated above, expenditures at each level of government are determined by that level's economic plan, not by the volume of revenues that are actually collected within the region. Thus, the first step in the planning and budgetary process at the provincial level is the

Table 2.9. *Central-provincial revenue-sharing rates, 1956 and 1957 (percent)*

Province	1956	1957
Northeast		
Heilungkiang[e]	−32.7	−48.3[a]
North		
Hopei[d,f]	−5.1	−21.7
Shantung[g]	−59.2	−51.6
Shansi[h]	−11.9	−10.8
Honan[i]	−40.2	−35.1
Inner Mongolia[j]	0	−11.5
East		
Kiangsu[k]	−63.4	−49.2
Anhui[l]	−10.5	−17.6
Chekiang[m]	−61.1	−55.0
Central		
Hupei[n]	−35.5	−41.1[a]
Hunan[o]	−41.0	−39.4
Kiangsi[p]	−34.0	−29.9
South		
Kwangtung[q]	−59.6	−56.3
Kwangsi[r]	−18.5	+8.6
Southwest		
Szechuan[s]	−62.5	−50.8[a]
Kweichow[t]	−30.3	−22.7
Yünnan[u]	−18.7	0[a]
Tibet[v]	+70 to 80[c]	—
Northwest		
Shensi[w]	−23.5	−23.4[a]
Kansu[x]	+11.0[b]	—
Tsinghai[y]	+61.5	+62.8
Sinkiang[z]	+5.2	+7.2

Note: Negative numbers show provincial net remittances to the center as a percentage of total revenues collected by the provinces. Positive numbers show net subsidies from the central government as a percentage of total provincial expenditure. All numbers are calculated on the basis of final accounts except as noted. Financial accounts are also available for Liaoning, Kirin, Peking, Tientsin, and Shanghai for this period. However, because these areas shared in fewer revenue sources with the central government, their remission rates are not comparable with those given above.

[a] 1957 final accounts are not available for these provinces. Number shown is calculated on the basis of 1957 budgetary figures.

[b] Value for Kansu is for the period 1953–7. Annual breakdown is not available.

[c] Value for Tibet is for the period 1952–5. Annual breakdown and values for 1956 and 1957 are not available.

[d] Excluding Tientsin.

center's determination of the level of expenditures permitted in each province. This determination is based on the outlays required to finance the centrally approved provincial economic development plan and to finance the approved levels of spending for local government administration and for social services. After estimating the total revenues that will be collected in each province, the center calculates a revenue remission rate for every province. These rates are set so that each province will be left with just enough revenue to finance the initially determined level of expenditure.

Because provincial fiscal capacity varies enormously and because provincial expenditure plans are centrally determined according to the priorities of a broadly conceived national plan rather than on the basis of the volume of revenues raised locally, revenue-sharing rates between the center and the provinces are far from uniform. The central government's desire to reduce the degree of interprovincial disparity in productive capacity and in the provision of social services is reflected in the relatively low rates of remission that prevail in most poorer provinces. On the other hand, more developed provinces, with revenues far in excess of centrally approved expenditures, are usually required to remit large amounts of revenue to the central government. This determination of remissions and subsidies is called the "adjustments of budgets" (*yü-suan t'iao-chi*). The size of the flows involved in this adjustment process are reported in provincial fiscal reports under the headings of "subsidy income from higher levels" (*shang-chi pu-chu shou-ju*) and "income remitted to higher levels" (*shang-chieh chih-chu*) (Ministry of Finance 1954, 70, 76).

Table 2.9 shows these revenue-sharing rates for 22 provinces for 1956 and 1957. Remittance rates ranged from roughly −60 to +80 percent. That is, some provinces relinquished over half the revenues they collected, whereas others retained all the revenues they collected and, in addition, received subsidies of up to 80 percent of their total expenditures.

Table 2.9. (*cont.*)

Sources: [e]Yang I-ch'en. [f]Hu K'ai-ming 1957, 1958. [g]Yüan Tzu-yang; Chang Chu-sheng. [h]Wu Kuang-t'ang 1957, 1958. [i]Ch'i Wen-chien 1957, 1959. [j]Wang I-lun 1957a; Wang Tsai-t'ien. [k]Ch'en Shu-t'ung 1957, 1958. [l]Chang Huo 1957, 1958. [m]Jen I-li; Li Wen-hao. [n]An Tung-t'ai. [o]Chang Po-shen 1957, 1958. [p]Hsü Kuang-yüan 1957, 1958. [q]Chang Yung-li. [r]Tung Ching-chai; Kuo Ch'eng. [s]Chang Hu-ch'en 1957. [t]Hsü Chien-sheng 1957, 1958. [u]Wu Tso-min 1957. [v]Ko Chih-ta 1956b, 76–7. [w]Chang I-ch'en. [x]Kansu Finance Department, 199. [y]Sun Chün-i 1957, 1958. [z]Liu Tzu-mo 1957, 1959.

A comparison of Tables 2.9 and 1.1 shows that, in general, revenue-sharing rates were inversely related to the level of provincial
industrial development. More industrialized provinces, such as Heilungkiang, Chekiang, Kiangsu, Kwangtung, and Shantung, remitted
from 50 to 60 percent of the revenues they collected. Their own
expenditures were financed from the funds they retained. Less-developed provinces remitted a smaller proportion of their revenues.
The poorest provinces retained all their revenues and received net
subsidies as well. During the First Five-Year Plan period, Sinkiang,
Tsinghai, Tibet, and Kansu usually received such subsidies.

Remission rates are not, however, perfectly inversely correlated
with the extent of industrialization. First, differential revenue-sharing rates are only one policy instrument used to redistribute resources geographically. Most important, these rates do not reflect
the distribution of expenditures undertaken directly by the central
government ministries. Honan and Shensi, for example, as shown in
Table 2.9, remit substantial portions of their revenue to the center.
They are also the beneficiaries of extensive centrally managed investment projects, particularly in the municipalities of Loyang,
Chengchou, and Hsian. On the whole, these provinces appear to
have been net recipients of central aid even though they remitted
funds to the center through the revenue-sharing system. Secondly,
the goal of achieving a more balanced pattern of industrial output
was only one of a number of objectives of central government policy. The geographic distribution of investment resources was also
influenced by the location of natural resources, defense requirements, and, particularly in the short run, the adequacy of the transportation system and other types of infrastructure. In spite of these
qualifications, the revenue-sharing system does appear to have had
a strikingly redistributive effect during the First Five-Year Plan
period.

Control of local expenditures

The redistributive character of the budgetary and planning process
was not confined to the provincial level but actually extended to the
lowest level of government administration. The redistribution of resources within each province was carried out by a system of intraprovincial revenue sharing that replicated the central–provincial pattern. Indeed, as will be shown below, redistribution among prov-

inces was made possible only by considerable redistribution of revenue within provinces.

Documenting the magnitude of this intraprovincial redistribution and analyzing its significance over time is difficult because subprovincial financial data are relatively scarce. Just as provincial budgets are required to trace revenue flows between the center and the provinces, subprovincial budgets are required to trace redistribution within each province. Because holdings of municipal and *hsien* newspapers in the West are quite limited, only a few of these financial reports are available.

However, data from scattered municipal budget reports confirm that substantial redistribution was carried out within some provinces. Major municipalities, which were key sources of revenues, typically were required to remit a very high proportion of their revenues to their respective provincial governments. The precise rate for each municipality was set annually by the province. Where data are available, these rates exceed the rate of remission for the province to the central government. This meant, of course, that the financial burden of the remaining portion of each province was correspondingly reduced.

This pattern is shown in Table 2.10. Canton, the capital of Kwangtung, had to remit between 75 and 80 percent of the revenues it collected. This supplied the provincial government with 25 to 40 percent of its remissions to Peking. In Szechuan, Chungking's remission rate to the provincial government always exceeded the province's rate of remission to Peking. In absolute terms the municipality, with less than 3 percent of the province's population, provided from about one-fifth to one-half of the province's remittances to Peking. Finally, intraprovincial revenue sharing in Shensi and Shantung was even more redistributive. Hsian and Tsingtao each remitted a portion of their revenues that was more than twice as great as that for their respective province as a whole. Municipal remissions provided these provinces with more than three-fourths of the revenue they were required to send to Peking.

This system of revenue sharing among and within provinces is only the most obvious means of central control of the budgetary and planning process. In addition, the center also exercises a great deal of control over how funds retained by provinces are actually used. In turn, provincial governments heavily influence the composition of local government expenditures.

Table 2.10. *Provincial–municipal revenue sharing (absolute numbers in millions of yuan)*

Year	Canton 1. Remissions to Kwangtung	Canton % of total revenues remitted	Kwangtung 2. Remissions to central govt.	Kwangtung % of total revenues remitted	1 ÷ 2 (%)
1955[a]	155,432	74	650,085	66	24
1956[b]	239,404	76	604,639	60	40
1957[b]	231,965	75	594,690	56	39

Year	Chungking 1. Remissions to Szechuan	Chungking % of total revenues remitted	Szechuan 2. Remissions to central govt.	Szechuan % of total revenues remitted	1 ÷ 2 (%)
1956[c]	108,126	65	639,261	63	17
1957[c]	109,241	64	593,243	51	20
1958[d]	361,313	66	776,050	38	47
1959[e]	321,630	45	990,810	33	32

Table 2.10. (cont.)

Year	Hsian		Shensi		
	1. Remissions to Shensi	% of total revenues remitted	2. Remissions to central govt.	% of total revenues remitted	1 ÷ 2 (%)
1956[f]	68,029	57	77,060	23	88

	Tsingtao		Shantung		
	1. Remissions to Shantung	% of total revenues remitted	2. Remissions to central govt.	% of total revenues remitted	1 ÷ 2 (%)
1958[g]	616,280	83	814,762	40	76

Note: Numbers are from final accounts except for 1957.
Sources: [a]Yü Mei-ch'ing; Chi Chin-chang 1957. [b]Chu Kuang; Chi Chin-chang 1956. [c]Ch'en Ch'ou 1957; Chang Hu-ch'en 1957. [d]Tuan Ta-ming 1959; Chang Hu-ch'en 1959. [e]Tuan Ta-ming 1960; Chang Hu-ch'en 1960. [f]Liu Keng; Chang I-ch'en. [g]Sun Kang; Li Yü-ang.

Control of the composition of provincial and local expenditures

Each year, the central government promulgates a system of budgetary accounts for use by local governments (Ko Chih-ta 1957b, 148).
Although provincial governments have some freedom to arrange
their own expenditures within this system of accounts, the level of
expenditures allowed within certain categories must be approved by
the central government. Thus, an examination of the degree of
specificity of these centrally approved expenditure levels and the
authority of provincial governments to make adjustments among
these components during the fiscal year provides a broad measure of
the degree to which the central government sought to control the
composition of provincial expenditures. This measure, of course, remains very imprecise because little is known about the central–
provincial negotiating process that must have established these expenditure ceilings. However, judging by the debate that was summarized in Chapter 1, there is little doubt that provincial governments
believed that this system of expenditure controls was a major re-
straint on their own plan and budgetary authority.

Detailed accounting categories are available for 1950, 1951, 1952,
1955, 1956, and 1959 (Ministry of Finance 1950b, c; Liu Hsi-shu
1951, 1952; Ministry of Finance 1954, 1955b, 1959b). Over time,
these categories became increasingly disaggregated as the central
government sought to exert greater and greater control over the composition of local expenditures. My discussion will be based on the
accounting system for 1955, which was somewhat less detailed than
that used in 1956.

The central government established six major expenditure categories (*ta-lei*) for 1955. These, in turn, were broken down into a total of
31 appropriation categories (*k'uan*). Table 2.11 shows this breakdown. The *k'uan* shown in Table 2.11 were further subdivided into
expenditure items (*hsiang*). Finally, all expenditures were further
divided into 13 functional classifications (*mu*).

For example, the most important provincial expenditure category
was culture, education, public health, and welfare. The central government specified the aggregate expenditure permitted for the category as a whole, and further allocated these expenditures among the
nine appropriations numbered 13 through 21 in Table 2.11. In turn,
each appropriation was subdivided further into 2 to 16 items (*hsiang*).
In 1955, the accounts included 62 items for social expenditures alone.

Table 2.11. *Local budgetary accounts, 1955*

Category (ta-lei)	Appropriation (k'uan)
I. Economic construction	1. local industry
	2. construction and engineering
	3. agriculture and animal husbandry
	4. forestry
	5. water conservancy
	6. meteorology
	7. transportation
	8. telecommunications
	9. commerce
	10. municipal construction
	11. public–private joint enterprise
	12. other economic construction
II. Culture, education, and health	13. culture
	14. education
	15. cadre training
	16. physical culture
	17. broadcasting
	18. publishing
	19. public health
	20. pensions
	21. social relief
III. Administration	22. administration
	23. political affairs
	24. people's democratic parties and organizations supplements
	25. justice and prosecutor
	26. public security
IV. Other	27. other
	28. recovery of previous year's expenditures
V. Reserves	29. budgetary reserves
VI. Adjustments to various levels' budgets	30. remissions to higher levels
	31. expenditures to subsidize lower levels

Source: Ministry of Finance 1954, 71–6.

The number of items listed within each appropriation was primarily a function of the degree of heterogeneity of the activities carried out under the category. Relatively simple programs, for example cadre training, had only 2 expenditure items, whereas education and public health were subdivided into 16 and 14 categories, respectively. The expenditure items for education are shown in Table 2.12.

Table 2.12. *Local budgetary account for education, 1955 (items included in category II, appropriation 14, Table 2.11)*

1. higher education expenses
2. expenses for sending students abroad
3. other higher education expenses
4. higher-level teacher education expenses
5. minority academies expenses
6. middle-level teacher education expenses
7. middle-level vocational school expenses
8. middle school expenses
9. workers' and peasants' intensive schools expenses
10. primary school expenses
11. nurseries expenses
12. educational expenses for the blind, dumb, and deaf
13. middle and primary school teacher refresher course expenses
14. assistance to privately established schools
15. other educational expenses
16. expenses for illiteracy elimination

Source: Ministry of Finance 1954, 73–4.

Table 2.13. *Local budgetary accounts, functional divisions (*Mu*), 1955*

1. wages
2. wage supplements
3. cadre living expenses
4. worker and staff benefit expenses
5. business expenses
6. expenditures for purchase of fixed assets and equipment
7. scholarships
8. welfare
9. administration
10. capital construction investment
11. working capital
12. expenses to cover planned losses
13. other expenses

Source: Ministry of Finance 1954, 77.

Each expenditure item was further characterized by function. Major functional divisions (*mu*) were investment, working capital, wages, and funds for the purchase of fixed assets and equipment. The 13 functional classifications used in 1955 are shown in Table 2.13. Not every expenditure item included funds in all 13 divisions. For example, under most of the items for education shown in Table 2.12 only eight of the functional classifications were used.

This system of budgetary accounts placed substantial limitations on provincial fiscal authority. Most important, the central government specified the level of expenditures within each major expenditure category and also for each appropriation. This meant in 1955, for example, that each province's approved level of aggregate expenditures was further allocated among 31 separate categories. Thus in the compilation of its budget, the province's authority was limited to determining the allocation of expenditures among various items within each of these appropriations. For example, although the total volume of expenditures for education was established centrally, the province had the responsibility for allocating this total among the sixteen items shown in Table 2.12. After the detailed provincial budget had been approved at the center, the province had limited authority to make adjustments among budgetary account components during the fiscal year. They were unable, for example, to shift funds among various appropriations categories without advance approval from the central government. Some sources suggest that toward the end of the First Five-Year Plan even adjustments among various expenditure items also required central approval once the budget had been approved (Ko Chih-ta 1957b, 154). Furthermore, in addition to the control of expenditure appropriations, the center also imposed additional constraints in the form of ceilings on certain functional classifications, such as wages and capital construction, that were independent of the appropriation category.

Provincial governments, in turn, used the same system and similar restrictions to control the composition of the expenditures of subprovincial governments. Local governments arranged their own expenditures within the appropriations ceilings set by the province. Once their budgets had been approved, subprovincial governments had only to receive approval from the province to make changes among various programs. But provincial governments could not approve them without receiving permission from the center if the change affected a provincial appropriation ceiling. Thus, in effect, unless the province could make compensating changes in the budget of another subordinate municipality or county it was not able to grant requests for changes in a county's expenditures for any appropriation without going to the central government for authorization.

This system of disaggregated expenditure controls clearly reveals the high degree of central economic control exercised from Peking. It shows that Peking's control was not limited to the high-priority industrial sector, where its power was exercised primarily through direct vertical administration of investment programs and commodity distribution. The unified fiscal system allowed the center to control a broad range of social programs which, because of their heterogeneity and peculiarly local nature, were less amenable to direct physical control.

This highly centralized system of fiscal control of local expenditures was a source of continuing central–provincial friction. Provincial governments objected to the detailed control of the composition of their approved level of expenditures as well as to the limits placed on their ability to utilize surpluses. Even the adjustment of subprovincial expenditures during the fiscal year was a difficult undertaking, because it invariably affected aggregates at the provincial level that could not be changed without central approval.

The 1956 fiscal decentralization

In response to the complaints of local governments, in 1956 Peking announced a new fiscal reform. To allow greater local initiative and flexibility in arranging budgets to suit local conditions, the system of controlling every category and each appropriation (*fen-k'uan fen-hsiang t'iao-t'iao hsia-tao ti pan-fa*) was replaced with the system of "control of budgetary totals" (*yü-suan tsung-o ti k'ung-chih*). Under this system, the center only stipulated the total expenditures and total revenues for each province. Each province was given the authority to arrange its total expenditures among various appropriations categories to suit its particular needs and interests. Furthermore, during the fiscal year, if revenues exceeded the planned level or expenditures savings in particular categories were realized, these funds could be expended under provincial authority rather than being subject to central control in the next fiscal year.

There is no extensive discussion in the Chinese press and financial journals of the precise implementation of this reform. It was mentioned briefly by Li Hsien-nien in his report on the national 1956 budget. But there are no major directives that deal with the exact means of implementing the new system. Furthermore, in marked contrast with the later 1957 reforms that were widely discussed in provincial publications, there is little discussion of the implications of the new system at the provincial level.

However, a variety of sources indicate that in practice the reform had little initial effect (Lin Yün, 37, 40; Ch'en Hsüeh, 11–12; Ch'eng Chang, 16). The new regulations gave provinces the authority to draw up their own expenditure plans, but provincial budgets still had to be approved by the Ministry of Finance. Actually, in 1956 the ministry itself compiled detailed provincial budgets, just as in previous years. When provincial budgets were first announced, they specified only the approved expenditure ceilings for each province without the detailed categorical breakdowns used to derive the totals. But according to one source, provincial governments demanded to know how their expenditure totals had been determined. To oblige provincial governments, the Ministry of Finance provided the expenditure breakdown, just as they had in the past. Although these figures were nominally provided for "reference" (*ts'an-kao*) purposes, provincial governments continued to regard these disaggregated expenditure targets as obligatory (Li Ch'eng-jui 1957, 6).

In addition to the detailed budgetary figures provided by the Ministry of Finance, other central government departments sent down financial control targets through their own communications channels to various local departments. As a result, provincial governments apparently were unable to utilize effectively their new authority to arrange their own expenditures.

Summary

During the First Five-Year Plan, the central government had successfully exercised a far-reaching degree of control over the entire economy. The scope of the budget had progressively expanded to encompass revenues that had previously been expended outside the budgetary process. Although output per industrial worker had increased more than 50 percent, the central government's control of industrial-sector wages limited wage increases to 30 percent (20 percent in real terms). The growth of value added was channeled through the budgetary process to increased social services and economic development programs. The rate of capital formation grew dramatically from 10 percent of gross domestic output in 1952 to 18–20 percent during the latter years of the plan (Field, 22). This rapid increase in capital formation was largely channeled to the producer-goods sector of the economy and to backward regions. The producer-goods sector of the economy received 86 percent of all industrial investment although it was the source of only 43 percent of industrial output (Niu Chung-huang, 45; State Statistical Bureau 1960, 87). Backward inland regions, which were the source of only one-third of industrial output, received about half of all investment funds. Finally, provincial and local planning commissions and finance departments had been established to insure that the rapid growth of local expenditures was channeled to programs consistent with the unified national economic plan.

Although this system of planning and budgetary administration was successful in accelerating the rate of capital formation and allocating investment resources to priority sectors and regions, even after several reforms it remained a source of friction between the provinces and the center. The high degree of external control of provincial and local expenditures reduced local initiative and decision-making authority. Furthermore, the unified budgetary process was cumbersome and frequently meant that local budgets were not approved until long after the fiscal year had begun.

The initial stages of the budgetary process occurred at an annual fall national financial conference, which brought together officials of the Ministry of Finance and each of the provincial finance departments. Debate at this meeting between central and provincial officials is said to have focused on the aggregate expenditure level to be permitted in each province (Ko Chih-ta 1957a; Lin Yün, 35). Because the central government always assigned a combination of shared, adjustment, and subsidy revenues sufficient to cover this approved expenditure level, the specific sources for financing these expenditures, from the point of view of the provinces, were a secondary consideration. The name of the system, "taking expenditures to determine [provincial] revenues" (*i-chih, ting shou*), indicated that the crucial decision was the annual determination of expenditure levels (Lin Yün, 38).

Provincial and local governments were interested primarily in establishing an independent fiscal base that would provide them with regularly increasing revenues to finance local programs. Although in theory each province's portion of income shared at a fixed rate was not to be changed, in practice sharing rates were subject to annual adjustment (Ch'en Hsüeh, 12). Provincial officials complained about these adjustments for two reasons. First, they introduced an additional element of uncertainty into provincial revenue sources and made planning more difficult. Indeed, one provincial official charged that because of the center's annual redetermination of revenues and expenditures, there was "no way for local finance to play any role in comprehensive long-run local economic planning" (Heng K'ai, 8). Secondly, annual readjustment of sharing rates upset financial arrangements between the province and subprovincial levels of budgetary administration. A Kwangtung official specifically stated that readjustment of central–provincial sharing rates caused the provincial finance department many difficulties because it, in turn, was forced to make changes in the revenue-sharing arrangements it had established with subordinate municipalities and *hsien* (Heng K'ai, 8).

In short, both because sharing rates were set low and because in practice the rates were subject to adjustment, provincial governments did not have a stable fiscal base from which to finance regularly increasing expenditures.

Finally, the lengthy process of approving the unified budget resulted in delays that undermined the ability of the center to control efficiently the structure of local expenditures. Following the fall national financial conference that established provincial expenditure ceilings, the Ministry of Finance in cooperation with the State Planning Commission established the expenditure ceiling in each of the budgetary categories. After the detailed provincial expenditure budget was drawn up by the province, it was resubmitted to the ministry. The ministry had to coordinate the provincial budgets with those of 89 different central government authorities that together formed the unified national budget (Ko Chih-ta 1956a). The process of coordinating these vertical and horizontal plans and budgets was extremely time consuming. The national draft budget did not become the official budget until after it had been approved by the national legislative body, the People's Congress. Only after this national approval was each provincial budget in turn submitted to Provincial People's Congresses for approval, after which it became the official operational budget.

In summary, the piecemeal reforms introduced since 1951 failed to satisfy the demands of provincial officials for a restructuring of the fiscal system. However, consideration of further reforms continued. Particularly after Mao's speech, "On the Ten Major Relationships," there was a new, more open effort to find a solution to the long-standing problems of the fiscal system (Mao Tse-tung 1977). This culminated in the promulgation of the 1958 reforms – the subject of the next chapter.

3

The 1958 decentralization

This chapter examines the detailed provisions of the economic reform that was initiated in 1958 and offers specific hypotheses to test the degree to which the decentralization reduced the ability of the central government to carry out the interregional resource transfers that were so characteristic of the First Five-Year Plan period. The results of these tests and supporting analysis suggest that although provincial and local governments gained considerable administrative authority, the central government continued to exercise far-reaching control over the interregional and intersectoral allocation of resources. Although it has frequently been suggested that the decentralization represented a deliberate policy choice favoring efficiency and growth over equity, these tests, as well as qualitative evidence presented in this chapter, suggest that the fundamental commitment of the leadership to a path of relatively equitable development was not abandoned after the First Five-Year Plan.

Elements of the decentralization

The economic reform announced in 1957 expanded the system of revenue sharing, gave provincial governments greater authority to determine the composition of their expenditure budgets, and generally provided for increased local authority in the management of local economic affairs, including for the first time a role in the management of central government enterprises.

Revenue sharing

The heart of the reform was the provision that provinces would receive a large fixed portion of a substantially broadened revenue-sharing base. Because the revenue-sharing rates were to be fixed over a

five-year period, provinces for the first time would automatically receive a share of increased revenues that would accompany rising
industrial and agricultural output.[1] In effect, the old system in which
revenues retained by each province were determined by the level of
expenditures necessary to underwrite the centrally approved provincial economic plan and in which revenue-sharing rates were adjusted
annually (*yi-chih ting-shou, yi-nien yi-pien*) was partially replaced by
a system in which expenditures were determined by revenues and
revenue-sharing rates were fixed for five years (*yi-shou ting-chih,
wu-nien pu-pien*). This combination of fixed sharing rates and the
adoption of the philosophy that revenues would determine expenditures was enormously important because it meant that provinces
would no longer have to bargain with the center for annual expenditure increases. As revenues grew over time, provincial governments
would automatically receive a proportionate share of the increase.

Equally important, the revenue-sharing base was broadened, including for the first time the profits of central government enterprises. Twenty percent of the profits of enterprises transferred to
local management and of many enterprises remaining directly under
the center was assigned as provincial government revenue. This allowed provinces to share the most important single source of state
revenue.[2] The industrial and commercial and agricultural taxes were
shifted from "revenue shared at a fixed rate" to the category of "revenue shared by adjustment." The categorization of other revenues was
not changed from that established in earlier years.

Each province was assigned shared revenues to cover all its normal expenditures. Provinces whose local fixed income was insufficient automatically received 20 percent of enterprise profits as local
income. Provinces whose normal expenditures were not met by
these two sources combined were assigned a share of adjustment
revenues. Only if 100 percent retention of adjustment revenues was
insufficient to finance local expenditures would the center provide
direct subsidies. Thus, the new system was designed to finance most
provinces' normal expenditures from shared revenues and end provincial dependence on central subsidies.

Local expenditure authority

Local governments simultaneously were given increased authority
over the disposition of these growing local revenues. Most important,

the center reiterated the provision initially introduced in the 1956 fiscal reform. This allowed provincial governments to arrange the structure of their own expenditures within an overall expenditure ceiling imposed by Peking. The 1958 reform, by fixing revenue-sharing rates over a period of several years, in effect meant that this ceiling would automatically increase each year rather than being fixed by the center annually.

Secondly, the long-standing complaint that year-end provincial surpluses were treated as part of provincial income in the following year was also resolved in favor of provincial interests. Beginning with 1957, retained surpluses were no longer to be offset by a reduction in shared revenues or central subsidies. In addition, the use of surpluses was to be arranged by the provinces themselves instead of being stipulated by the center.

Finally, provincial governments' sources of extrabudgetary income were increased. The reform called for local retention and management outside the budget of the agricultural surtax, the municipal public utility surtax, and a 1 percent surtax on the industrial, commercial and commodity taxes. Although the agricultural surtax was already a source of extrabudgetary income for local governments, the public utilities surtax previously had been included in budgetary revenues. The other surcharges were also new because they had been abolished in earlier years. Local governments managed all these funds independent of central control.

These provisions of the decentralization represented concessions to provincial interests. Provincial governments wanted additional financial resources assigned to them on a more permanent basis to reduce their dependence on adjustment revenues and central subsidies and to facilitate local planning. In addition, they wanted freedom to utilize the surpluses they had accumulated either through overfulfillment of revenue quotas or economizing on expenditures.

These provisions for revenue sharing and for increased local fiscal authority, summarized above, have been widely noted in Western studies of the decentralization. The fiscal reform and the subsequent dramatic increase in the provincial share of total national expenditures, the devolution of most central government enterprises to local management, as well as other changes in the system of economic planning announced in 1957 and 1958 have been cited in many Western studies as marking the effective end of centralized economic planning in China. These studies advance the hypothesis that the direction of national economic development since 1957 has been determined through independently compiled provincial economic plans, rather than through a nationally integrated economic plan in which major spatial and sectoral allocation decisions reflect the preferences of the central political leadership.

However, I believe this view overlooks the limits that were placed on provincial and local governments by the decentralization. Just like earlier reforms, the 1958 decentralization provided a series of policy instruments through which the center could continue to control the overall level of expenditures of provincial governments. Although allowing some greater freedom for local governments to control the structure of their expenditures, the reform reflected an acute Chinese perception of the increased interregional inequality that would result if resource-allocation powers were devolved in a wholesale fashion. This concern was directly reflected in several reform provisions.

First, although the directive initially appears to have transferred important new revenues to provincial governments and removed restrictions on aggregate provincial expenditures, in fact, the center continued to restrict expenditures of more developed provinces to levels far below the revenues they collected. Secondly, although the directive seems to remove any remaining central controls over the composition of local expenditures, the basic mechanisms of central government control were only marginally modified by the formal decentralization measures. Finally, although most have argued that the decentralization had profoundly inegalitarian results, the new system had several provisions militating against this development.

Continued control of aggregate provincial expenditures.   Key features of the reform undercut the operational significance of the seemingly generous revenue-sharing provisions of the decentralization. The essential point of the decentralization in this respect was the definition of "normal expenditures" (*cheng-ch'ang chih-chu*) (State Council 1957c; Lin Yün (no. 10), 42). This was crucial because the normal expenditure base was used to calculate the sharing rates for taxes that were in the category of "adjustment revenues." The lower this base, the lower the provincial retention rates necessary to finance "normal expenditures."

Normal expenditures in each province were based on 1957 budgetary outlays for local economic construction; health, education, and

Table 3.1. *Provincial investment, 1955 and 1957 (millions of yuan)*

Year	Total budgetary investment (including central government)	Provincial budgetary investment		
		amount	as % of total investment	as % of total provincial expenditure[c]
1955	8,630[a]	1,500[a]	17	23
1957	11,905[b]	2,500[b]	21	28

Note: All data are based on final accounts.
Sources: [a]Li Hsien-nien 1956, 7. [b]Li Hsien-nien 1958, 9. [c]Calculated based on provincial expenditure data in Table 1.4.

welfare; and local government administration. Funds for capital construction, relief of natural calamities, and large-scale migration were specifically excluded. These programs were to be funded through special appropriations from Peking rather than from locally retained revenues.

The crucial exclusion was capital investment. As noted in Chapter 2, prior to 1958 investment was preponderantly centrally financed. Even so, provincially financed investment was not an insignificant portion of total provincial expenditures. Data on the division of budgetary investment between the central and provincial governments are given in Table 3.1. These data show that in 1955 and 1957 about one-fourth of total provincial expenditures consisted of capital investment. Because provincial investment was not included in the normal expenditure base, the revenue-sharing system established in 1958 did not put provincial finance on a fully independent basis.

In effect, because the sum of local, shared, and adjustment revenues covered only about three-fourths of their expenditures, the provinces' position had not improved significantly from the 1954–7 period, when these same categories of revenue covered 60 to 80 percent of their expenditures (Government Administrative Council 1953, 82). As in the past, most provinces still depended on Peking's subsidies to finance a substantial portion of their total expenditures. Because these subsidies were adjusted annually, provinces did not have an assured means of regularly increasing their total expenditures. Actually, as will be shown later in this chapter, the position of the provinces deteriorated because the decentralization of enterprise management increased their required expenditures.

Continued control of the composition of provincial expenditures. A key element of the 1958 reform was the provision authorizing provincial governments to arrange their own expenditure budgets. However, in practice the central government continued to influence the composition of provincial expenditures through a system of unified revenue and expenditure accounts. There was, however, some reduction in the degree of disaggregation of local expenditure targets that reduced the inflexibility of the pre-1958 system of budgetary control and reflected marginally increased local fiscal authority. For example, as discussed in Chapter 2, social expenditures in each province in 1955 were divided into nine appropriations (*k'uan*). In 1959 there were still nine divisions that were almost identical to those that had existed in 1955 and 1956. There was, however, some simplification and consolidation of accounting categories at lower levels of disaggregation. The appropriation for education was no longer divided into sixteen items as in 1955, but was instead broken down into only six categories. For example, the four higher education items (higher education expenses, expenses for sending students abroad, other higher education expenses, and expenses for minority academies) were consolidated into a single higher education expenditure item. Comparable consolidations were made within other appropriations. The number of functional expenditure divisions, the lowest level of disaggregation, was reduced from thirteen to six (Ministry of Finance 1959a, b).

On purely theoretical grounds one would, of course, predict that the use of more aggregated expenditure targets would enhance the autonomy of local governments (Montias). One might hypothesize that this enhanced autonomy would be reflected in greater variations among provinces in the pattern of educational expenditures, perhaps reflecting educational philosophies and priorities that differ across regions of China. This of course remains conjecture because provincial expenditure data are rarely published in fully disaggregated form.

Formally, however, the somewhat simplified system of budgetary accounts appears to have still imposed substantial constraints on the ability of local governments to arrange their own expenditures. Rather than allowing provincial governments to utilize their authority to arrange their own expenditure budgets within the limit imposed by the sum of their local and shared revenues, the central government continued to stipulate the composition of local expenditures and restrict the authority of provincial governments to make significant adjustments once these expenditure ceilings had been established. In 1959, expenditure ceilings were established for forty-seven appropriation (*k'uan*) items, compared with thirty-one in 1955. The increase in the number of categories was concentrated under the heading of economic construction. This facilitated control of the expenditures of industrial enterprises that had been transferred to local management. Prior to the decentralization, industrial enterprise expenditures were carried under a single appropriation entitled "local industry." However, in 1959 there were eleven separate appropriations to cover various types of industry managed by local governments.

Once the provincial budget had been approved by the center, additional expenditures required specific advance approval from the Ministry of Finance. Local governments could make adjustments within each of the appropriations, as long as they did not increase the expenditure within the appropriation as a whole and as long as they did not influence the overall ability of the Ministry of Finance to carry out the planned budget (Ministry of Finance 1959a, 65). The ability to make these adjustments represented an expansion of provincial authority compared to the First Five-Year Plan period when, as pointed out in Chapter 2, even adjustments among items within a single appropriation were not permitted without central approval. After the decentralization, for example, the provinces could increase their expenditures for higher education while decreasing outlays on primary and middle school education, if they remained within the overall limit on social expenditures placed by the central government.

The decline in the degree of disaggregation of local expenditure targets and the increased authority to adjust expenditure plans gave provincial governments increased ability to modify their expenditure programs during the fiscal year. This undoubtedly enhanced incentives to reduce expenditures to transfer the saved funds to other programs.

Decentralization and regional inequality.   In addition to continued control of the level and composition of provincial expenditures, several specific elements of the reform reflected Peking's concern over the potential trade-off between decentralization and interregional equality. This concern stemmed primarily from the geographic concentration of central government enterprises. Despite a substantial allocation of investment resources for inland provinces in the First

Table 3.2. *Planned central enterprise profits, 1958 (millions of yuan)*

Province	Profits
Shanghai	1,300
Liaoning	1,200
Anhui	100
Kweichow	23
Tsinghai	14

Source: Lin Yün (no. 11), 46.

Five-Year Plan period, most central government enterprise revenues still came from a few key coastal provinces. Uniform rates of profit sharing would thus provide some areas with enormous increases in revenues, while in others there were few profits available for sharing. Table 3.2 shows that the level of planned profits of central government enterprises ranged from well over a billion (American billion) yuan in Shanghai, to about one-hundredth of this amount in Tsinghai. The potentially inegalitarian consequences of profit sharing in this highly dualistic environment were alleviated by two means.

First, Shanghai, Liaoning, Peking, and Tientsin, the areas with the greatest concentration of central government enterprises, were not allowed to retain any share of enterprise profits (Ministry of Finance 1957a; Hsü Fei-ch'ing 1957, 4). This applied to both enterprises that remained under direct central control and enterprises that were transferred to local management. Thus local management did not always mean that a share of enterprise profits was retained locally. These four provinces were also denied any share of the industrial and commercial and agricultural taxes collected in their areas. All these revenues remained under direct central control.

Secondly, the center set the sharing rate on enterprise profits relatively low. During the formulation of the decentralization, higher rates of sharing had been considered (Lin Yün (no. 10), 45; Hsü Fei-ch'ing 1957, 4). But it was found that if the rate was set above 20 percent many provinces, in addition to the four mentioned above, would be able to finance all their normal expenditures without any adjustment revenues or subsidies. Because the central government wanted to retain some leverage over local aggregate expenditures, and to provide incentives for local governments to collect industrial and commercial and agricultural taxes, they set the rate at 20 percent. They then could set sharing rates for adjustment revenues and subsidies to determine each province's total retained income.

Finally, the central government made several special concessions to autonomous regions (Ministry of Finance 1957c, 1958e; Hsü Fei-ch'ing 1957, 4; Wen Cheng-i 1958a, b). Because of their relative backwardness and higher expenditure requirements, autonomous regions were automatically assigned all revenues from the shared and adjustment categories. That is, they were allowed to retain not 20 but 100 percent of enterprise profits, and all revenues in the adjustment category. On the expenditure side, local capital construction expenditures were included in their normal expenditure base.

Extrabudgetary funds.   The decentralization directive outlined three sources of extrabudgetary funds for local governments. Although these funds were not subject to central budgetary control, their significance should not be overemphasized. The agricultural surtax, which was by far the most important of the three, had actually been a source of extrabudgetary funds for local governments since 1950. The surtax rate continued to be controlled by the central government. The basic surtax in 1958 was set at 15 percent, the same as in 1957. However, the directive increased the maximum surtax to 30 percent in areas specializing in commercial, as opposed to grain, crops (State Council 1957d, 13; 1957e). As a result, agricultural surtaxes increased from about 400 million yuan in 1957 to about 440 million yuan in 1958 and 1959 (Li Hsien-nien 1959, 22).

The municipal public utilities surcharge and industrial and commercial surcharges were both new sources of extrabudgetary funds. Although the utilities surtax had been collected since 1953, prior to the decentralization it was included within the scope of the state budget and was carried under the category of "other revenue." Evidence from scattered local budgets suggests that these funds may have amounted to 110 to 120 million yuan annually after the decentralization.[3] The industrial and commercial surtax provided local governments with an additional 140 to 145 million yuan in extrabudgetary funds in 1958 and 155 to 160 million yuan in 1959.[4]

The expansion of the sources of local extrabudgetary funds increased their volume from about 400 million yuan in 1957 to about 690 to 705 million yuan in 1958 and about 705 to 720 million yuan in 1959. Because local governments had complete freedom in determining the uses of these funds, the expansion enhanced the ability of local governments to pursue programs independent of central government control. However, the significance of these funds should not be overestimated. They were, for example, equivalent to about 3 percent of local budgetary expenditures in 1958 and 1959.[5]

Summary

The discussion above suggests that the economic reform instituted at the end of the First Five-Year Plan did not represent a deliberate policy choice favoring efficiency and growth at the expense of equity. The reform provided for continued central government control of each province's total expenditures as well as for some influence over the composition of those expenditures. In addition, specific measures were instituted to assure that revenues available in the less-developed areas would be adequate to maintain the level of their locally financed programs.

Although the reform itself seems to provide potential mechanisms for continued central government control over major resource-allocation decisions, it is not clear that the center actually was able to exercise these powers. Indeed, frequent wide discrepancies between official regulations and actual practice have led Western commentators to assume that formal economic regulations and directives are sometimes either ignored or distorted in practice from their original intent (Perkins 1968, 624).The empirical data presented in the following section are designed to determine if the center did exercise the powers outlined in the formal decentralization directives and to test whether or not the economic reform did in fact have important consequences for interprovincial inequality.

Hypotheses and empirical tests

As noted in Chapter 1, many studies have argued that the decentralization substantially diminished the ability of the central government to control basic resource-allocation decisions. After the decentralization, the share of national budgetary revenues collected directly by the central government declined from 40 to 20 percent. As a result, Peking became increasingly dependent on fiscal remittances from more-developed provinces both for revenues to subsidize poorer provinces and for revenues to finance programs managed directly by the central ministries. Wealthier provinces are believed to have increased their ability to resist the demands of the center for the remittance of revenues. As a result, it is believed that the ability of the central government to utilize national planning to achieve its economic goals was substantially impaired.

The fundamental economic implication of this line of analysis is increasing interprovincial inequality. As noted in Chapter 2, during the First Five-Year Plan the central government consistently transferred income and wealth from many well-developed provinces to more backward areas. A significant diminution of this redistributive power would have important implications for the pattern of Chinese social and industrial development. It would lead to a relative decline in the level of social services provided in the less-developed areas and a tendency for investment and industrial growth to become more concentrated in the areas of greatest existing industrial capacity. Indeed, proponents of the view that the decentralization substantially blunted the redistributive policies of the central government and led to a considerably more autarkic pattern of development agree that "reliance on local resources, whether material or managerial, for investment to expand output is inevitably a system of 'to him that hath shall be given' " (Donnithorne 1972b, 613).

Because this view is not supported by my analysis of the provisions of the decentralization, an examination of the actual changes in the pattern of resource allocation may provide an additional perspective from which to evaluate the distributive consequences of the reform. The remainder of this section develops two specific empirical tests that can be used to examine the validity of the hypothesis that economic development after 1957 was marked by increased provincial autarky. The subsequent sections present the empirical tests of the hypotheses and an analysis of the results.[6]

The social expenditure hypothesis

If the decentralization led to greater provincial control of revenues collected, it would have resulted in a markedly different pattern of social expenditures beginning in 1958. More-developed provinces that had remitted most of their revenues to Peking in the predecentralization period would have vastly greater resources at their disposal. They could use these to maintain or increase the level of social services, which as we saw in Chapter 2 were primarily provided from local budgets.[7] Because the hypothesis of increased provincial autarky holds that the remittances of the wealthier provinces to the center were reduced, the central government would no longer have the resources necessary to subsidize backward areas that were previously dependent on net central government subsidies. Thus I hypothesize that social expenditures in these areas would decline *as compared with* less dependent (i.e., more developed) provinces.

This hypothesis does not depend solely on an increase in social expenditures in more developed areas, but rather a rise *relative* to less-developed areas. This could arise from a larger increase in expenditures in less-dependent provinces, a fall in expenditures in more-dependent provinces, or a combination of these two factors. Reduced expenditures in more-dependent provinces would be more important if the decentralization dramatically diminished the central government's fiscal resources and redistributive powers. This is, of course, the central contention of those subscribing to the "autarky hypothesis."

The investment hypothesis

The second test focuses on the distribution of fixed investment. If the hypothesis of increased autarky is valid, there would be a sharp decline in the interprovincial mobility of capital. Given the absence of long-term capital markets and the short-term nature of bank loans in China, the budget of the central government was the only available policy instrument for redistributing significant investment funds among regions. A diminution of central fiscal authority and a concomitant rise of provincial autarky would result in a marked increase in the share of total national investment in provinces with proportionately greater fiscal resources and a concomitant decline in the investment shares of the less-developed provinces.[8] Provinces that previously lost most of their revenues to the center, either through remission or through direct central government collection, would now be able to use these resources to increase substantially their own investment expenditures. For example, as pointed out in Chapter 2, even a modest increase in the ability of Shanghai to convert its resources to local use would have produced a substantial increase in total investment within the municipality. Investment in many less-developed provinces, on the other hand, was more dependent on central government subsidies or on projects directly managed by

Table 3.3. *Provincial per capita social expenditures, 1953–9 (yuan)*

Province	1953	1954	1955	1956	1957	1958	1959
Average for all all provinces			3.9	5.1	5.4		
Northeast							
Liaoning		7.3		7.7	7.5		
Kirin			6.1	8.5	9.0	9.4	12.2
Heilungkiang			6.0	8.2			
North							
Hopei[a]			4.3	7.0	6.6		7.8
Shantung			2.7	3.6		4.4	
Honan			2.9	3.7	4.1	4.1	
Shansi			5.1	6.7	6.5		9.2
Inner Mongolia	6.5	5.4	5.0	8.7	9.1	9.2	
Peking			20.0	22.9	19.2		
East							
Kiangsu			3.3	4.7	5.0	5.2	6.5
Anhui			3.6	4.9	4.6	4.0	5.6
Chekiang			2.8	4.2	4.2		
Shanghai		11.1	10.2	15.5	19.9	20.1	20.4
Central							
Hupei				4.3			
Hunan				3.5	3.7	3.4	3.9
Kiangsi	3.8	3.9	4.1	4.8	5.0	5.2	
South							
Kwangtung	3.4	3.9	3.9	5.1		5.4	
Kwangsi		3.1	3.1	5.0	5.6		
Fukien		4.5					
Southwest							
Szechuan			2.3	2.8		3.1	3.4
Kweichow			2.1	3.2	3.3	3.4	4.3
Yünnan			2.7	3.6		4.2	4.4
Northwest							
Shensi			4.9	6.2			
Kansu					5.5	5.7	7.7
Tsinghai			7.9	14.9	14.6	19.0	
Sinkiang	7.9	8.9	10.3	14.5	11.9	13.9	13.9

Note: All data are based on final accounts. Provincial data and average for all provinces included only expenditures financed through provincial budgets. Discussion of centrally financed social expenditures is in Chapter 2. [a] Includes Tientsin for 1957 and 1959.
Sources: Calculated from expenditure data in Appendix Table A.3 and population data from Teiwes, Table 16 (p. 169), which are based on official data for 1953 and 1957 with the following exceptions: For Kwangtung, I have used the adjusted growth rate suggested by John S. Aird (1974, 13). For municipal population data (not given in Teiwes), I have used data based on official sources adjusted for boundary changes that occurred in Peking and Shanghai in 1958 and 1959. These changes, which were rather substantial, are discussed in Ullman, Appendix D (pp. 42–4). I have adjusted the provincial population data given by Teiwes for Kiangsu and Hopei to reflect the population transferred to Shanghai and Peking, respectively.

central ministries. A diminution of Peking's redistributive powers would cut sharply their levels of investment.

It is important to recognize that confirmation of this hypothesis of increased provincial autarky requires a significant increase in the share of national investment in more-developed regions. That is, simply a shift in the level of control of investment projects from the center to the provinces without a change in the overall distribution should not be interpreted as a trend toward provincial autarky. The shift in the level of management of investment projects did have important implications that will be brought out in Chapter 4, but this is to be distinguished from an increase in the ability of more-developed provinces to withhold their resources from central government redistribution.

Data and test results

The social-expenditure test.   Table 3.3 summarizes social expenditure data from provincial fiscal reports. All the data represent final account figures rather than planned budgetary expenditures. Prior to decentralization, the pattern of interprovincial variation in per capita social expenditures did not vary significantly from year to year. This pattern is not noticeably changed in the postdecentralization years of 1958 and 1959. Although provinces experienced differential rates of increase in per capita social expenditures, they were not appreciably larger than those of the 1955–7 period. Consequently, the ranking of provinces by expenditure level showed little change. Moreover, the ratio between the highest and lowest expenditure levels did not increase.[9] In short, there is little initial reason to suspect that wealthier provinces were able to increase their expenditures more than backward provinces.

More precise statistical tests also support the view that the center apparently continued to control at least total outlays for social expenditures on a province-by-province basis and that preventing increased interprovincial inequality was a significant policy goal. In particular, provinces that were more dependent on central government subsidies to finance their local expenditures in the First Five-Year Plan were actually quite successful in maintaining or even increasing the level of social services in 1958 and 1959. For example Kansu, Sinkiang, and Tsinghai, which were shown in Table 2.9 to be the regions most dependent on central government subsidies, were

Table 3.4. *Provincial per capita output, 1957 (national average = 100)*

Province	Industry and agriculture	Industry	Agriculture
Northeast			
Liaoning	200	401	81
Kirin	132	157	117
Heilungkiang	185	219	166
North			
Hopei	93	56	115
Shantung	74	62	82
Honan	70	29	95
Shansi	97	95	98
Inner Mongolia	115	68	143
Peking	191	73	21
Tientsin	391	1,101	21
East			
Kiangsu	86	83	88
Anhui	74	37	97
Chekiang	93	78	103
Shanghai	587	1,550	12
Central			
Hupei	104	75	122
Hunan	80	41	103
Kiangsi	90	52	111
South			
Kwangtung	95	82	102
Kwangsi	74	34	97
Fukien	79	69	85
Southwest			
Szechuan	77	56	90
Kweichow	75	30	102
Yünnan	82	48	103
Northwest			
Shensi	106	58	135
Kansu	89	36	119
Tsinghai	137	40	194
Sinkiang	132	65	171

Source: Appendix Tables A.1, A.2, and official provincial population data.

able to increase their expenditures for social programs 28 percent in 1958 while total national outlays on social programs actually fell by 6 percent (Li Hsien-nien 1958, 1959). The growth of the social expenditures of these provinces continued to outstrip the national average in 1959.[10] Thus some provinces that were more dependent on the central government prior to 1958 actually were able to increase their social expenditures more, on the average, than were those richer provinces that historically had remitted part or even most of their revenue to the center.

Similarly, the level of provincial economic development in 1957, shown in Table 3.4, is a very poor predictor of changes in social expenditure after 1957. Provinces with higher levels of per capita agricultural and industrial output did not succeed, on the average, in increasing their social expenditures relative to the less-developed provinces.[11]

The outstanding characteristic of these results is the absence of the systematic shift in resource allocation predicted by the hypothesis of provincial autarky. Peking's continued control of the fiscal system assured that despite the substantial interprovincial variation in the level of economic development, the decentralization did not result in a relative decline in the level of social services provided in less-developed areas. In short, there appears to be little support here for the hypothesis that the decentralization undermined the ability of the central government to achieve important distributive objectives.

It has been argued that increased extrabudgetary outlays for social programs, which are not included in Table 3.3, vitiate this empirical test of the change in the distribution of social expenditures. In response, it should be pointed out that social programs financed outside the budget in the 1950s were quite limited. The health and welfare benefits provided through the labor insurance program of the All-China Federation of Trade Unions were the most important source of extrabudgetary funds devoted to social programs. These funds, however, were only about 3 to 6 percent of budgetary outlays for social programs during the First Five-Year Plan[12] and available evidence, discussed in Chapter 4 suggests that they were incorporated into the state budget in 1958 or 1959. Extrabudgetary funds of local governments, discussed above in this chapter, were also relatively limited, under 5 percent of their total budgetary expenditures.[13] Consequently, although there was certainly some increase in

Table 3.5. *Provincial investment, 1953-9 (in millions of yuan and as a percent of national investment)*

Province	1953–7 (cumulative) million yuan	% of nat. invest.	1957 (cumulative) million yuan	% of nat. invest.	1958 (cumulative) million yuan	% of nat. invest.	1959 (cumulative) million yuan	% of nat. invest.
Northeast								
Liaoning[a]	7,770	14.1	1,300	9.4	2,043	7.7		
Kirin[b]	2,150	3.9	325	2.3	650	2.4	878	2.8
Heilungkiang[c]	3,300	6.0	1,430	10.3	1,570	5.9	1,600	5.0
North								
Honan[d]	2,590	4.7	694	5.0	1,735	6.5		
Shansi[e]	2,139	3.9	724	5.2	1,293	4.8	1,342	4.2
Inner Mongolia[f]	1,139	2.1	339	2.4	925	3.5	1,277	4.0
Peking[g]					1,230	4.6		
East								
Kiangsu[h]	1,080	2.0	365	2.6	915	3.4	960	3.0
Anhui[i]	1,186	2.2	268	1.9				
Shanghai[j]	1,371	2.5	372	2.7	1,101	4.1	1,395	4.4
Central								
Hupei[k]	2,210	4.0	668	4.8	1,250	4.7	1,600	5.0
Hunan[l]	1,217	2.2	310	2.2	790	3.0	1,300	4.1
Kiangsi[m]	631	1.1			472	1.8	632	2.0
South								
Kwangtung[n]	1,438	2.6	490	3.5	980	3.7	1,275	4.0
Kwangsi[o]	446	.8						
Fukien[p]	375	.7	118	.9	437	1.6		
Southwest								
Szechuan[q]			547	4.0				
Kweichow[r]	370	.7	130	.9	520	1.9	580	1.8
Yünnan[s]	791	1.4	280	2.0	555	2.1	633	2.0
Northwest								
Shensi[t]	2,200	4.0	575	4.1	815	3.1	1,100	3.4
Kansu[u]	2,175	4.0	725	5.2	1,015	3.8	1,052	3.3
Tsinghai[v]	603	1.1	166	1.2	380	1.4		
Sinkiang[w]	2,049	3.7			690	2.6	860	2.7

Note: The Chinese investment aggregate reported in this table, "basic capital construction investment" (chi-pen chien-she t'ou-tzu), includes expenditures for building and installation, purchase of equipment, tools and fixtures, and ancillary expenses. Functionally, it includes the following sectors: industry, agriculture, water conservancy, forestry, transportation, post and telecommunications, culture, education, health, and urban public utilities. The data in this table generally include all investment irrespective of the source of funds. That is, these numbers include local investment financed through the provincial budget; direct central government investment undertaken within a province financed through the center's budget; and extrabudgetary investment. However, in a few cases it is not possible to determine from the Chinese sources whether or not extrabudgetary investment funds are included within re-

extrabudgetary expenditures for social programs, they appear to have been relatively small in relation to the budgetary data on which the empirical tests are based.

One might suspect, however, that had more-developed regions gained increased control of the disposition of their revenues they would have chosen to allocate most of them for productive investment rather than for providing increased social services. This is particularly likely to have been the case because the policy of the pe-

Table 3.5. *(cont.)*

ported investment aggregates. The sum of provincial totals shown above is, however, less than aggregate national investment for two reasons. First, I have not been able to locate data for all provinces in all years. For example, for the period of the First Five-Year Plan data are not available for six important provinces: Chekiang, Hopei, Peking, Shantung, Tientsin, and Szechuan. However, even after allowance for these provinces is made, aggregate provincial investment falls 10 to 15 percent short of total national investment. This arises because some extrabudgetary investment probably is not included and some investment occurs that apparently is not distinguished by area. [State Planning Commission, National Economic Summary Planning Bureau, Methods Office, "Kuan-yü 1958 nien-tu kuo-min ching-chi chi-hua piao-ke chu-yao pien-tung ch'ing-k'uang ti shuo-ming" (An explanation of important changes in 1958 national economic plan forms), *Chi-hua ching-chi,* no. 8, 1957: 26]. Although I have not found any discussion in Chinese sources of the nature of this investment, presumably it includes railroad rolling stock and other types of investment that are not allocable to a specific province.

Sources and methods: The numbers reported in this table come directly from or are calculated on the basis of a very large number of individual provincial reports on capital investment. Numbers from different sources frequently appear to be in conflict. For example, it is frequently not clear whether or not reported provincial investment aggregates (1) are inclusive or exclusive of direct central government investment; (2) are inclusive or exclusive of extrabudgetary investment. However, when all the reports for a single province are examined it is generally possible to resolve any apparent discrepancies and to determine the coverage of the reported investment magnitude. The sources cited below include only those used to derive the numbers in the table, rather than all the reports examined for each province.

[a]*Liao-ning jih-pao,* 3 December 1958, 26 September 1959. Foreign Broadcast Information Service, Daily Report, 14 February 1958. [b]*Chi-lin jih-pao,* 11 November 1957, 6 June 1959, 25 May 1960. [c]*Hei-lung-chiang jih-pao,* 6 February 1959, 25 January 1960. [d]*Cheng-chou jih-pao,* 4 January 1958; *Ho-nan jih-pao,* 1 January 1959. [e]*Shan-hsi jih-pao,* 12 May 1958, 10 October 1959, 24 May 1960. [f]*Hu-pei jih-pao,* 31 December 1957, 11 September 1959. [g]*Pei-ching jih-pao,* 11 September 1959. [h]Ch'en Shu-t'ung 1959. [i]*Anhui jih-pao,* 30 April 1958, 29 September 1959. [j]*Chieh-fang jih-pao,* 7 June 1959, 18 May 1960. [k]Inner Mongolia Statistical Bureau, 67; *Nei-meng-ku jih-pao,* 23 August 1960. [l]Shang Tzu-chin 1959; *Hsin Hu-nan pao,* 4 May 1958, 23 December 1960. [m]Hsü Kuang-yüan 1959; *Chiang-hsi jih-pao,* 1 January 1958, 29 June 1960. [n]Wei Chin-fei 1959; *Nan-fang jih-pao,* 22 March 1959, 5 October 1959, 4 April 1960. [o]*Kuang-hsi jih-pao,* 24 July 1956, 29 December 1960. [p]*Fu-chien jih-pao,* 16 January 1959, 11 February 1959. [q]*Szu-ch'uan jih-pao,* 17 August 1957. [r]Chang P'ing; *Kuei-chou jih-pao,* 30 September 1959. [s]*Yün-nan jih-pao,* 5 October 1957, 8 October 1958, 3 December 1959. [t]*Hsi-an jih-pao,* 29 September 1957; *Shansi-hsi jih-pao* (Hsian), 22 July 1959, 5 February 1960. [u]*Kan-su jih-pao,* 12 June 1958, 1 February 1959, 4 June 1960. [v]*Ch'ing-hai jih-pao,* 30 September 1958, 21 May 1959. [w]*Hsin-chiang jih-pao,* 1 February 1959, 29 May 1960.

riod called for a reduction in the share of funds allocated for social programs and government administration and an increase in the proportion used for productive investment, particularly in industry. The evidence that increased provincial autarky was reflected in investment expenditures, rather than social programs, is examined in the discussion below.

The investment test.   If the hypothesis of increased provincial autarky is valid, one would expect to find a marked shift in the flow of investment resources in favor of more-developed provinces with greater fiscal resources after 1957. Although investment data are not available for all provinces, Table 3.5 includes nineteen provinces for which information on investment before and after the decentralization has been found. These data show that more-developed provinces were not able, on the average, to increase significantly their share of total national investment.[14] Specifically, level of economic development is actually a very poor variable to use to try to predict changes in investment after the decentralization. As in the case of social expenditures, there is a diverse pattern of change. However, the relatively backward provinces of Kweichow and Fukien experienced the largest increases in their shares of national investment. At the same time, several of the most-developed provinces, most notably Liaoning and Heilungkiang, experienced dramatic declines in their investment shares.

These results, then, also do not seem to support the hypothesis of significantly increased provincial autarky. Some more-developed provinces were able to increase their shares of national investment, but as a group they do not appear to have been able to reinvest a substantially higher portion of their revenues after the decentralization of the fiscal and planning system. Although a few less-developed provinces experienced declines in their shares of national investment, as a group they appear to have at least held their own relative standing in the allocation of investment resources. In short, no simple variable such as level of development can successfully explain the shifts in resource allocation. However I believe that, in broad outline, the changes in the pattern of investment allocation can be explained by modifications to Chinese development strategy that were discussed before the decentralization measures were introduced. The modified investment strategy and a more detailed examination of the pattern of provincial per capita social expenditures is presented in the next section of this chapter.

Analysis of statistical tests

The provincial social expenditure and investment data raise a number of important questions. This section examines several of these with the hope that the general empirical results of the previous section will be strengthened by a discussion of central government policy regarding the distribution of social expenditures and the pattern of regional investment.

The pattern of provincial social expenditures

One finding of this study is that the central government used the fiscal system to redistribute substantial amounts of income. Why, then, wasn't the center more successful in reducing the per capita social expenditure differentials shown in Table 3.3? Moreover, what qualitative evidence is there to support the view that the system for financing local social expenditures was motivated in part by equity considerations?

I believe that it is difficult to judge the degree to which differences in provincial social expenditures represent differentials in the level of real services. Because of the relative stability of prices during this period, I am confident that changes over time in provincial social expenditures reflect changes in the level of real services provided. It is doubtful, however, that cross-provincial comparisons of expenditures are a reliable indicator of interprovincial differences in real services. This doubt arises because urban–rural expenditure differentials and regional wage variations are embodied in the expenditure data in Table 3.3. At the same time, qualitative evidence suggests that the system of financing social expenditures through the unified budgetary system was motivated primarily by a desire to mitigate the potentially inegalitarian consequences of local self-financing.

Urban–rural expenditure differentials.   Part of the differentials shown in Table 3.3 should be interpreted as urban–rural, rather than interprovincial, expenditure differentials. Educational, health, and other social facilities are concentrated in major urban centers.[15]

Table 3.6. *Municipal per capita social expenditures, 1953–9 (yuan)*

	1953	1954	1955	1956	1957	1958	1959
Provincial-level municipalities							
Peking[b]			20.0	22.9	19.2		
Shanghai[b]		11.1	10.2	15.5	19.9	20.1	20.4
Ordinary municipalities							
Amoy[c] (Fukien)					12.4		
Anshan[d] (Liaoning)					8.3	9.8[a]	
Canton[e] (Kwangtung)	12.0		12.2	17.1	16.3	16.5[a]	
Ch'angsha[f] (Hunan)					11.0	9.1[a]	
Ch'engtu[g] (Szechuan)				10.5	12.1		
Chungking[h] (Szechuan)		12.2	10.3	12.7	13.7[a]		12.3
Harbin[i] (Heilungkiang)			12.0	13.0	10.5[a]		
Hsian[j] (Shensi)			12.5	11.9	11.8	9.1[a]	
Loyang[k] (Honan)				13.8			
Lüta[l] (Liaoning)				11.8			
Paot'ou[m] (Inner Mongolia)					19.2	14.4[a]	
Shenyang[n] (Liaoning)					10.7	9.1[a]	
Tsingtao[o] (Shantung)				10.7	15.3	14.9	16.8[a]
Wuhan[p] (Hupei)			15.5		15.9	15.3[a]	

Note: All data are based on final accounts except as noted.
[a] Based on budgeted expenditures.
Sources: [b] Table 3.3. Ordinary municipalities, expenditure data: [c] Shih Neng-hao. [d] Wang I-hsin. [e] Wei Chin-fei 1954; Yü Mei-ch'ing; Chu Kuang; Chiao Lin-i. [f] Yang Ju-p'eng. [g] Feng Ching-ch'uan 1957, 1958. [h] Ch'en Ch'ou 1956, 1957; Tuan Ta-ming 1959. [i] Kao Yün-fan 1956, 1958. [j] Yang Hsiao-ch'u 1956, 1958; Liu Keng. [k] T'ien Yao-ch'i. [l] Li Tung-ch'ao. [m] Chang Ting-an. [n] Ch'en Wei-kan. [o] Chang Yün-shan; Sun Kang. [p] Wuhan Municipal People's Congress; Wu Neng-kuang. Ordinary municipalities, population data: Ullman, Appendix Table 3, pp. 35–6.

Therefore, the high per capita expenditures in Peking and Shanghai shown in Table 3.3 partly reflect the unique provincial-level administrative status of these municipalities.

This argument is supported by an examination of social expenditures in major urban centers that did not have provincial-level administrative status. Table 3.6 shows per capita social expenditures for Shanghai and Peking and for 14 major urban centers that did not have provincial-level status. Comparison of Tables 3.6 and 3.3 shows that per capita expenditures in these 14 major urban centers were three to six times the level for their respective provinces. For example, in 1956 per capita social expenditures in Chungking were 4.5 times the level of expenditures in Szechuan. Comparison of ordinary municipalities with provincial-level municipalities shows that, although expenditure levels in Shanghai and Peking were usually higher than those of most ordinary municipalities, the margin of their expenditure differentials substantially diminished compared with the interprovincial differentials as shown in Table 3.3. For example, Shanghai's per capita social expenditures were 5.5 and 6 times those of Szechuan in 1956 and 1959, respectively. However, in the same years Shanghai's per capita expenditures were only 1.2 and 1.7 times those of Chungking, a major municipality in Szechuan.

More generally, differing degrees of provincial urbanization, shown in Table 3.7, appear to partly explain variations in the level of social expenditures among all provinces. Above-average per capita social expenditures in Liaoning, Kirin, Inner Mongolia, and Hopei are partly explained by their comparatively high levels of urbanization. Relatively low rates of urbanization in Kweichow, Honan, Anhui, and Hunan undoubtedly partially account for below-average social expenditures in these provinces.

Regional wage differentials.   Substantial regional price and wage variations also make it difficult to draw general conclusions concerning the degree of interprovincial inequality in the level of real social services. Because the largest component of social expenditures is salaries and because regional salary schedules are tied to local price levels, part of the expenditure differentials shown in Table 3.3 are due to interprovincial wage variations, rather than differences in real services.

Interprovincial price and wage differentials in China are substantial. Since 1956 the entire country has been divided into 11 basic

Table 3.7. *Urban population as a percent of total population by province, 1953 and 1958 (midyear)*

Province	1953	1958
National	13.3	14.7
Northeast		
Liaoning	42.0	42.4
Kirin	29.0	29.7
Heilungkiang	31.1	35.3
North		
Hopei	12.2	13.1
Shantung	6.9	9.1
Honan	6.5	7.9
Shansi	12.9	14.3
Inner Mongolia	10.7	21.3
East		
Kiangsu	18.4	17.6
Anhui	6.7	7.1
Chekiang	9.8	9.4
Central		
Hupei	8.6	11.1
Hunan	7.0	7.1
Kiangsi	7.6	8.3
South		
Kwangtung	12.2	13.4
Kwangsi	4.8	4.9
Fukien	12.0	11.8
Southwest		
Szechuan	9.7	9.3
Kweichow	3.9	6.3
Yünnan	7.4	7.9
Northwest		
Shensi	9.9	13.6
Kansu	8.6	13.3
Tsinghai	7.0	8.4
Sinkiang	10.8	14.1

Note: Urban population total for Hopei excludes Peking and Tientsin; total for Kiangsu excludes Shanghai.
Source: Ernest Ni.

wage districts (State Council 1956a). Wage standards in each district are based primarily on regional differentials in prices of typical consumption goods. Regional differentials, which reach a maximum of 30 percent, are constant across all wage grades based on skill level and also across all types of industry. For example, in a region such as Peking, which is classified in the sixth wage standard, the mayor (a position classified in grades 5 through 9 on a 30-grade wage scale) and an engineer in the Shihchingshan iron and steel plant (classified in grades 9 through 13 on an 18-grade scale) would both receive a 15 percent salary differential compared to identical jobs in a region classified in the first wage standard. In some remote areas where the required cost-of-living adjustment is greater than the 30 percent differential provided by the eleventh standard, a special cost-of-living allowance is also paid. This differential is expressed as a percentage addition to the basic differential for the eleventh classification and ranges from 2 to 93 percent.

The geography of wage regions is complicated. The eleven basic regions invariably cut across provincial boundaries. Most provinces are divided into three or four basic wage areas. One province, Szechuan, is divided into ten. This means that wages frequently vary from *hsien* to *hsien* even within a single special district. The additional cost-of-living differentials are also specified on a *hsien* by *hsien* basis. Even within a single basic wage area, five or more special cost-of-living allowances may be applied. However, in most areas of the country there are no special cost-of-living allowances. This area includes Peking, Tientsin, Shanghai, Hopei, Liaoning, Kirin, Heilungkiang, Shensi, Shantung, Kiangsu, Anhui, Chekiang, Fukien, Honan, Hupei, Hunan, Kiangsi, Kwangsi, Kweichow, and Yünnan. In frontier areas, the special cost-of-living differentials are quite high. Table 3.8 shows the highest differential in areas where cost-of-living allowances were paid.

It is difficult to judge what proportion of the variation in provincial social expenditures arises from regional wage diversity. First, there is no precise information on a province by province basis (or even for the nation as a whole) on the share of wages in social expenditures. Wages were, however, the single largest component of these expenditures. Secondly, the Chinese have not published wage indexes on a provincial basis and it is difficult to construct such wage indexes with available information. Although data on the wage differentials are given on a *hsien* by *hsien* basis, corresponding *hsien*-level em-

Table 3.8. *Regional special cost-of-living wage differentials*

Province	Area with highest wages	Differential (% above 11th standard)
Inner Mongolia	O-chi-na Banner	46
Kansu	Ma-ch'ü *hsien* in Southern Kansu-Tibetan Autonomous *Chou*	50
Tsinghai	Yu-shu and Kuo-lo Tibetan Autonomous *Chou*	97
Sinkiang	Fu-yün *hsien* in A-lo-t'ai Special District	84
Kwangtung	Ch'ang-kan *hsien* in Hainan Administrative District. Yai, Pao-t'ing, Tung-fang, Pai-sha, Ch'iung-chung, and Lo-tung *hsien,* all in Hainan Li and Miao Nationalities Autonomous *Chou.*	8
Szechuan	Kan-tsu, Tao-cheng, Pa-t'ang, Li-t'ang, Se-ta, Pai-yü, Te-ko, I-tun, and Hsiang-cheng *hsien,* all in Kansu-Tibetan Autonomous *Chou.*	50

Source: State Council 1956a.

ployment or even *hsien* population data that could be used as weights to aggregate this data on *hsien* wage differentials in order to derive provincial wage indexes have not been published.

However, it is possible to estimate crudely a province by province index of wages based on very general information on population density and the data on regional wage differentials. This estimate, which incorporates both the basic differential and the special additional cost-of-living differential, is shown in Table 3.9. Wages in remote Sinkiang and Tsinghai were 50 to 60 percent above those paid in the lowest wage areas – Szechuan and Kweichow. Szechuan and Kweichow, as shown in Table 3.3, had the lowest per capita social expenditures whereas Sinkiang and Tsinghai had the highest expenditures with the exception of the provincial-level municipalities.

Two factors, urban–rural expenditure differentials and interprovincial price differentials, were the major sources of interprovincial variation in per capita social expenditures. Expenditures were very high in Shanghai and Peking relative to the rest of the country pri-

Table 3.9. *Estimated interprovincial wage differentials*

Province	Estimated overall wage standard (including special cost-of-living allowances)	Wage index (with regional wage standard #1 = 1)
Northeast		
Liaoning	5.5	1.13
Kirin	4.5	1.11
Heilungkiang	5	1.12
North		
Hopei	4	1.09
Shantung	3	1.06
Honan	3	1.06
Shansi	4	1.09
Inner Mongolia	6	1.15
Peking	6	1.15
Tientsin	6	1.15
East		
Kiangsu	4	1.09
Anhui	3	1.06
Chekiang	3.5	1.07
Shanghai	8	1.21
Central		
Hupei	2.5	1.05
Hunan	2	1.03
Kiangsi	2.5	1.05
South		
Kwangtung	7	1.18
Kwangsi	3.5	1.07
Fukien	6	1.15
Southwest		
Szechuan	1.5	1.01
Kweichow	1.5	1.01
Yünnan	4	1.09
Northwest		
Shensi	7	1.18
Kansu	11	1.30
Tsinghai	11 + 20%	1.63
Sinkiang	11 + 25%	1.63

Source: Author's estimate, based on data on regional wage standards (State Council 1956b), special cost-of-living allowances by region (State Council 1956a), detailed administrative maps (U.S. Central Intelligence Agency), and population data in Ullman.

marily as a result of their unique status as provincial-level municipalities. Expenditures were very high in Tsinghai and Sinkiang relative to the rest of the country primarily because of their high price
levels. On the other hand, provinces where social expenditures were
relatively low were usually regions with both a very low level of
urbanization and a relatively low price level. This group in particular
includes all of the Southwest, Honan and Shantung in North China,
and Anhui and Chekiang in East China. This suggests that the data
in Table 3.3 largely reflect regional price and wage variations and
urban–rural differentials rather than pure interprovincial variation
in the provision of social services.

The data also show, however, that the central government's commitment to reducing inequality in the provision of education and
health care services had not eliminated the gap between urban and
rural areas. In most provinces during the 1950s, the urban–rural gap
appears to have been 2:1 or higher.[16] Most of the more sophisticated
medical centers as well as institutions of higher education were concentrated in major urban centers. Although some of these urban institutions provide services to an entire province or even to the nation as
a whole, rather than only to local residents, apparently some bias in
the delivery of services remained after taking this factor into account.
Quite explicit criticism of this urban bias in the delivery of social
services was made during the Cultural Revolution, and vigorous efforts have been made since then to reduce this urban–rural imbalance. The results of this shift in policy are discussed in Chapter 5.

In spite of these remaining differentials in services between urban
and rural areas, the leadership's commitment to reducing interprovincial variation in the provision of social services in the 1950s was
quite real. A major goal of the expansion of the unified state budget
in the early 1950s, which was discussed in Chapter 2, was to provide
a mechanism for the redistribution of resources at the lowest levels
of government. Through differential revenue-sharing rates at each
level of budgetary administration, the center was able to mitigate
inequalities that would have arisen had social expenditures been
financed exclusively by locally generated resources.

Although this system of incorporating the expenditures of each
level of government in a unified budget facilitated central control of
local expenditures, it also placed a heavy fiscal burden on the central
government. This burden was increased, particularly after 1953,
when township expenditures were incorporated into the national

budget. Consequently, the central government began to look for a formula that would allow a substantial degree of self-finance of local expenditure programs while at the same time providing some leverage to assure that this devolution of the financing did not exacerbate interregional inequality in the provision of social services.

An experiment in local self-finance.   In 1956 Peking initiated an experimental program for financing school expenditures that was designed to meet these twin objectives. The plan called for the shifting of one-half of expenditures for rural primary schools from the state budget to purely local, nonbudgetary financing. To provide local governments with the funds necessary to finance these additional expenditures outside the budget, the State Council in 1956 increased the local agricultural surtax from 12 to 22 percent (State Council 1956d; Li Hsien-nien 1956, 6; Li Shu-te, 3; Wu Kuang-t'ang; Shantung People's Congress). The remaining half of rural primary school expenditures was still to be financed from the state budget. The plan was attractive because it called for a 268-million-yuan reduction in budgetary expenditures without a reduction in budgetary revenues (Feng Ch'i-hsi 1957b, 32). *Hsiang* governments had strong incentives to collect the increased surtax because it financed local services. The plan, however, hardly attempted to shift all local social services to self-financing. The planned shift of funds represented only 7 percent of all social expenditures.[17]

In spite of its modest scope, the experiment in self-finance was unsuccessful. Because 1956 was a year of exceptionally bad weather in many provinces, some localities were unable to collect the full amount of the agricultural tax, not to mention the surtax (Union Research Institute, 183–4; MacFarquhar, 91; Tung Ching-chai; Chang I-ch'en). Consequently, during the fiscal year Peking had to provide unforeseen subsidies to many areas to prevent the collapse of the rural primary school system (Li Shu-te, 3; Ts'ao Ti-ch'iu 1956). This unanticipated expenditure was acknowledged as one cause of the national budgetary deficit in 1956 (Li Hsien-nien 1957, 17). In some areas not adversely affected by severe weather, self-finance was apparently successful. In both Shantung and Szechuan, for example, substantial primary school expenditures were financed outside the budget and state subsidies were not required. These two provinces spent 30 and 25 million yuan, respectively, in extrabudgetary funds for social expenditures. These amounts represented 16 and 21 per-

cent of all expenditures for social programs in Shantung and Szechuan (Yüan Tzu-yang; Chang Hu-ch'en 1957).

Overall, however, the central government found that the policy of
local financing was inconsistent with its desire to improve the equality of access to social services. Major programs requiring significant
continuing expenditures could not be financed from the margin of
local revenues without giving rise to potentially large and variable
interregional differences in the level of services actually provided.
As a result, the experiment in local financing was ended in 1957. The
State Council reduced the maximum agricultural surcharge from 22
to 15 percent. Beginning in 1957, primary level education was again
financed entirely from the state budget (State Council 1956c, 210).
Provincial reports confirm that this policy was followed (Ts'ao Ti-
ch'iu 1956; Chang I-ch'en).

The pattern of investment expenditures

The investment test does not support the view that more-developed
provinces were able, on the average, to retain and control more resources relative to less-developed provinces, after the decentralization. This section offers an alternative explanation of the changes in
the pattern of investment expenditure shown in Table 3.5. In general
terms, I believe the changes can be explained by modifications in
Chinese development strategy that were apparent before the decentralization measures were introduced.

Coastal versus inland industrial development.   The most important
modification concerned the relative priority assigned to inland as
opposed to coastal industrial development. In the early years of the
First Five-Year Plan, the leadership placed great emphasis on the
development of inland industrial centers for several reasons. First,
they believed that the inherited concentration of industry in a few
coastal centers was a highly irrational pattern existing primarily because of previous foreign exploitation. In 1949, 77 percent of total
industrial output originated in coastal areas (Liu Tsai-hsing and
Chang Hsüeh-ch'in, 10). Because capital investment in the recovery
period (1949–52) was concentrated on the reconstruction of existing
industrial enterprises damaged during the Sino-Japanese and Civil
wars, 73 percent of industrial output still originated in coastal areas
in 1952 (Liu Tsai-hsing and Chang Hsüeh-ch'in, 11).

The Chinese leadership felt that this pattern of industrial concentration was unwise from the point of view of defense, raw material supply, transport, and areas of consumption (Wu Chun-yang; SSST Editor). Some plants were located so far from domestic sources of raw materials that imported materials were cheaper. Development of inland industry would take advantage of available domestic raw material supplies and reduce transport costs for the distribution of goods to inland areas.

Another closely related factor was the domination of coastal industry by private firms. Although the government inherited a substantial state-controlled sector from the Nationalists in 1949, well over half of industrial output was produced by privately owned firms (State Statistical Bureau 1960, 38). These firms were concentrated in a relatively small number of urban coastal industrial centers. The leadership was unwilling to allow significant expansion of private enterprises because a major goal was the conversion of privately owned firms to state ownership. In fact, private firms suffered from discriminatory price and tax policies designed to hasten the willingness of their owners to convert to joint state – private ownership (Jung Tzu-ho 1959, 19–20). This policy depressed investment in existing firms in coastal areas. Furthermore, the state was unwilling to invest substantial amounts of resources in new state-managed enterprises in these urban areas because new firms would have to depend to some degree on inputs and services from existing private firms.

A third factor influencing industrial location policy was defense. At the beginning of the First Five-Year Plan, the leadership decided to build up several key heavy industrial centers in relatively remote inland areas that were less vulnerable to foreign attack than existing coastal industrial centers such as Shanghai and Tientsin. The inland cities selected for development included Lanchou (Kansu), Wuhan (Hupei), Hsian (Shensi), Harbin and Ch'ich'ihaerh (Heilungkiang), Paot'ou (Inner Mongolia), Ch'engtu (Szechuan), T'aiyüan and Tat'ung (Shansi), and Chuchou (Hunan), Chengchou and Loyang (Honan), and Ch'angch'un (Kirin) (Chang Yen-hsing). These cities were designated as "key-point" (*chung-tien*) areas and received generous infusions of funds from Peking (Yün Chung, 37–40). Many of the 156 Soviet aid projects which formed the core of the First Five-Year Plan, were located in these municipalities (Institute of the Study of Chinese Communist Problems, 850–3).

Provincial and municipal officials were well aware of the impact of defense considerations on investment allocations and their own budgets. In Kwangtung's plan it was acknowledged that the province's share of national investment was quite low. "During the First Five-Year Plan period the national effort will be concentrated on key-point construction. Therefore Kwangtung must not, and cannot, demand additional economic appropriations from the central government" (T'ao Chu, 11). The mayor of Canton, Chu Kuang, specifically linked Canton's lack of key-point status to national defense. "Because Canton is a coastal city in the front line of our nation's defenses, it is not a key-point city for state economic development."[18] Other areas openly acknowledged that their "key-point" status meant larger investment allocations from the central government (Chao Shou-shan).

As a consequence of defense and other considerations, inland areas in the early years of the First Five-Year Plan received large investments. In 1953–5, 55.2 percent of all investment was in inland areas (TCKTTH Data Section, 6).

By 1956, several factors had coalesced to modify Chinese regional investment policy. The change was signaled by Mao's speech, "On the Ten Major Relationships," which urged increased priority for coastal industry. This speech, and a subsequent series of articles published in the journal of the State Planning Commission, candidly discussed the reasons for the shift in policy. The major reasons were the completion of the socialist transformation of private industry, improved information on low rates of capacity utilization of coastal industry and the high capital-output ratios inherent in inland industrial development, and a reevaluation of the external military threat.

The initial impetus came from the completion of the socialist transformation. In the last half of 1955, the ground was laid for the early conversion of remaining private firms to joint state–private ownership. Conversion was completed in most large industrial cities by the end of January 1956 (MacFarquhar, 19–24). This eliminated the last remnants of capitalist ownership and placed virtually all industrial enterprises under direct state control, substantially reducing the reluctance of the leadership to allocate new investment resources for coastal areas (Chang Feng-chi, 25–6).

Second, Chinese economic planners and political leaders were becoming increasingly aware of the high costs of inland industrial development, perhaps due partially to continued improvements in the statistical system. Most notably, the rapid expansion of inland productive capacity, particularly in some branches of light industry, had resulted in a diversion of raw material supplies from previously established manufacturers in coastal regions. By mid-1956 articles in economic journals gave examples of numerous industries in Shanghai and Tientsin where rates of capacity utilization were below 50 percent (Chang Feng-chi; Chu Jung-chi; Liu Tsai-hsing).

In addition, because of a lack of adequate transportation and communications facilities, housing, and urban public utilities, development of inland capacity required substantially larger investment than construction of similar plants in coastal areas where substantial overhead capital already was in place. The lead times involved in site selection, survey and design work, and other preparation were substantial, and construction work itself also took longer in inland areas. Because of the importance of these factors, it was asserted that the strategy of emphasizing inland industrial development had actually led to a lower rate of industrial growth than that which could have been attained under an alternative investment strategy (Chu Jung-chi, 22–3).

Finally, the leadership's perception of the external military threat also changed at this time (MacFarquhar, 68–74). The conclusion of the U.S.–Taiwan Defense Treaty in December 1954 and the realization in 1955 that the U.S. had the capability to utilize tactical nuclear weapons in the Taiwan Straits area had previously heightened the leadership's perception of defense requirements. This, of course, reinforced the emphasis on inland industrial development that had been pursued since 1953.

But, by early 1956 the leadership had apparently fundamentally reappraised the external threat. As a result, defense expenditures, which had been increased by 10 percent in 1955, were reduced in 1956 (Li Hsien-nien 1955, 25; 1956, 1; 1957, 17). The argument that defense considerations should influence the relative priorities assigned to inland and coastal industry was abandoned. Indeed, in 1956 it was said that previous accentuation of defense considerations had resulted in an overemphasis on inland industrial development (Chu Jung-chi, 25; Chang Feng-chi, 73). The new view was that the overall defense interests of the country would be best served by more rapid growth of aggregate industrial output and that this was most easily achieved through the "full utilization of coastal industry" (Editorial 1956).

The combination of these three factors – the completion of the socialist transformation of private enterprises, the realization of the high costs in terms of growth foregone that was inherent in the inland development strategy, and the reassessment of defense requirements – led to a marginally increased emphasis on the development of coastal industry. This trend is evident in Table 3.5, which shows that investment shares in 1957 for Fukien, Kwangtung, Shanghai, and Kiangsu – all coastal provinces – were well above their shares for the First Five-Year Plan as a whole. The increases are, however, modest because aggregate national investment in 1957 was reduced in comparison with 1956 and because a substantial portion of investment funds was committed to the completion of projects begun prior to 1957. Furthermore, the shift in investment strategy appears to have been quite marginal – it did not constitute a reversal of the general priority of more rapid development of backward regions.

Other changes in regional investment strategy.   In addition to the increased priority for coastal industrial investment, two other changes in regional investment priorities were discussed in 1956 in connection with the formulation of the Second Five-Year Plan (1958–62). First was a reduction in the investment share for the Northeast (Liu Tsai-hsing). This actually was part of a long-run trend evident since 1953. The Northeast received more investment than any other region during the First Five-Year Plan period, but its share was less than during the recovery period (when the bulk of state investment went to the reconstruction of the war-damaged Manchurian industrial base) and was well below the proportionate contribution of the region to industrial output. In addition to the overall reduction, there was to be a geographic shift of emphasis within the Northeast. A larger portion of investment in 1958–62 was planned for Kirin and Heilungkiang, rather than Liaoning. Data for these provinces confirm that this pattern was, in fact, followed. In 1958, the investment share of the region as a whole was reduced by one-third of the level allocated during the First Five-Year Plan period and, within the Northeast, Liaoning's share was significantly reduced.[19]

A second change was the increased investment in the Southwest beginning in 1957. In the early years of the First Five-Year Plan, the Southwest had a low investment priority. Natural resource exploration was undertaken to determine which industries were most suitable for the Southwest. In addition to a lack of knowledge of the raw material base, the region lacked a rail link to the rest of China. One of the key railroad construction projects in the First Five-Year Plan was the Paochi–Ch'engtu line, which linked the Szechuan Basin with the rest of China. After it was completed in 1956, additional investment projects were begun in Szechuan (Shabad, 219; Wu Chun-yang; Liu Tsai-hsing).

Postdecentralization investment data for Szechuan do not appear in Table 3.5 because I have not found data on the magnitude of direct central investment in Szechuan after 1957. However, the increase in local investment alone was sufficient to increase the province's share of national investment in 1958 and 1959.[20] Increased investment in Yünnan and Kweichow, the other two provinces in the Southwest, shown in Table 3.5, confirms the increased investment priority enjoyed by the region as a whole after 1956.

Summary.   The actual allocation of investment funds in the years immediately after the First Five-Year Plan appears broadly consonant with the changes in investment strategy that were articulated by central government policymakers prior to the initiation of economic reform. This modified investment strategy called for more investment in the coastal provinces (except Liaoning) and the Southwest and reduced allocations for the Northeast.

On the whole, these changes do not appear to have favored either more- or less-developed regions. The beneficiaries of the changes were a very mixed group. The coastal regions of Shanghai, Peking, and Hopei (including Tientsin) were well above the average level of per capita development, whereas other coastal provinces were relatively less well developed. The Southwest, the other region that gained as a result of the modified investment policy, was also a relatively backward region. The Northeast provinces, which received reduced investment allocations, were well above the average level of development.

In short, because the modified investment strategy did not substantially increase the investment priority of more-developed regions as a group, the actual pattern of investment continued to involve considerable redistribution of resources from rich to poor regions. Shanghai continued to be a major source of these centrally redistributed funds, and as the northeastern provinces lost the relatively favorable investment status that they enjoyed during the First Five-Year Plan, they too provided the center with a growing volume of revenues that could be transferred to less-developed regions.

Institutional changes in 1958 and 1959

In broad terms, then, the central government continued to achieve
its major distributive goals. In particular, the pattern of expenditures
after the decentralization shows little if any tendency for relatively
advanced provinces to gain an advantage over less-developed regions, at least in the first years following the decentralization. Beyond this statistical evidence, additional modifications of the fiscal
system that were undertaken in 1958 and 1959 give broad support to
the hypothesis that equity goals remained salient in the collective
preference function of the leadership. These reforms reflect continued central government control of the fiscal system and also the
perception that even the limited devolution of resource-allocation
powers initiated in late 1957 could eventually have unfavorable distributive implications.

This view of the leadership carefully weighing the consequences
of alternative approaches to economic decentralization is not consistent with most published Western accounts of this period. By and
large, these analyses have been heavily influenced by the hectic
campaign atmosphere that prevailed after the Great Leap Forward
was announced in mid-1958. During the latter half of the year and
well into 1959 the Chinese press was filled with inflated claims of
achievement in all fields of endeavor. In response to the surge in
production, enterprise plans were repeatedly revised upwards. Normal planning procedures appeared to have been thrown to the
winds, particularly as inflated local reports of tremendous break-
throughs in agricultural production were accepted.

Beneath this frantic pace, however, the fiscal system appears to
have functioned with a semblance of normalcy. Provincial fiscal reports published during this period suggest that established procedures and regulations continued to be followed. Several tax and
fiscal reforms, to be discussed below, worked their way through the
usual bureaucratic channels and were approved and promulgated by
the State Council and the Ministry of Finance. Although these documentary materials inevitably provide only a partial view that tends to
emphasize rationality, continuity, and stability, this normalcy is also
related by a former ministry official. This informant, who left China
via Honk Kong in the very early 1960s, reports that the budgetary
process itself in 1958 and 1959 was basically unchanged from earlier
years (Vogel n.d., 12).

The unified fiscal system and the system of revenue sharing both continued to be important mechanisms for controlling the allocation of resources after 1957. Although the decentralization directive dealing with the tax system appeared to vest local governments with increased tax authority (State Council 1958e), most evidence suggests the central government continued to impose a unified tax structure. Provincial governments appear to have been unable to use tax reform as a means of raising revenues that they could control outside the centralized budgetary process. The central government in 1958 and 1959 implemented a number of specific tax reforms that demonstrate this continued control of the fiscal system.

The relative stability and continuity of the budgetary and financial processes even during periods of political instability appears to be due partly to the unusual continuity of leaders and administrators and the resiliency of the related institutions. The Ministry of Finance was headed by Li Hsien-nien from its inception in 1949 until January 1975. After 1954, Li was not only minister of finance but also simultaneously director of the State Council's Office of Finance and Trade, which controlled the activities of the People's Bank, and the Ministries of Food, Commerce, and Foreign Trade as well as Finance. The day-to-day operations of the Ministry of Finance were actually in the hands of the ranking vice-minister. Up until the mid-1960s, this post was held successively by only three individuals: Jung Tzu-ho (1949–53), Chin Ming (1954–8), and Wu Po (1958–67).[21] All had long experience in fiscal administration. The People's Bank appears to be characterized by similar continuity of leadership.

Equally important, both the Ministry of Finance and the People's Bank appear to have been somewhat immune to the periodic bureaucratic reorganizations that have occurred since 1949. Both were established in 1949 and have remained as coequal subordinates of the state's highest administrative organ (initially the Government Administrative Council and after 1954 the State Council), which in turn was under the leadership of Premier Chou En-lai from its inception until his death in 1976. This institutional continuity and the enduring influence of high-ranking officials such as Li Hsien-nien and Chou En-lai explains much of the apparent stability of budgetary practices even during periods of political turmoil.

Tax reform

In mid-1958, Peking announced a major agricultural tax reform (State Council 1958a; Editorial 1958b; Wu Po 1958a). The new system

Table 3.10. *Agricultural tax rates, by province
(agricultural tax as a percent of the normal yield)*

Province	Rate
Northeast	
Liaoning	18.0
Kirin	18.5
Heilungkiang	19.0
North	
Hopei	15.0
Shantung	15.0
Honan	15.0
Shansi	15.0
Inner Mongolia	16.0
Peking	15.0
East	
Kiangsu	16.0
Anhui	15.0
Chekiang	16.0
Shanghai	17.0
Central	
Hupei	16.0
Hunan	16.0
Kiangsi	15.5
South	
Kwangtung	15.5
Kwangsi	14.0
Fukien	15.0
Southwest	
Szechuan	16.0
Kweichow	14.0
Yünnan	14.0
Northwest	
Shensi	14.0
Kansu	13.5
Tsinghai	13.5
Sinkiang	13.0
Ninghsia	13.5

Source: Li Ch'eng-jui 1959, 325.

fixed progressive tax rates on a regional basis. Although progressive rates had been applied to individual peasant households in most areas of China since 1950, this was the first time they were established on a regional basis. The new rates, shown in Table 3.10, ranged from a high of 19 percent in Heilungkiang to a low of 13 percent in Sinkiang.[22] Because provincial authorities were instructed to implement nonuniform tax rates within their provinces to take account of differing land and other conditions, the effective differential between the highest and lowest rates was probably in excess of 100 percent. That is, tax rates on the most-developed portions of some provinces were over twice the rates that applied in the provinces where agriculture was less developed.

Because the tax rates shown in Table 3.10 are positively correlated with the level of per capita grain output (Donnithorne 1967, 339), the differentiation in tax rates tends to reduce real rural consumption differentials across provinces. At the same time, because the expenditures financed from the agricultural tax were largely controlled by the central government, the differential in the basic rates further reflects the power of the center to extract greater resources from more-developed areas.

In 1958, Peking also overhauled the structure of industrial and commercial taxes (State Council 1958k; Editorial 1957; Wu Po 1958b). The new consolidated industrial-commercial tax combined several taxes previously collected at different stages of production into a single tax paid on final sales. Taxes on most intermediate goods were eliminated. Although the overall burden of the new tax was designed to equal the collections from the four taxes that it replaced, rates for many individual commodities were adjusted. Furthermore, the new tax incorporated the stamp tax, which had previously been assigned exclusively to local governments. Similarly, in 1959 the tax on interest income, which had been a local revenue source since 1950, was abolished (State Council 1958j). Thus, even after the decentralization Peking retained the ability to redesignate local revenues as shared revenue or to abolish certain local taxes altogether. In summary, although the major goal of the reform was to simplify the overall tax structure, the actual implementation demonstrated the central government's continued control of the structure, scope, and rates of the single most important tax.

The 1959 fiscal reform

In 1959, the central government launched another reform of the fiscal system. Although partly stimulated by the desire to simplify further the revenue-sharing apparatus, there is reason to believe that the reform also reflected the desire to assure a continuing high degree of central control of the fiscal system. The thrust of the changes was to reduce significantly the possibility that provincial governments might eventually be able to turn the features of the 1958 decentralization to their own advantage. Although the detailed provisions of the reform are not known, its main outlines can be determined from a variety of sources (Ministry of Finance 1958a,b; Hsü Fei-ch'ing 1959).

Most important, the reform abandoned fixed revenue-sharing rates between the center and the provinces. As pointed out above, this was potentially the most significant aspect of the 1958 reform because it would have assured provincial governments of automatic increases in revenues available to finance local expenditures. The abolition of fixed sharing ended any possibility that individual provinces might establish genuinely independent revenue sources.

The division of revenues into four categories was also ended. Instead, all income, with the exception of local fixed income, was pooled and subject to an overall sharing rate. This was called the "method of sharing the total amount" (*tsung-o fen-ch'eng ti pan-fa*). The artificial category "normal expenditures" was eliminated. Instead, each province's sharing rate was set annually to cover the investment and increases in working capital necessary to carry out the plans of enterprises that had been transferred down, as well as to finance all other approved local expenditures. Revenues collected in excess of approved expenditures had to be remitted directly to Peking.

In addition, provinces that had previously not shared enterprise profits and adjustment revenues began to receive a portion of these revenues in 1959 (Ma I-hsing 1958). Because provincial expenditures continued to be controlled by the center, this caused enormous increases in their remission rates. In Shanghai, for example, the rate rose from 8 percent in 1958 to over 80 percent after enterprise profits and industrial-commercial tax revenues began to be channeled through the municipal budget in 1959. Similar changes occurred for Tientsin (Sung Ching-i 1959, 1960), Peking (Ch'eng Hung-i; Wan Li), and presumably Liaoning as well.[23]

These changes signaled an end to the system in which provincial expenditures would be limited only by their revenues. The crucial factor thus continued to be central government approval of expenditure levels. Only the system of revenue collection and the sources subject to sharing had changed from the First Five-Year Plan period. Now all revenues, with the exception of customs taxes and earnings of enterprises remaining under exclusive central government control, were collected through provincial budgets and shared partially with each province. But, as previously, collection did not imply control over the allocation of revenues.

Continued central government control of provincial expenditures included the usual provincial programs and also control of the expenditures for enterprises that had been transferred to local management. This is borne out not only by the statistical tests, which failed to reflect any increased provincial control of locally collected revenues, and the continued existence of a system of comprehensive expenditure controls, but also by the revenue-sharing rates established in 1959.

Under the system of sharing total revenues, provinces collecting revenues in excess of approved expenditures had to remit the excess portion to Peking. Under this arrangement, in 1959 half of all provinces had revenues in excess of approved expenditures. The other 14 provinces' revenues were less than their expenditures, so they received subsidies from the center. The planned rates of remission for surplus provinces for the first quarter of 1959 are shown in Table 3.11.

These rates can be compared with the annual remission rates for 1959 calculated from available provincial financial correspondence between the first-quarter planned rate and the observed annual rate for those provinces for which I have actual data.[24] Thus, the planned first-quarter rate is an acceptable approximation of the actual annual rate for those provinces for which I have not been able to locate fiscal reports in the postdecentralization period. The planned figures do include several important provinces for which this is the case. For example, Liaoning, the second-largest industrial center, does not appear in Table 3.12, but from Table 3.11 it can be seen that Liaoning's planned remission rate was second only to Shanghai's. Heilungkiang, another highly developed industrial center for which actual data are not available, also had a very high planned rate of remission.

Comparison of Tables 3.11 and 3.12 is also useful because the

Table 3.11. *Planned central-provincial revenue-sharing rates, first quarter, 1959 (percent)*

Province	Rate
Northeast	
Liaoning	−63.9
Heilungkiang	−50.5
Kirin	−16.8
North	
Hopei[a]	−50.8
Shantung	−52.2
Honan	−17.2
Peking	−42.0
East	
Kiangsu	−47.7
Chekiang	−31.0
Shanghai	−80.2
Central	
Hupei	−4.2
Hunan	−15.3
South	
Kwangtung	−38.8
Southwest	
Szechuan	−25.1

[a] Includes Tientsin.
Source: Ministry of Finance 1958a, 61.

source for Table 3.11 makes clear that the other 14 provinces had approved expenditures in excess of their planned revenues and were to receive subsidies from the central government to make up the difference. From provincial reports summarized in Table 3.12, it is clear that Anhui, Kweichow, Shansi, Sinkiang, Tibet, Tsinghai, and Yünnan did, in fact, receive central subsidies. Thus the official source confirms that Fukien, Inner Mongolia, Kiangsi, Kwangsi, Shensi, and Kansu, all provinces for which I do not have actual data, also received subsidies.

Finally, Table 3.12 makes it clear that fixed sharing rates were actually abandoned. For the twelve provinces for which actual 1959 and planned 1960 sharing rates are available, the rates are different for the two years in all provinces. Four provinces were to receive proportionately greater subsidies (less outflow) in 1960, while eight were to receive proportionately reduced subsidies (greater outflow).

Table 3.12. *Central-provincial revenue-sharing rates, 1959–60 (percent)*

Province	1959	1960[a]
Northeast		
Kirin[c]	-27.4	-24.0
North		
Hopei[b,d]	-28.8	-36.4
Shantung[e]	-44.8[a]	—
Honan[f]	-22.0[a]	—
Shansi[g]	7.9	—
Peking[h]	-51.2	-62.0
Tientsin[i]	-69.2	-70.8
East		
Kiangsu[j]	-45.6	—
Anhui[k]	30.7	16.7
Shanghai[l]	-80.2	-83.3
Central		
Hunan[m]	-19.6	-5.9
South		
Kwangtung[n]	-43.3[a]	—
Southwest		
Szechuan[o]	-33.2	-30.1
Kweichow[p]	18.2	23.8
Yünnan[q]	18.0	10.3
Tibet[r]	83.5	60.0
Northwest		
Sinkiang[s]	25.9	10.3
Tsinghai[t]	56.7[a]	—

Note: Negative numbers show provincial remissions to the central government as a percent of total revenues collected by the province. Positive numbers show net subsidies from the central government as a percent of total provincial expenditures. Numbers for 1959 are calculated on the basis of final accounts except as noted. Data for 1960 are planned, not actual.
[a] Budgeted sharing rate, final account not available. [b] Exclusive of Tientsin.
Sources: [c] Wang Huan-ju 1960. [d] Chou Cheng-hsin. [e] Li Yü-ang. [f] Ch'i Wen-chien 1959. [g] Wu Kuang-t'ang 1960. [h] Wan Li. [i] Sung Ching-i 1960. [j] Ch'en Shu-t'ung 1959. [k] T'ien Lei. [l] Ma I-hsing 1960. [m] Shang Tzu-chin 1960. [n] Wei Chin-fei 1959. [o] Chang Hu-ch'en 1960. [p] Hsü Chien-sheng 1960. [q] Wu Tso-min 1960. [r] Wang Yung-k'uei. [s] Liu Tzu-mo 1960. [t] Yüan Jen-yüan.

The striking inverse relationship between level of development and central–provincial revenue sharing is brought out in Table 3.13. The systematic redistributive influence of the center's fiscal program is unmistakable. The most-developed provinces, shown at the top of Table 3.13, generally have the highest remission rates. Indeed, all the provinces that are above the median level of industrial output, with the exception of Shansi, Fukien, Sinkiang, and Inner Mongolia, were required to remit part of their revenues to Peking. These remission rates ranged from 4 to 80 percent. On the other hand, most of the provinces below the median level of development retained all their revenues and in addition received subsidies from the central government.

The data contained in Table 3.13 do not appear to support the hypothesis of increased provincial autarky. They show that the central government continued to extract proportionately more resources from the more-developed provinces predicted to have gained the most as a result of the decentralization. Most noticeably, provinces such as Heilungkiang, Shantung, Kiangsu, Chekiang, and Kwangtung, which were shown in Table 2.9 to be among the major sources of central government revenue during the First Five-Year Plan, continued to have proportionately higher remission rates to the central government. Furthermore, compared with the First Five-Year Plan period, central government subsidies to backward areas have increased and more provinces have moved into a subsidy position.[25]

Thus, the empirical evidence on both the revenue side, presented immediately above, and the expenditure side, as discussed earlier in this chapter, support the same conclusion – that the central government continued to exercise relatively centralized control over resource allocation. This control was used to redistribute a substantial volume of real resources on an interprovincial basis. As a result, there is little evidence of the development of a pattern of provincial self-sufficiency or autarky.

One final example reinforces the view that provincial governments had minimal tax authority in the postdecentralization period. In 1958, Peking announced that it would no longer issue national economic construction bonds, but that provincial governments could sell their own local bonds (National People's Congress Standing Committee; Editorial 1958c). The revenues were to be retained entirely by each province. This was undoubtedly the most important additional tax authority given to provincial governments after 1957. De-

Table 3.13. *Central–provincial revenue-sharing rates, 1959 (percent)*

Province	Rate
Shanghai	−80.2
Peking	−51.2
Liaoning	−63.9[a]
Heilungkiang	−50.5[a]
Kirin	−27.4
Hopei[b]	−44.7
Shansi	+7.9
Kiangsu	−45.6
Kwangtung	−43.3[c]
Hupei	−4.2[a]
Chekiang	−31.0[a]
Fukien	+[d]
Sinkiang	+25.9
Inner Mongolia	+[d]
Shantung	−44.8[c]
Shensi	+[d]
Kiangsi	+[d]
Szechuan	−33.2
Yünnan	+18.0
Hunan	−19.6
Tsinghai	+57.7[c]
Anhui	+30.7
Kansu	+[d]
Kwangsi	+[d]
Kweichow	+18.2
Honan	−22.0[c]
Ninghsia	+[d]
Tibet	+83.5

Note: Provinces are listed in descending order of 1957 per capita industrial output. Negative numbers show provincial remittances to the center as a percentage of total revenues collected by the province. Positive numbers show subsidies from the center as a percent of total provincial expenditures. All rates were calculated on the basis of final accounts, except as noted.
[a] Planned revenue-sharing rate for the first quarter of 1959. Annual data were not available.
[b] Including Tientsin.
[c] Planned revenue-sharing rate for the full year.
[d] A + indicates that the province retained 100 percent of its revenues and in addition received a subsidy from the central government but that the size of this subsidy in relation to expenditures is not known.
Sources: Tables 3.11, 3.12.

spite this opportunity, only a few provinces actually issued economic construction bonds.[26] This may reflect the realization of provincial authorities that, under the system of "sharing the total amount," increased tax revenues from this source would be offset by a reduction in shared revenues. Thus, issuing provincial bonds would only result in a higher local tax burden, not more retained revenues.

Shanghai's fiscal role

Up to now, the analysis of the redistribution of resources has not focused on any particular region but rather has been couched in terms of relatively advanced versus relatively backward provinces. A more detailed analysis of a single province will both demonstrate more vividly the far-reaching powers of the central government over resource-allocation decisions as well as offer a more general explanation of the degree to which revenue sharing rates shown in Table 2.9 and 3.13 actually understate the center's fiscal powers. Understatement arises because provincial remission rates reflect only revenues collected by the provinces. In addition, the center also collects some tax revenues directly within each province that are not reflected in provincial budgets. The most important of these revenues was the profits of centrally managed industrial enterprises. As was shown in Table 3.2, these enterprise revenues were concentrated in major industrial centers. Thus, the structure of revenue sharing shown in Tables 2.9 and 3.13 underestimates the degree of resource redistribution. The downward bias in Table 3.13 is less because, after the decentralization, the share of national revenues collected by provincial governments rose from about 60 to 80 percent.

For one provincial unit, Shanghai, data on both revenue collected directly by the central government and revenues remitted to the center from local collections are available. These data are shown in Table 3.14. During the First Five-Year Plan period, revenues generated in Shanghai and collected directly by or transferred to the central government by municipal remissions financed almost one-fifth of central government expenditures. Some of these revenues were used by the central government to finance its activities within Shanghai. The most important of these central government expenditures was investment. As shown in lines 4 and 5, however, direct central government investment in Shanghai was only about one billion (American bil-

Table 3.14. *Shanghai's fiscal role (absolute numbers in billions of yuan)*

	1953–7 (cumulative)	1958
1. Revenues from Shanghai to central government[a,c]	17.79	6.20
2. Total central government expenditure[d]	101.13	18.69
3. Shanghai's contribution as a percent of total central expenditure	17.6%	33.2%
4. Direct central government investment in Shanghai[b,e]	1.0	.12
5. Central investment in Shanghai as a percent of Shanghai revenues to center	5.6%	1.9%

[a] Includes revenues collected directly by the central government and remissions through the municipal budget.
[b] Does not include investment financed through the municipal budget.
Sources: [c] 1953–7, P'an Hsüeh-min, 304; Ma I-hsing 1958. 1958, *Wen-hui pao,* 14 June 1959.
[d] Table 1.4. [e] 1953–7, *Chieh-fang jih-pao,* 11 August 1956, 28 August 1957, 7 June 1959.
1958, *Chieh-fang jih-pao,* 7 June 1959; *Wen-hui pao,* 14 June 1959.

lion) yuan during the First Five-Year Plan period or about 6 percent of the revenues that the center extracted from the municipality.

Shanghai's importance as a revenue source for the center was hardly diminished by the decentralization. In 1958, revenues collected directly by or transferred to Peking financed one-third of the center's expenditures. The return of revenues to the municipality in the form of central government investment was reduced to less than 2 percent of the revenues that had been extracted. And, as will be shown in Chapter 4, Shanghai has continued to make comparable contributions in the 1960s and 1970s.

Summary

The expenditure tests, the pattern of central–provincial revenue sharing, and a comparative analysis of the decentralization and earlier reform efforts, all suggest that after 1957 the center retained substantial power to determine the expenditure of local governments. There was a modest increase in local fiscal authority because of some reduction in the degree of disaggregation of expenditure targets and an increase in local extrabudgetary funds. However, the center continued to impose a unified tax system and to implement a broad nationally integrated economic plan that required the redistribution of substantial resources from rich to poor provinces. As a result, there is little evidence of the emergence of autarkic provincial planning and increasing interprovincial inequality during the 1950s. It is, however, likely that certain kinds of evidence suggesting an adverse effect of decentralization on interregional inequality would not become available until after a significant time lag. Thus Chapter 4 analyzes the distributive implications of Chinese planning since the 1950s.

4

Economic planning since the First Five-Year Plan

A central finding of this study is that the decentralization introduced at the end of the First Five-Year Plan period did not significantly reduce the ability of the central government to achieve broad distributive objectives. This view is supported by specific expenditure tests and the pattern of central-provincial revenue sharing, as well as by a more careful examination of the provisions of the decentralization measures themselves. Particularly when compared with earlier reforms, the decentralization seems less extensive than many have supposed. Equally important, as will be shown in this chapter, the redistributive investment policy of the central government has led to a significant reduction of interregional inequality in the distribution of industrial output, both during the First Five-Year Plan and during the 1957–74 period.

However, this is not meant to suggest that the decentralization did not have important implications for the nature of economic planning in China. Although the leadership has not either deliberately sacrificed equity for the achievement of more rapid growth or allowed the emergence of de facto provincial autarky, the system of economic planning that was initiated in the closing years of the 1950s decade did provide improved mechanisms for coordinating the partially overlapping horizontal and vertical hierarchical elements of the planning process. This enhanced the economic management powers of provincial governments and introduced a new degree of flexibility in economic and budgetary planning that became the foundation of the system of planning in the 1960s and 1970s.

This chapter explores how the modified system of economic planning emerged and explains the changing distribution of resource-allocation powers in the period following the First Five-Year Plan. In particular, it focuses on the mechanisms of the new system that enhanced the authority of provincial and local officials while simultaneously preserving basic resource-allocation power at the central level. The closing sections of the chapter will analyze the distributive implications of the new system. Most important, it will be argued that the central government's policies with respect to interprovincial economic balance were not only well intentioned, but that they have contributed to a pattern of regional industrial growth that is distinctly different, not only from other less-developed market-oriented economies but from some socialist planned economies as well.

It must be borne in mind that the analysis presented here is necessarily somewhat more tentative than that contained in earlier chapters. Since 1960, the Chinese government has not only severely restricted the release of data necessary to judge accurately the overall performance of the economy but has also imposed a virtually complete blackout on information concerning the planning process. Annual national and provincial economic plans are no longer released and, more important, qualitative information comparable to the lively discussion of the merits of alternative approaches to economic planning that was published in the 1950s is no longer available. Consequently, documenting the nature of the improved mechanisms for coordinating economic plans at the provincial level and precisely delineating the extent to which lower levels of planning administration have replaced higher levels is an extremely difficult task. Fortunately, there has been some improvement in the availability of data that reflect broad distributive outcomes and this information to some extent can be used to interpret the nature of the planning process itself.

Economic planning versus economic management

The reform initiated at the end of the First Five-Year Plan can perhaps be most usefully understood as an attempt to decentralize operational decision-making power to the enterprise level and coordinating functions to the provincial level while retaining a high degree of centralized control of the economic policy instruments that could be used to achieve distributive goals and to prevent the emergence of what Peter Wiles calls "subordinate autarky" (Wiles, 58). The latter phenomenon arises when territorial decentralization allows all regions to attempt to manufacture all products regardless of cost. This reform was thus designed to alleviate the inefficiencies arising from the inflexibility of the vertically organized hierarchical planning system without giving rise to significantly increased inequality or to losses of interregional specialization and economies of scale associated with provincial autarky.

Perhaps the most significant long-run change introduced by the decentralization is the expanded scope of provincial economic plans. Economic planning during the First Five-Year Plan period was characterized by lack of effective coordination between locally and centrally managed production units. For example, at the end of the First Five-Year Plan period almost one-half of all industrial output and 60 percent of all producer goods originated in centrally managed firms (Hai Ch'ü-niao). The production, investment, supply, and labor plans of these firms were determined by central government ministries and planning agencies with little or no coordination with other production units managed by local governments. As discussed in Chapter 1, the absence of adequate mechanisms to coordinate locally the vertical and horizontal plans, particularly for investment, commodity distribution, and labor supply, led to considerable economic inefficiency.

After 1957, the authority of provincial officials in the planning process was enhanced via two mechanisms. First, many enterprises were transferred to local management. As a result, the share of industrial output originating in centrally managed enterprises fell from 46 percent in 1957 to 16 percent in 1959. More recent evidence suggests that this proportion has not changed substantially since the late 1950s. Barry Richman reports that in the mid-1960s significantly fewer than 10 percent of all enterprises were centrally managed, although their share of output was undoubtedly somewhat larger (Richman, 676). In some regions the shift has been even more dramatic. In Shanghai, for example, the central government share of output was reduced from 46 percent in 1957 to less than 7 percent in 1970 (Bettelheim, 46). Following this transfer, the plans of these enterprises were, for the first time, included within the scope of the provincial plan.

Secondly, provincial plans were further expanded, at least in theory, to include the enterprises remaining under direct central government administration. The inclusion of both central and local enterprises within local plans, particularly at the provincial level, has created enormous opportunities for improved economic coordination within each province.

For example, local labor bureaus are better able to coordinate the supply of labor and carry out wage planning because of the broadening of the scope of local plans. Provincial and municipal labor bureaus were organized in early 1950 to carry out the policies of the Ministry of Labor. Although the local labor bureaus were initially confined to dealing with welfare issues, unemployment relief, and labor mediation, after the initiation of the First Five-Year Plan manpower planning loomed increasingly important in the functions of the bureaus. The role of provincial and municipal bureaus was particularly important because at this time there was still no effective manpower planning at the national level. Local bureaus controlled the hiring of labor and met the demand for labor in the public sector, if necessary through interregional labor transfers. Labor plans for centrally administered enterprises were, however, compiled by central industrial ministries without consulting the local labor bureau. As a result, the local bureaus were unable to carry out effective manpower planning and control. "Labor plans were compiled separately according to both the vertical system [for centrally managed enterprises] and the horizontal system [for locally managed enterprises]. This method of compilation made it very difficult to carry out unified arrangements for the distribution of the labor force and to correctly determine wage levels within one region. In one city, two identical factories, separated only by a wall (one enterprise of the central government, one of the local) could have different wage levels and welfare benefits" (Wang Kuei-wu, 13).

Following decentralization, the authority of local labor bureaus was considerably enhanced. Local labor plans were expanded to include all enterprises, even those remaining under central management. As a result, hiring powers were unified under local organizations "whose territorial span of control was approximately coterminous with effective local labor markets" (Howe, 142). Although the Ministry of Labor was formally abolished during the Cultural Revolution and had still not formally been reestablished by the end of 1977, the work of labor planning at the local level appears to have been maintained. There appears to have been no substantial change in the wage structure in different provinces nor uncontrolled growth of employment in the modern sector, as one might have expected in the absence of continuing central controls on wages and employment. Since the Cultural Revolution, Provincial Labor Departments have continued to play a central role in the allocation of labor to even the largest industrial plants (Eckstein 1975, 363).

The decentralization also significantly improved the system of material-supply planning. During the First Five-Year Plan period, central government enterprises received their material supplies through a vertically organized central supply system, while local enterprises were supplied by a horizontally administered local supply system. In the absence of effective coordination between the two systems, commodity distribution was inherently inefficient. It frequently meant, for example, that commodities were subject to unnecessary cross-hauls simply because of a lack of sharing of information between the two systems (Ch'en Ta-lun, 34). Since decentralization, the system of material-supply planning has been improved because of the expansion of the scope of provincial plans and a substantial reduction in the number of commodities subject to the unified supply planning of the center.

The expansion of the scope of provincial plans has made it possible for local governments to coordinate the supply arrangements of all enterprises within a province. Under the new system, even centrally managed enterprises receive their inputs through the locally managed commodity distribution system and these commodities are included in the provincial distribution plan. The interprovincial distribution of a large number of important commodities is still determined by the central government, but the actual administration of commodity supplies within each province has, to a significant degree, been unified under the control of local planning agencies. This has allowed a substantial reduction in the number of central supply agencies and associated commodity warehouses and material stockpiles (She I-san, 34).

In spite of increased provincial authority in economic planning, particularly in manpower and commodity distribution, there has been substantial continuing central government control of basic resource-allocation decisions, particularly planning of production, commodity supply, and investment. This control was implicit in the decentralization directives, which specified that the center would continue to control such plan targets as output of principal agricultural and industrial products; investment; interprovincial transfers of raw materials, equipment, and consumer goods; the value and structure of exports and imports; financial revenue and expenditure targets, including the transfers of revenues between the center and each province; the enrollment plans of institutions of higher education; total wages of labor; volume of freight; and the detailed plans of the enterprises under the direct control of the central ministries (State Council 1958c).

Despite the decentralization of substantial authority to provincial governments, the center retained several important means of assuring that these centrally determined components of the economic plan were in fact carried out by lower levels of government administration.

Most important, the central government is intimately involved in the planning process at the local level. The first round of the planning process, which is described with the phrase "sent down twice, reported up once" (*liang-tz'u hsia-ta i-tz'u shang-pao*), begins with the preliminary plan targets (so-called control numbers) that are sent from the State Planning Commission to provincial governments. Although the provincial planning authorities have considerable flexibility in arranging the precise details of the plan, the process is one in which the initial targets are supplied from above rather than coming from the local level (State Council 1957a; Eckstein 1975, 360; Berger, 559–61). These centrally specified targets include the value of output of principal agricultural and industrial products, the amount of investment, the number of workers, and the total wage bill. These preliminary targets are then further divided by provincial authorities and assigned to administrative regions and factories under direct provincial control. These targets are, in turn, disaggregated again and serve as the preliminary targets for the plans of towns and counties under the administrative region level of government. After discussions at the lowest levels, suggestions for revised targets are assembled at each level and transmitted upward. At the national level, the State Planning Commission coordinates the plans of the provinces, autonomous regions, and municipalities. Nominally there are no longer vertically organized plans covering individual sectors, but it is clear that the unified national plan that emerges has also been integrated with the overall sectoral priorities of the central government. Once the plan has been centrally approved, final plan targets are issued to provincial and, in turn, lower levels of government and of course to the enterprises under their jurisdiction.

In addition to this general central role in determining the major targets of provincial plans, the center also maintains much more specific policy instruments for intervening at lower levels. Among the most important of these mechanisms are the systems of dual rule of enterprises, and of continued control of interprovincial transfers of both fiscal and material resources.

The system of dual rule is perhaps the most innovative of these mechanisms and the one that best exemplifies the center's attempt to delegate administrative and managerial authority to lower levels while retaining control of major resource-allocation decisions. Prior to the late 1950s, state enterprises were controlled by a single level of government. About one-half of all industrial output originated in enterprises under central government control. Particularly in heavy industry, most of the important plants were directly managed by central industrial ministries. This meant, for example, that any expansion of an enterprise was authorized by and financed from the budget of the controlling ministry. Enterprises of lesser importance were usually managed by provincial or municipal governments. Investment in a provincial enterprise would be arranged by the provincial government and financed from the province's centrally approved investment allocation. However, enterprises devolved to local management after 1957 were usually placed under a system of dual rule. Under the system of dual rule, enterprises are managed jointly by the central government and a subordinate level of government administration, usually a province or municipality. Dual rule provides a flexible framework that allows the central government to intervene in the planning process at the enterprise level, while delegating most administrative authority to local government officials. This flexibility was, in fact, alluded to by Chou En-lai when he first discussed dual leadership as a means of enhancing local economic power. In his speech to the Eighth Party Congress in the fall of 1956, Chou explained that in some cases of enterprise decentralization the center was to continue to play the "main role," whereas in others the local government was to assume greater responsibility (Chou En-lai 1956b, 311). However, Chou did not specify how this determination would be made.

In practice, the system of dual rule provided a continuing role for the central industrial ministries. This contrasts sharply with the Soviet decentralization of 1957, in which the ministerial system in the industrial sector was abolished. The Chinese government not only retained the ministerial system but repeatedly warned industrial ministries that decentralization could not be used as an excuse for failing to continue to supervise enterprises nominally transferred to local management. In the fall of 1957, when the first directive on decentralization of enterprise management was promulgated, central government departments were told to strengthen their planning work and were warned that they "should never think that since authority has been decentralized they can now adopt a hands-off attitude" (Editorial 1957).

This was reiterated in April 1958, when the number and variety of enterprises transferred down was increased. "Central government departments, after their enterprises have been transferred to local control, should not give up their responsibility for improving the management of these enterprises. Generally speaking the duty of the various central government departments should be to . . . devote 60 to 70 percent of their strength to helping the localities manage their enterprises successfully" (State Council 1958g, 332). The central government ministries were only too happy to comply with the spirit of these instructions.

How was vertical control from the center exercised once enterprises were managed by local governments? In particular, how were they able to play a role in determining the plans for output, for increases in working capital, and for fixed investment?

The mechanisms of continued central control of enterprises nominally devolved to local control are most obvious in 1958. Before each enterprise was transferred down, a central government department had already determined the basic elements of the enterprise plan. When enterprises were transferred downward, local governments became directly responsible for the fulfillment of these predetermined plans. Because the revenues retained by local governments were based on their normal expenditures of 1957, they did not have the resources necessary to manage transferred enterprises. Consequently, local governments received special subsidies specifically earmarked for both increasing the working capital and financing the fixed-investment plan for each enterprise transferred down. In most provinces, the bulk of the increase in expenditures was financed from central subsidies (Lardy 1975a, 165–6).

The limited ability of provincial governments to change enterprise appropriations is not only implicit in fiscal arrangements, but also specifically acknowledged in provincial financial reports. In Liaoning's 1958 provincial budget it was explained that it was not even necessary to discuss expenditures of 360 million government before the start of the decentralization" (Liaoning Provincial People's Council).

Continued direct central government control of investment in decentralized enterprises was also explicitly discussed in Peking's 1958 budget (Chang Yu-yü 1958). The total planned expenditures approved by the Municipal People's Congress were about 475 million yuan. However, in the budget message, the Congress was asked to delegate the responsibility for adjusting this amount to the Municipal People's Council–a body that met throughout the year rather than annually like the Congress. This was necessary, it was explained, because the central government was turning over large numbers of enterprises to local management. Because this was accompanied by the transfer of sizable budgetary appropriations, it required large adjustments in the Peking municipal budget. Even though the Congress did not meet to approve the budget until eight months into the fiscal year, the final accounts showed that expenditures were about 760 million yuan, about 60 percent above the planned level. The transfer of enterprises to municipal control was specifically acknowledged to be the reason for most of this increase (Ch'eng Hung-i).

The central ministries not only controlled the investment plans of enterprises but could, if necessary, reestablish their direct control over all aspects of management. This was evident in 1959, when the central government reasserted direct control over some important projects that had been transferred to local management the previous year. Although there is little, if any, discussion in national publications of this direct reassertion of central management, it was specifically acknowledged by provincial authorities.

For example, in Sinkiang the director of the Finance Department explained that the level of expenditure authorized by the Region's People's Congress in January 1959 had subsequently been substantially reduced when the central government had reassumed management of the petroleum industry in the region (Liu Tzu-mo 1960). Because the provincial budget had originally included 167 million yuan for petroleum-sector investment, when the projects were transferred back the center deducted this amount from the region's approved expenditures.

Similarly, in Peking the deputy mayor, Ch'eng Hung-i, in discussing a planned 50 percent reduction in expenditures for 1959 compared with actual expenditures in 1958 said, "it must be explained that a portion of the capital construction investment in the 1958 budget of the city, such as the Mi-yün reservoir and some municipal construction projects, will be transferred to the budget of the central government in 1959" (Ch'eng Hung-i).

In spite of this reversion of some enterprises to direct central management, most of the enterprises decentralized in the late 1950s remain under dual rule. In addition, some enterprises, most noticeably the Anshan iron and steel works, which were not transferred in the late 1950s (Ministry of Finance 1957b, 17), have been subsumed within the system of dual leadership in recent years (Donnithorne 1974b, 773–4).

In addition to influencing enterprise plans through the system of dual rule, the center retains control of the interprovincial distribution of most important producer goods. Although provincial governments exercise increased administrative responsibility for the intraprovincial distribution of all commodites, the system of unified distribution of many industrial goods has been retained. As noted in Chapter 1, the number of commodities whose distribution is directly controlled by the central government increased steadily during the First Five-Year Plan period. The number of centrally allocated commodities rose from 28 in 1952 to 417 in 1958. However, beginning in 1959 the number was to be reduced to 132. Of these, 45 were under the jurisdiction of the State Economic Commission and 87 were controlled by the central government ministries (She I-san, 34). Reports of recent visitors to the People's Republic suggest that the number of commodities subject to unified distribution remains in the range of from 100 to 200 (Eckstein 1975, 361).

The reduction in the number of centrally distributed commodities expands provincial authority, but the center retains the ability to control directly the distribution of many important producer goods. For example, under the provisions of the reform almost the entire output of the machinery industry remained within the sphere of central control. The Ministry of Metallurgy is responsible for the distribution of pig iron, steel products, and metallurgical materials and equipment; the Ministry of Hydroelectric Power for electric power generation equipment; the Ministry of Petroleum Industry for oil drilling and refining equipment; the Ministry of Textile Machinery for textile machinery, etc. (State Council 1958c). While individual firms are known to strive to develop the capability to produce their own machinery in order to reduce their dependence on outside suppliers (Rawski 1975a, 183), the central government, through the ministerial system, continued to exercise significant monopoly power over the distribution of the capital goods that were crucial to the expansion of output in most sectors.

Finally, the center retained the right to exercise control over the interprovincial distribution of products that they did not control directly through the system of unified distribution. The initial decentralization directive contained an explicit clause authorizing central planning agencies and ministries to convene material production and marketing conferences to exercise control over products for which provincial governments were formally responsible (State Council 1958c, 100).

Material-allocation conferences have emerged as a particularly important means of administering commodity distribution in the 1960s and 1970s (Richman, 712–18; Eckstein 1975, 362; Reynolds). Corresponding with neither the traditional Soviet bureaucratic methods nor with flexible price, free market methods of resource allocation, these meetings are perhaps most usefully thought of as a quasimarket mechanism. By bringing final users and suppliers face to face to agree on delivery times, product specifications, etc., they introduce a degree of flexibility and rationality into the distribution of intermediate products and capital goods that has been absent from the usual bureaucratic approach of centrally planned economic systems. They clearly result, for example, in a significant increase in horizontal flows of information between enterprises that previously would have been formally linked only indirectly through a pair of vertical hierarchical systems.

Meetings are convened once or twice a year to bring suppliers of important raw materials and intermediate goods together with major enterprises that require these goods for meeting their production targets or investment plans. Significantly, however, in the early stages of the planning process these meetings are typically arranged on a functional, vertical basis rather than on a geographic basis, and national planning agencies and ministries play a key organizing role. Thus, initially they usually bring together all major suppliers and users of a limited range of commodities from throughout the nation rather than suppliers and users of all commodities within a single geographic region. In the later stages of the process, the meetings are frequently carried out on a provincial basis. Although there is little information available describing how the contracts between enterprises are actually arranged at these conferences, the continuing role of national agencies and predominantly vertical lines of administration suggest that these conferences provide a mechanism for continued central government control of interprovincial resource transfers.

Provincial governments, however, do have a greater role in the administration of the material supply arrangements worked out at these conferences, particularly when compared with the 1950s, when major enterprises received all their material inputs through a system of vertically administered supply agencies.

This combination of relatively decentralized day-to-day management of enterprises and relatively centralized control of planning functions is a balance that satisfies several ends. The ability of local governments to carry out horizontal, geographic coordination of economic activities has been enhanced by the widespread implementation of dual rule and the enlarged scope of provincial economic plans. However, the center has maintained control of many basic resource-allocation decisions. This control is used to insure a high rate of overall investment, to allocate a large share of investment resources to the producer-goods sector, and to achieve important equity and distributional goals.

In fact, the economic reforms of the late 1950s, which decentralized economic administration while basically retaining control of resource-allocation functions, increased the ability of the central government to achieve these goals. That is, by ridding themselves of many time-consuming onerous management tasks, the central planning agencies and ministries were able to concentrate their talents and energies on overall economic planning. As suggested in Chapter 3, ministries were, in fact, continually exhorted to focus on "comprehensive planning work." The *People's Daily* editorial that accompanied the announcement of the decentralization was even more explicit, saying that "in order to have effective centralization it is necessary to decentralize a portion of authority and give it to the localities; this decentralization of authority on the surface seems to be a weakening of centralization, but it actually strengthens centralization" (Editorial 1957).

I would postulate that it was primarily this continuing central control of overall economic planning, exercised largely through the ministerial system, that accounts for the apparent longevity of the Chinese reform. The Soviets, by contrast, abolished industrial ministries in their reform of 1957 and substituted a horizontal system of planning based on about 100 sovnarkhozy. Subsequently, the center was apparently unable to prevent the phenomenon of territorial subordinate autarky. With fewer constraints imposed from above, many sovnarkhozy attempted to become as self-sufficient in as broad a range of products as possible, irrespective of the higher costs associated with losses in specialization and economies of scale. Although the former problem of ministerial autarky was eliminated, the inefficiencies of the territorial principle appear to have been even larger. Within a short time, the sovnarkhozy were stripped of their resource-allocation power and by 1964 the production principle was formally readopted.

The Chinese, on the other hand, retained the ministerial system, while at the same time introducing new forms of enterprise management and commodity distribution. The continuing role of the ministries largely prevented the emergence of subordinate autarky, while dual rule and new commodity distribution systems allowed local governments to capture the efficiency gains from improved horizontal information flow and coordination.

Efficiency gains presumably resulted from a reduction in the number of levels of administrative control that linked interdependent activities within a region. A larger number of commodity-supply and labor-allocation decisions could be made at the provincial level on the basis of more complete, detailed, and timely information than could be made available in Peking at the ministerial level or within the central planning apparatus. On the other hand, the center's control of investment funds and its capability to redistribute commodities interregionally appears to have prevented the efficiency losses associated with the emergence of territorial subordinate autarky in the Soviet Union.

It is also probable that the large size of China's provinces contributed significantly to the overall success of the reforms. The 1957 decentralization of economic management to geographic units with a median population of about 20 million persons and median land mass of about 70,000 square miles still permitted the capture of economies of scale in production and distribution in most industries while at the same time it reduced the costs of coordination among enterprises within each region. By contrast, the 100-plus sovnarkhozy to which decentralization occurred initially in the Soviet Union were substantially smaller in geographic and population size. Furthermore, the potential for efficiency gains from improved horizontal communication in China may have been greater because prior to decentralization a relatively large share of industrial output was manufactured in plants that were not directly controlled by ministries of the central government. The problems of regional coordination of interdependent activities are presumably greater when a larger portion of interenterprise exchanges occur between centrally and locally controlled plants, rather than when the overwhelming majority of plants are centrally managed, as was the case with plants in the Soviet Union prior to their experiment with the territorial principle.

While I believe that the above analysis captures the broad outlines of the system of economic planning as it has emerged since 1957, particularly the increased emphasis on the territorial principle, the issues raised in the decentralization discussion of the mid-1950s were certainly not resolved conclusively by the reform decrees of 1957 and 1958. Rather, these issues appear to have been the subject of continuing debate and conflict within the leadership. As a result fluctuations in policy continue, although as pointed out earlier in this chapter they can be seen only dimly with currently available information. It would appear, for example, that in the early 1960s in the aftermath of the Great Leap Forward the planning authority of the provinces was somewhat eroded. Not only had implementation of the principle of integrated horizontal plans encountered considerable operational difficulties, but significant opposition to the principle of comprehensive local planning had emerged. The National Economic Planning Group of the Hupei Provincial Economic Studies Association reported that some people argued that "since the distribution and utilization of the important raw materials and most of the financial resources are arranged according to the unified plan of the central government, that localities have no means of compiling a comprehensive balance plan before the state plan has been completed" (Hupei Economic Studies Association National Economic Planning Group). Although the article goes on to argue for the importance of local planning, it concludes by recognizing that the original goal of compiling local plans that would include centrally managed enterprises in order to integrate systematically the sectoral and the local plans "has not yet been completely solved."

Similarly, Li Ch'eng-jui, in an important article in 1964, stated that plan management was still divided into vertical and territorial systems and that the latter did not include all central government enterprises. His discussion also suggests that the center had begun to encroach systematically on the authority that had been devolved to provincial planning authorities (Li Ch'eng-jui 1964).

Finally, and most intriguingly, a recent long article commemorating the achievements of Chou En-lai refers to a formal economic reform that was undertaken in 1970. The article, which appeared in the official journal of the Chinese Communist Party *Hung-ch'i* (Red Flag) and was reprinted in the *Peking Review,* states that "in 1958 and 1970 he [Chou] twice handled the issue of vesting units at the lower levels with greater power to run and build certain enterprises and the reform of the system of economic management . . . " (State Council 1977, 16). Although it is clear that reference to 1958 concerns the decentralization decrees discussed in detail earlier in this study, there is little qualitative evidence that sheds light on the nature of the decisions made in 1970. Like 1957, 1970 marked the end of a five-year-plan. However, unlike the period prior to 1958, when there was a public discussion of the shortcomings of the system of planning as it had evolved during the First Plan, we know little about the specific planning techniques used during the Fourth Plan (1966–70). This period was dominated by the turmoil of the Cultural Revolution (1966–8), which significantly depressed the rate of industrial growth. It is commonly believed that this period of political divisiveness enhanced the power of provincial governments vis-à-vis the center. Most important in this regard are the charges of regionalism leveled against some provincial leaders who were purged during the Cultural Revolution.

For example, Chiang Hua, the First Party Secretary in Chekiang, is reported to have refused to transfer certain commodities to Shanghai, saying "Chekiang is not a colony of Shanghai."[1] Requests for the transfer of food grains to other provinces were also allegedly refused on the grounds that feeding of livestock within Chekiang took a higher priority.

It is usually argued that the powers of the central government were enhanced as political normalcy returned in the late 1960s and that this type of subordinate autarky was reduced if not eliminated. This would suggest that the 1970 decisions referred to in the *Peking Review* were an attempt to devolve greater authority to local governments in the wake of the increased centralization following the close of the Cultural Revolution. This interpretation would appear to be supported by continuing Chinese rhetoric advocating an economic development policy based on local self-sufficiency. Many western analysts have argued that the campaign for local self-sufficiency, particularly the verbal emphasis on the development of local small-scale industry, reflects an attenuation of the redistributive role of the central government (Sigurdson, 212; Donnithorne 1972b, 607–13; Harding, 5).

The uncertainty surrounding the nature of the 1970 reform as well as conflicting opinions concerning the meaning of the local small-scale industry campaign naturally lead one to ask how effectively the planning mechanisms described earlier in this chapter have been in achieving distributive goals. Does Peking continue to exercise wide-ranging powers over resource allocation? If so, does it continue to redistribute resources from more- to less-developed provinces? Has the degree of redistribution been as significant as that of the 1950s, or has the center implicitly sanctioned growing inequality as a means of achieving improved overall growth performance? Furthermore, is the center unable to prevent, or does it overlook, the efficiency losses that accompany subordinate autarky or has it continued to impose an optimal degree of regional specialization?

These are difficult questions to answer with the limited information available since 1960. The absence of empirical data comparable to the rich provincial data of the 1950s makes it impossible to undertake precise statistical tests to answer these questions. Furthermore, although there has been some improvement in recent years, there is still relatively little qualitative information available that clarifies these issues. The sources of information that are most useful for understanding central-provincial fiscal relations and the nature of the budgetary process have been published since the late 1950s.

Despite the relative lack of data and qualitative information, I believe that it is possible to give preliminary answers to these important questions. Although based on partial information, this analysis is strengthened by a more complete understanding of the fiscal system in the earlier years. That is, more limited fragmentary information and data for the years since 1960 can be evaluated in light of the evidence presented in Chapters 2 and 3.

The pattern of resource allocation

Three principal types of evidence bear on the evolution of the redistributive powers of the central government since 1960. The first is a comparison of the patterns of provincial industrial growth during the pre- and postdecentralization periods. Secondly, there is some qualitative evidence on the nature of the tax system and central-provincial revenue-sharing rates. Finally, there is evidence concerning the

Table 4.1. *The pattern of provincial industrial growth, 1952-7*

| Rate of industrial growth 1952-7 | Level of per capita industrial output (1952) | |
	Above median	Below median
Above median	Peking Liaoning Shansi Sinkiang Hupei	Fukien Inner Mongolia Szechuan Shensi Tsinghai Kansu Anhui Yünnan Ninghsia
Below median	Shanghai Tientsin Heilungkiang Kirin Kiangsu Chekiang Kwangtung Shantung Hopei	Kiangsi Hunan Kwangsi Honan Kweichow

Source: Lardy 1977, Table 3.

scope of the state budget and central government control of the composition of provincial expenditures.

The pattern of provincial industrial growth

1952-1957. China's average annual rate of industrial growth during the First Five-Year Plan was 18 percent, according to official statistics (State Statistical Bureau 1960, 19). However, this aggregate growth rate disguises substantial regional variation in the pace of industrial development. The average annual rates of provincial growth actually ranged from a high of about 32 percent in Inner Mongolia to a low of only 12 percent in Kiangsu.[2] Overall, the most striking aspect of China's pattern of provincial industrial development is the relatively slow growth of most of its leading industrial centers. As is shown in Table 4.1, nine of the fourteen provinces where per capita industrial output was above the median level experienced below-median rates of industrial growth. This group included seven of China's ten most industrialized areas: Shanghai, Tien-tsin, Heilungkiang, Kirin, Kiangsu, Chekiang, and Kwangtung. As a group, these regions of above-average development but below-average rates of growth not only produced over half of China's industrial output in 1952 but, as discussed in Chapter 2, they also served as major sources of government revenues during the First Five-Year Plan period. They had been required to remit the vast majority of the revenues they collected to the central government, and in most cases the return flow of resources to these areas in the form of direct central government investment was relatively limited. For example, as shown above for Shanghai, during the period central government investment was equivalent to only about 6 percent of the outflow of revenues from the municipality. Comparable if not quite as extreme situations existed in Kiangsu, Kwangtung, Shantung, and Chekiang.

This relatively unfavorable treatment by the central government and the resulting slow rate of industrial development in these provinces is not surprising. With the exception of Heilungkiang and Kirin, these regions of above-average development were coastal provinces. The declared goal of the First Five-Year Plan was to change "the irrational concentration of industrial enterprises along the coastal areas" and "to restrict the development of big coastal cities in favor of furthering medium and small cities in the interior" (Li Fu-ch'un, 21).

On the other hand, two-thirds of the provinces that ranked below the median level of per capita industrial output in 1952 experienced rates of industrial growth that were above the median level. These provinces are shown in the upper right quadrant of Table 4.1. The members of this group, with the exception of Fukien, were all inland regions. Because of the goal of developing the interior comparatively rapidly, these provinces, for the most part, benefited from favorable fiscal treatment, that is, low remission rates or net subsidies from the central government. They were also the major beneficiaries of the central government's policy of transferring skilled labor away from places like Shanghai to newly emerging industrial centers in inland China. Between 1950 and 1956 the central government, through its direct control over labor allocation, transferred 270,000 workers out of Shanghai. Of this number, 28,000 were specifically identified as technicians and another 170,000 as skilled workers (Liu Chih-ch'eng, 61). These redistributive government programs made substantially more capital and labor inputs available for local growth in less-developed regions than would have been the case under more autarkic policies.

Although less-developed inland regions did not benefit uniformly from this central government investment strategy and a substantial portion of the large-scale investment projects of the First Plan were not completed until after 1957 and thus did not affect the pattern of industrial growth until somewhat later, the degree of interregional inequality was actually reduced during this period. The population-weighted coefficient of variation, which measures the overall degree of dispersion of provincial per capita industrial output from the mean, declined from 1.01 in 1952 to .92 in 1957 (Lardy 1977, 19).[3]

1957–1974. Was this pattern of industrial growth substantially altered by the decentralization? Proponents of the hypothesis of increased provincial autarky believe that the transfer of resource-allocation powers to provincial governments inevitably led to relatively faster rates of industrial growth in more-developed areas that had previously transferred most of their resources to the center. At the other end of the development spectrum, however, provinces that previously financed most of their growth with central government subsidies and direct central government inputs would experience drastic declines in their relative rates of industrial growth. Thus, those who adhere to the hypothesis of increased provincial autarky predict that the previous inverse relationship between the level of development and the rate of industrial growth would be substantially weakened after 1957.

What is the empirical evidence? How does the pattern of provincial industrial growth after the decentralization compare with the pattern during the First Five-Year Plan period? Although the pace of national industrial growth since 1957 has been substantially below that of the First Five-Year Plan period, there continues to be substantial variation in provincial industrial performance. Average growth rates during the period 1957–74 ranged from about 18 to 8 percent per year. As shown in Table 4.2, there continued to be a general inverse relation between level of development and rate of growth. Again over two-thirds of the provinces where per capita industrial output was initially below the median level experienced above-median growth rates. This group included several provinces that had also been less-developed but rapidly growing during the 1952–7 period–Ninghsia, Tsinghai, Kansu, and Shensi. Of the more-developed provinces, over two-thirds experienced rates of growth that were below the median level. Several of these areas, notably

Table 4.2. *The pattern of provincial industrial growth, 1957–74*

Rate of industrial growth 1957–74	Level of per capita industrial output (1957)	
	Above median	Below median
Above median	Peking Kiangsu Kwangtung Inner Mongolia	Shantung Hopei Shensi Hunan Tsinghai Kansu Kwangsi Honan Kweichow Ninghsia
Below median	Shanghai Tientsin Liaoning Heilungkiang Kirin Chekiang Shansi Hupei Fukien Sinkiang	Kiangsi Szechuan Yünnan Anhui

Source: Lardy 1977, Table 3.

Shanghai, Tientsin, Heilungkiang, and Kirin, were also relatively slow growing during the 1952–7 period.

Of course, the pattern of provincial industrial growth since 1957 is not precisely the same as that observed during the First Five-Year Plan period. For example, among the provinces with above-median levels of industrial output, Kiangsu and Kwangtung have moved from the low- to the high-growth category, while Liaoning, Shansi, and Hupei have moved from the high- to low-growth category. Similarly, among the less-developed provinces Szechuan, Yünnan, and Anhui have shifted from the high- to low-growth category, while Hunan, Kwangsi, Honan, and Kweichow have moved from the slow- to the fast-growth category.[4]

These changes in the pattern of provincial industrial growth since 1957 appear to reflect a complex mix of forces. These include exogenous shocks to the economic system, such as the withdrawal of Soviet engineers and technicians in 1960 and the Cultural Revolution (both discussed further below); shifts in sectoral priorities that have had important consequences for industrial location strategy; the emergence of crucial location-specific industries, such as petroleum, in new regions (i.e., the Shengli and Takang fields in Shantung and Hopei, respectively); and perhaps the increased importance of commune- and brigade-operated industries that are financed outside the state budget. An analysis of the precise contribution of these and other forces would require detailed studies of the realtionship between the changing structure of industrial output nationally and within each of the provinces, as well as more complete data on provincial industrial output (particularly for the years 1960–4 and 1966–9) than are currently available.

However, there has been no significant shift of provinces toward the configuration suggested by the hypothesis of provincial autarky – the combination of rapid growth with high levels of output and slow growth with low levels of development. As a result, the pattern of regional convergence has continued in the years following the reform of the system of economic management. The population-weighted coefficient of variation of per capita provincial industrial output has fallen from .92 in 1957 to .87 in 1974 (Lardy 1977, 19).

Implications of the pattern of growth.   What are the implications of this pattern of provincial industrial growth for the redistributive powers of the central government? In the absence of a vigorous and enduring central government role in national economic planning, characterized by a strong redistributive commitment, would one predict a positive or a negative correlation between initial levels of provincial development and subsequent rates of growth? If each area had similar incremental capital-output and savings and investment ratios, an equal rate of return on existing productive capacity, and equal access to labor and other factors of production, one would expect provinces to grow at roughly the same rate.

There is every reason to believe, however, that these conditions did not generally apply and that the more-developed provinces enjoyed significant advantages. As suggested in Chapter 3, incremental capital-output ratios in more-developed regions were lower, on the average, than in less-developed areas where the existing industrial infrastructure was less adequate. Furthermore, existing centers of industrial output enjoyed substantial comparative advantages from their disproportionate concentrations of skilled manpower and greater access to modern technology. They also enjoyed substantial economies of scale and some locational advantages. Peculiarities of China's pricing policies for industrial products, probably also raised the rate of return on existing capacity in more-developed provinces far above that in less-developed areas. That is, the Chinese preference for setting industrial-product prices high enough to allow even relatively inefficient producers to remain in operation without relying on subsidies meant that profit rates for well-established firms tended to be quite high (Eckstein 1977, 147–8). All these conditions support the a priori presumption of a positive correlation between initial levels of development and subsequent rates of growth.

Jeffrey Williamson's study of the relationship between level of development and rate of growth also supports the view that richer provinces would be relatively faster growing in the absence of central government redistribution. Following the suggestions of John Hicks, Albert Hirschman, and Gunnar Myrdal, Williamson tested the hypothesis that the early stages of economic growth tend to be characterized by increasing regional disparities, whereas later stages of development lead to regional convergence (Hicks, 162–6; Hirschman, 187–90; Myrdal). Locational advantages, historical accident, resource endowment, and other considerations may give certain regions within a country an initial advantage when the process of modern economic growth begins. Hirschman hypothesized that when national growth accelerates, the greater importance of "polarization effects" as opposed to "trickle-down effects" would lead to more rapid growth in more-developed areas and increasing interregional inequalities. Capital would be attracted from backward areas to the more rapidly growing regions of the country, and skilled labor would tend to migrate to advanced regions in response to greater employment opportunities. Government policies favoring maximal aggregate economic growth rather than balanced regional development might further compound growing regional disparities.

Only at substantially higher levels of per capita income, Hirschman suggested, would the trickle-down effects of growth become increasingly important and tend to neutralize the polarization effects. The combination of increasing costs of growth in advanced regions with deliberate government policy to insure more balanced regional development would lead to a decline and eventually a reversal of the differential rates of growth between backward and advanced areas. Thus, the interaction of these forces over time gives rise to what is sometimes called an "inverted U-shaped" pattern of economic growth, in which interregional inequality first rises and later falls as per capita income increases.

Williamson, using both time-series and cross-section data for a large sample of countries, was able to confirm empirically the hypothesis of Hicks, Hirschman, and Myrdal. In his cross-section sample of twenty-four nations, low-income countries exhibited relatively small interregional disparities. Middle-income countries had the most extreme interregional inequality, whereas the highest-income nations revealed considerably less interregional disparity. These findings were corroborated by time-series data for the United States. Less-complete long-term data for Sweden, Italy, Brazil, and France analyzed by Williamson, and subsequent intensive investigations of Canadian and Japanese regional growth over periods that include the early stages of industrialization, also give support to the classic inverted U-shaped pattern of regional development (Green; Cleaver).

Quantitative studies of Chinese economic growth suggest that the pattern of regional development conforms to this classic inverted U-shaped pattern. The record shows that, although there was no sustained increase in per capita income for the country as a whole in the first half of the twentieth century (Perkins 1975b, 122–3), there was considerable growth in Manchuria and in a few coastal cities (Eckstein, Chao, and Chang). As a result, the fifty years prior to the formation of the People's Republic were undoubtedly marked by growing interregional inequality. However, the reduction of interregional income variation in China began at a substantially earlier stage of economic development than other countries for which historical time-series data are available.

Regional convergence in Japan, Canada, and the United States did not begin until after three to six decades of sustained growth of per capita gross national product. By contrast, the Chinese pattern of development after 1949 is one in which the reduction of interregional income inequality and the initiation of sustained growth of per capita gross national product appear to have begun simultaneously. Furthermore, the levels of per capita income from which convergence began in Japan, Canada, and the United States were a severalfold multiple of the Chinese level in 1949. In short, although China conforms to the inverted U-shaped pattern of regional development, the timing of the convergence phase has been distinctly different from the historical experience of the currently developed countries.

It is quite clear that the pattern of convergence during the First Five-Year Plan period was the result of a distinct central government policy that favored the development of inland industry at the expense of the initially developed coastal cities and the Northeast. The persistence of this general pattern of regional convergence since 1957 suggests that, although there have been fluctuations over time in the degree to which the regime has been committed to the comparatively rapid growth of less-developed regions, the broadly redistributive nature of central government economic planning has not been reversed. That is, convergence has been achieved despite the marginal shift in investment policy in favor of more-developed regions after 1956, discussed in Chapter 3, and despite the crippling effect that the withdrawal of Soviet economic assistance must have had on the industrialization of inland regions. Most Soviet-aided projects had been located in these less-developed regions, and the long delays in completing these projects after the Soviets withdrew probably depressed industrial growth in these regions for many years (Richman, 857).

Much less is known about the pattern of regional growth within provinces. Some provincial planners explicitly embraced improved intraregional balance as a goal for the Second Five-Year Plan (Lü Chün-chieh), but it is difficult to measure the extent to which this objective has ever been realized. Quite scattered evidence suggests that inequality is being reduced within provinces, at least in the core areas of China and parts of the Northeast. In these relatively more industrialized regions industrial output growth, both since 1949 and during the 1965–75 decade, has been most rapid in intermediate-sized cities rather than provincial capitals. Cities such as Hsinhsiang (Honan); Ch'angchou (Kiangsu); Chuchou and Hsiangt'an (Hunan); Hunchiang and Ssup'ing (Kirin); and Kweilin and Wuchou (Kwangsi), while still contributing only a small share of total provincial output, have experienced rates of industrial growth that are well above their respective provincial averages. All these are prefecture (*ti-ch'ü*) or county (*hsien*) level cities but none are provincial capitals. They appear to represent the most successful examples of the group of forty medium-sized and rapidly growing cities referred to in the Chinese media. On the other hand, in the less-industrialized peripheral areas for which data are available, provincial (or autonomous region) capitals continue to grow either more rapidly than the provincial average, as in Kweiyang (Kweichow), or at roughly the same rate as the provincial average, as in Yinch'uan (Ninghsia) and Lanchou (Kansu). Presumably, in peripheral areas capital cities continue to contribute a preponderant share of total provincial industrial output. In short, within areas that encompass the great bulk of the Chinese population the reduction of inequality in industrial output has occurred within as well as among provinces.[5]

Continuing convergence among provinces, of course, does not imply that interregional inequality will soon be eliminated in China. Although a reduction in relative income inequality is quite unusual at this early stage of development, *absolute* levels of inequality continue to increase. Because the initial differences in the level of development were so large, growing gaps in the absolute level of output among provinces result even when there is a generally inverse relationship between the level of development and rate of growth. Although these absolute gaps may be of interest for some purposes, for drawing inferences about the ability of the central government to redistribute resources among regions, we must clearly focus on relative rates of growth. For it is really the ability of the center to sustain a *rate* of investment in a given province above that which could be financed with local revenues that will, in the long run, lead to relatively higher *rates* of growth for that region.

In short, the long-run pattern of regional economic growth supports the empirical finding discussed in Chapter 3 – that the decentralization of economic planning did not lead a marked increase in the ability of more-developed regions to retain and reinvest an increased share of their own resources for local economic and social development. Furthermore, this hypothesis is supported by scattered direct evidence of the continuing redistributive role played by the central government. This evidence comes both from recent interviews of Western visitors to the People's Republic and scattered data released by the Chinese.

Central-Provincial revenue sharing since 1957

Provincial governments have continued to play a significant role in revenue collection since 1960. In 1972, for example, they collected 80 percent of all government revenues – the same share they collected in 1958 and 1959 (Robinson 1975, 29). Given this continued

Table 4.3. *Central-provincial revenue-sharing rates*

			Post-1960	
	1957^d	1959^e	Year	Rate
Shanghai	n.a.	−80.2	1972	-90^f
Liaoning	n.a.	−63.9	1972	-82^f
Kiangsu	−49.2	−45.6	1972	-70^f
Yünnan	-18.7^a	+18	1974	$+15^g$
Inner Mongolia	−11.5	$+^c$	1972	$+^c$
Kwangsi	+8.6	$+^c$	1972	$+^c$
Sinkiang	+7.2	+25.9	1955–72	$+35^h$
Ninghsia	n.a.	$+^c$	1958–74	$+52^i$
Tibet	$+70-80^b$	+83.5	1960–73	$>50^f$

Notes: Provinces are listed in descending order of industrial development in the mid-1970s. Negative values show provincial remittances to the center as a percentage of total revenues collected by the province. Positive values show subsidies from the center as a percentage of total provincial expenditure. N.a. indicates not available.
[a] For 1956.   [b] For the period 1952–5.
[c] Expenditures in these provinces were greater than anticipated revenues, resulting in a subsidy from the central government. However, the size of this subsidy in relation to expenditures is not known.
Sources: [d] Table 2.9. [e] Tables 3.12, 3.13. [f] Lardy 1975c, 111. [g] *China Trade and Economic Newsletter*, no. 238: 6. [h] NCNA, 25 and 27 September 1975, in British Broadcasting Corporation, *Summary of World Broadcasts, Far East Weekly Economic Report*, W 847, p. A/3.
[i] NCNA, 26 January 1976, in Foreign Broadcast Information Service, *Daily Report, PRC*, 26 January 1976, p. M-5.

preeminence of provincial, as opposed to central, revenue collection, the extent to which physical resources are redistributed interregionally by the central government can be measured by the degree of differentiation in central-provincial revenue-sharing rates. That is, the central government will not be able to redistribute a significant volume of materials from more-developed to backward areas unless it succeeds in extracting proportionately greater resources from the former.

The pattern of central-provincial sharing of revenues in the 1950s, shown in Tables 2.9 and 3.13, continues in the 1960s and 1970s. Although comprehensive information on provincial remission rates is not available, specific rates for a number of provinces have been released in recent years. These rates, given in Table 4.3, show that more-developed provinces still give up a disproportionately large share of the revenues they collect, while poorer provinces retain all their revenues and frequently receive additional subsidies from the center as well.

Shanghai, the most important industrial center, remits 90 percent of its revenues. Liaoning and Kiangsu, the second and third most important sources of industrial output in the mid-1970s, also remit the vast majority of their revenues. Their remission rates, 82 and 70 percent respectively, are substantially above those of 1959. The five autonomous regions, which with the exception of Inner Mongolia are still among the least-developed areas of the country, retain all their revenues and receive additional direct government subsidies. Chinese sources indicate that central subsidies have been equivalent to from one-third to more than one-half of local expenditures in Sinkiang, Ninghsia, and Tibet.

In short, the central government continues to utilize its fiscal powers to redistribute considerable resources from rich to poor areas. The revenue-sharing data in Table 4.3 suggests that the magnitude of this redistribution is as great in the early 1970s as it was in the 1950s. The most-developed provinces continue to surrender about three-fourths of their revenues to the center and the poorest areas receive subsidies equivalent to over half their expenditures. In several cases, these subsidies have been sustained for periods of from fourteen to twenty years.

This pattern of systematic redistribution in favor of less-developed regions is confirmed by data on the ratio between investment and total budgetary revenue released in Shanghai. Accumulated capital (*chi-lei tzu-chin*) is a term used to describe the sum of tax revenues, enterprise profits, and depreciation funds. Because accumulation includes all budgetary revenues originating in a given area, regardless of their sector of origin or whether they are collected by the provincial government or directly by the center, it is the most comprehensive measure of the fiscal resources of a region. The ratio of industrial investment to accumulation is a measure of the extent to which the area is able to channel its revenues to capital investment projects that will contribute to further local economic growth. Nationally, this ratio is simply the ratio of capital investment in industry to total national budgetary revenues. During the First Five-Year Plan period, for example, it ranged from a low of 13 percent in 1953 to a high of 24 percent in 1956 (State Statistical Bureau 1960, 23, 55).

Shanghai has recently released comparable data for the 1949–73 and 1966–75 periods. The ratio of industrial investment to accumulation from 1949 to 1973 was 6.7 percent, whereas the reinvestment rate has been 6.9 percent since 1966.[6] The long periods over which these extremely low rates of reinvestment have been sustained show that the large outflow of revenues from Shanghai has not been limited to 1959–60 or 1972, the years shown in Tables 3.12 and 4.3, but has been a consistent pattern since 1949. In an analogous manner, Shanghai has continued to supply significant human capital to other regions. By the early 1970s, over half a million skilled workers trained in Shanghai had been transferred to other provinces (Eckstein 1977, 364). The similar size of the ratio of investment to accumulation during the 1949–73 and 1966–75 periods and the continued outflow of human resources suggest that Shanghai's large contribution to national economic growth has not been substantially reduced since the economic reform of the late 1950s.

The scope of the national budget since 1957

Evidence of a reduction in the scope of the state budget since the 1950s would tend to diminish the significance of the central-provincial revenue-sharing rates for recent years that are shown in Table 4.3. A reduction in the scope of the state budget would mean a greater portion of total national product was being distributed outside the direct control of the budgetary mechanism, giving rise to the possibility of a diminution in the redistributive powers of the fiscal system. However, both quantitative and qualitative evidence suggest that the scope of the state budget remains comparatively broad and that while the absolute volume of extrabudgetary funds available to enterprises, local governments, and particularly agricultural communes has grown, their share of gross national product does not appear to have risen.

Most important, recent Chinese statements place the growth of aggregate budgetary revenues since 1957 at a rate that is slightly in excess of the best Western estimates of the growth of China's gross domestic product. As shown in Table 4.4, the average annual rate of growth of budgetary revenues since 1957 has been 7.0 percent. This is in excess of the rates of growth of Chinese gross domestic product estimated by Robert M. Field, 5.2 percent (Field, 131) and Dwight Perkins, 5.6 percent (Perkins 1976, 9).[7] This suggests that the share of the total resources that is allocated through the budgetary mechanism in the 1970s exceeds the unusually high level achieved in 1957 and remains far above the share achieved in most less-developed countries.

Table 4.4. *Chinese budgetary revenues, 1952–73 (billions of yuan)*

Year	Budgetary revenues	Average annual rate of growth (%)
1950	6.52	
1952	17.56	
1957	31.02	
1970	65.2	
1973	91.3	
1952–57		12.1
1957–73		7.0

Notes: Budgetary revenues are in current year prices. Budgetary revenues for 1970 and 1973 are calculated on the basis of statements that revenues had increased "more than 9 times" between 1950 and 1970 and had increased "about 13 times" between 1950 and 1973. Because the data in the table for 1970 and 1973 are calculated on the basis of these rounded numbers, they probably overstate the increase in revenues between 1970 and 1973. The long-run rate of growth between 1957 and 1973 would not, however, be significantly affected.
Sources: 1950, 1952, 1957: State Statistical Bureau 1960, 21. 1971: *Cheng-chih ching-chi hsüeh chi-ch'u chih-shih* (Fundamentals of political economy), 1st ed. (Shanghai: Shanghai People's Publishing House, 1974), vol. 2, p. 195. 1973: *Cheng-chih ching-chi hsüeh chi-ch'u chih-shih* (Fundamentals of political economy), 2d ed. (Shanghai: Shanghai People's Publishing House, 1975), p. 406.

Furthermore, qualitative evidence suggests that many of the sources of extrabudgetary funds that existed in the 1950s have since been reduced in importance. As discussed in Chapter 2, the most important sources of funds in the First Five-Year Plan period not subject to direct budgetary allocation were bonus funds and above-plan profits retained by enterprises. Prior to the decentralization, these funds averaged about 900 million yuan, or 7 percent of total enterprise profits.[8] The decentralization not only expanded bonus funds and retained profits, but also allowed enterprises to retain funds to cover some expenditures that had previously been financed from the state budget.[9] Total enterprise retentions in 1958 were three billion yuan (American billion), or 16.7 percent of profits (T'ao Sheng-yü and Tan Ya-sheng, 13). In 1959, retained profits rose to 3.99 billion yuan but were reduced to 11.6 percent of total enterprise profits (Obolenskiy 1961a, 76).

The evidence on enterprise retentions for more recent years is limited to reports on specific enterprises by Western visitors. It is thus not as comprehensive in scope as the published national data for the 1950s. The only study of a significant number of enterprises is Barry Richman's. He found that many of the thirty-eight enterprises he visited in 1966 did not retain either above-plan profits or bonus funds. Among enterprises that retained any funds, the average rate of profits retained was only 5 percent (Richman, 503, 814). Reports of a large number of more recent Western visitors also suggest that retained profits remain quite limited. After modest deductions to finance the enterprise welfare programs, virtually all remaining profits, including depreciation funds, are remitted to the state and reallocated through the budgetary mechanism. Consequently, enterprises continue to depend primarily on direct budgetary allocations for both investment funds and for increases in permanent working capital (Cassou, 561). Thus the Chinese system for financing investment remains significantly more centralized than in either several of the planned economies of Eastern Europe or the Soviet Union, where since the mid-1960s the principle of self-financing is increasingly accepted and enterprises are allowed to retain from 20 to 40 percent of their profits (Wilczynski, 51–4).

Another major source of extrabudgetary funds in the First Five-Year Plan period was the labor insurance funds administered by the trade union system. These funds were probably put under budgetary management in 1958 or 1959.[10] This policy had been urged by several officials in the Ministry of Finance, and in 1959 labor insurance funds were specifically listed as a component of budgetary expenditures for worker and staff welfare programs.

This evidence would suggest that extrabudgetary funds controlled by enterprises and trade unions since 1960 are probably a smaller portion of total budgetary revenues than they were in the 1950s. A further source of extrabudgetary resources, the investment funds of joint state-private enterprises, came under budgetary management in 1957 (State Council 1956c; Ch'en Shu-t'ung 1957; Wang I-lun 1957a, Chi Chin-chang 1957; Chang Yu-yü 1957). Information on other sources of extrabudgetary funds is more limited. For example, although Barry Richman found that in the 1960s enterprises continued to have major repair funds comparable in scope to those of the 1950s, there is no specific information on the size of these funds (Richman, 742).

On the other hand, there has clearly been a substantial increase in the volume of funds expended outside the budgetary process at the commune level. Since the early 1960s, when state priorities were modified to place much more emphasis on the expansion of agricultural output, there has been an enormous increase in the flow of funds to rural development. A substantial further improvement in the terms of trade between the agricultural and industrial sectors, a continuing decline in the tax burden as a share of agricultural output (both discussed in detail in Chapter 5 below), and an increase in budgetary expenditures on agriculture have all channeled significant funds to the rural sector (Perkins 1975a, 365). However, only about one-half of these funds appear to have been allocated through the state budget (Perkins, 1975a, 365).

Although the growth of these expenditures reflects the increasing significance of the commune as a level of economic administration, the national budget still plays a significant role in the allocation of resources in the countryside. Many teachers in rural primary schools, as well as some commune-level cadres, are paid through the county budget which, of course, remains an integral component of the unified national budget. In addition, although many Western visitors have the impression that the system of communal health care is totally self-financed, it is clear that the state underwrites a very large portion of rural health expenditures, particularly for equipping commune hospitals and brigade health stations with relatively expensive equipment such as x-ray machines. Many provinces report that 70 to 80 percent of all budgetary funds expended for health are allocated to rural areas, clearly indicating the importance of the county-level budget in the delivery of medical care in rural areas.[11]

Perhaps the most important use of local extrabudgetary funds is to finance the development of rural small-scale industry. Unlike the state-owned sector, which is required to pay its profits into the state budget, commune- and brigade-level industries are collectively owned and are required only to pay state taxes.[12] These enterprises are typically founded with capital from commune internal accumulation funds and their subsequent profits are reinvested rather than being handed over to the state. Furthermore, unlike state-owned enterprises, which are more closely tied to the national economic plan, commune enterprises are much more autonomous. They are not usually dependent on the state either for their investment funds or for the distribution of their products. Unlike the relatively specialized state enterprises, whose production plans are specified in the plan and whose products are much more likely to enter state distribution channels, commune enterprises produce a more heterogeneous range of services and products, primarily in response to local needs. Employees of commune enterprises are also less subject to state control and are paid in work points whose value varies widely, rather than according to standardized state wage scales. This rapidly growing rural small-scale sector thus mobilizes local resources and produces inputs such as chemical fertilizer and agricultural machinery that are increasingly important for the growth of agricultural output.

Although this relatively autonomous rural small-scale sector has received considerable attention in the West, its importance should not be exaggerated. Most important, only a small portion of what is known as "rural small-scale industry" is actually managed by agricultural communes or their subordinate levels, the brigade and team. The largest, most well-equipped plants producing the most sophisticated output are managed at the county level and are much more fully integrated into state economic plans. County industries are not collectively but rather state owned. Thus, they pay their profits into the state budget and are largely dependent on the state budget for investment funds. For those counties where evidence is available it appears that although county-level plants constitute a third or less of rural small-scale enterprises, they produce 50 to 60 percent of rural small-scale industrial output (Perkins et al., 63–71). In Kwangtung, one of the few places for which provincewide data are available, commune- and brigade-level industry accounted for less than 10 percent of the province's industrial output in 1975.[13] The comparable figure for Kansu is well under 5 percent.[14]

In summary, the share of national income that is allocated through the budgetary process in the 1970s is at least as high as during the First Five-Year Plan period. Thus, in comparative terms, the budget remains an extremely powerful resource-allocation instrument. The growth of nonbudgetary funds at the commune level, however, provides additional flexibility in the system of economic management and provides greater opportunities for local initiative.

Unified tax system and expenditure controls

The unified tax system remains an important element of central control in recent years. The redistributive thrust of the center's fiscal programs could have been undermined if provincial governments had been able to make substantial adjustments to the coverage and rates of taxes. It would have led to geographic variations in the gross tax burden, enormously complicating the entire redistributive calculus and giving rise to the possibility of local governments manipulating tax rates to their own advantage. However, the tax structure and rates, even for so-called local revenue sources, are still determined by the central government (Robinson 1975, 31; Wei Min, 24).

The center still imposes a unified tax system and also continues to control the budgetary expenditures of local governments. This is apparent in aggregate terms from the central-provincial revenue-sharing rates shown in Table 4.3. In addition, as in the 1950s, the center restricts the freedom of local governments in the use of their retained funds. There continue to be disaggregated expenditure targets determined by the center. Provincial governments appear to have a greater role in the determination of these detailed expenditure targets than they did in the 1950s. However, they have little authority to reallocate funds among disaggregated expenditure categories once the budget has been approved by the center. As in the 1950s, adjustments among expenditure categories require the approval of higher levels (Eckstein 1975, 357). Finally, contrary to the specific provisions of the decentralization directives, provincial governments are apparently unable to retain all their budgetary surpluses for unrestricted use in the following fiscal year. Revenues collected in excess of those approved in the provincial budget must be shared with the central government. In 1972, for example, 50 percent of all above-plan revenues were to be turned over to the central government. Even the use of the remaining funds required prior central government approval if it would increase the number of employees or the wage bill of the province or require materials subject to unified distribution (Eckstein 1975, 357; Robinson 1975, 28).

Resource allocation and Chinese economic policy formulation

What does this evidence of considerable continuity of resource redistribution imply about the character of the economic policymaking process in China? Should one conclude that a strong consensus has always existed in support of a broadly redistributive government expenditure policy? Or has redistribution been rather a highly contentious policy sustained only by shifting coalitions of certain central government policymakers with specific regional interest groupings?

And if coalitions have been largely responsible, have these been formed on the basis of a single shared objective or on the basis of a more complex mix of overlapping and changing interests?

I believe, but will not attempt to show here, that the empirical findings presented in this study, particularly those in the latter half of the present chapter, could be consistent with several quite different models of the Chinese economic policymaking process. In short, the highly aggregate and indirect measures of the nature of resource allocation since 1960 are simply not sensitive enough to be used to discriminate among alternative hypotheses of the character of Chinese economic policymaking. One simply cannot assess year-to-year fluctuations in either investment strategy or the degree of commitment to the achievement of equity goals on the basis of the long-term pattern of provincial industrial growth or a few observations of central-provincial revenue-sharing rates for a small sample of provinces. The rates of provincial industrial growth in the short run reflect variations in the level of agricultural output, which in turn are induced both by the weather and by Chinese agricultural development policy, as well as by the repercussions of several political campaigns, each of which appears to have had an exaggerated effect on the rate of industrial growth in a few provinces. As suggested above, the aftermath of the Great Leap Forward and the withdrawal of Soviet economic assistance presumably had more detrimental effects in regions where Soviet-aided projects were concentrated. However, because no provinces have released data on industrial growth for the 1960–4 period this remains a plausible hypothesis rather than an established proposition. The Cultural Revolution, a largely urban phenomenon, also appears to have affected provincial industrial performance in a highly skewed fashion, but again incomplete data for the 1967–9 period make it impossible to examine this hypothesis carefully.[15] Similarly, a series of political campaigns that began in the latter half of 1974 sharply increased the variation in industrial performance among individual provinces. The national *rate* of industrial growth in 1975 and 1976 fell sharply, largely because the campaigns caused sharp drops in the *level* of output in a few provinces (Field, Lardy, and Emerson, 16–17).

I have attempted to minimize the effects of these short-run disturbances by examining the pattern of provincial industrial growth over a relatively long period, 1957 to 1974, and by comparing this pattern with the pattern of growth established in a period in which the economic system was less disrupted by political campaigns. The base year for the more recent long period, 1957, was a year of normalcy, whereas 1974 is long enough after the Cultural Revolution to avoid its distorting effects while missing the effects of the more recent campaigns. Thus I believe that the pattern of industrial growth from 1957 to 1974 does reflect long-run central government investment strategy in a rather crude fashion, but these data cannot be used to infer anything about the year-by-year or even medium-term fluctuations in development strategy. One could not, for example, test the hypothesis that planning in the 1960–6 period was run along highly "rightist" lines in which growth maximization was pursued to bring the country out of a sharp depression while equity goals were temporarily submerged.

Similarly, the revenue-sharing data, although suggestive, are far from complete. Data for only a few provinces are available for the 1960s and 1970s and the Chinese have not released year-by-year data that could serve as the basis for analyzing short-term fluctuations in the degree of redistribution carried out through the fiscal system.

Finally, we have almost no qualitative information that might allow us to assess the changing degree of informal decentralization of China's planning system. Many hierarchies, which are formally rather centralized and bureaucratic, operate effectively only by tolerating a high degree of what might be called informal decentralization. For example, although the formal rules may call for a high degree of centralized decision making, the center may be merely ratifying decisions that have been initiated at lower levels of the hierarchy. Without more information on the nature of the interaction that occurs between provincial planners and the central planning apparatus, which ultimately leads to the plan and fiscal targets for each province, it is difficult to even guess the extent to which the formal structure permits increased provincial decision-making power compared to the 1950s. Of course, the same remarks apply with even greater force to the economic relations between the provincial authorities and lower levels of the administrative hierarchy.

In summary, although I believe that the data suggest some degree of continuity in the redistribution of resources, the empirical evidence is not sufficiently detailed and sensitive either to test alternative models of policy formulation or to reveal changes in the degree of informal decentralization. In particular, one cannot assume, on the basis of this highly aggregate long-term evidence, that resource redistribution and the degree of central control of economic planning and management have not been highly contentious interrelated policy issues. Publications in the early 1960s suggest that the more decentralized horizontal planning envisaged in the reform directives of 1957 and 1958 had encountered profound difficulties and that some officials were arguing for a return of the status quo ante, in which the formal primacy of the vertical system would be reestablished. The recent oblique reference to a further reform of the system of economic management in 1970, referred to earlier in this chapter, suggests that after the Cultural Revolution the whole issue of the proper degree of central control of economic management was subject to a further systematic review. Although one well-informed Chinese economist has said that the reforms initiated by Mao in 1957 and 1958 were not systematically implemented until this time (Perkins et al., 277), we have very little independent information concerning the nature of the reform that emerged from this reexamination.

The further debate that emerged in 1976 during the transition to a new political leadership implies that the central issues remain unresolved. One of the charges leveled against Vice-Premier Teng Hsiao-p'ing after his second fall from grace in 1976 was that he had favored restoring the primacy of the vertically organized hierarchical system emphasizing industrial ministries. Because the information released during 1976 on this issue was quite cryptic and in any case presumably distorted by Teng's opponents, it is difficult to assess how significant his proposals may have been. Teng's rehabilitation as vice-premier in mid-1977 at least carries the suggestion that the charges aired against him in the media were distorted or represented a minority view. Nevertheless, the renewed discussion of these matters suggests that the Chinese are still striving to find a long-term solution to the basic underlying centralization-decentralization dilemma.

And what of the motives of those who have supported the use of relatively centralized economic policy instruments to implement a redistributive government expenditure policy? Again, the broad aggregate evidence is probably consistent with more than one hypothesis. I believe that this assessment is best undertaken in the more explicitly comparative framework of the next chapter.

5

China's distributive policies in comparative perspective

Although the decentralization of the economic system since 1957 has substantially enhanced the role of local governments in economic management, the empirical evidence presented in this study suggests that many basic planning decisions have remained relatively centralized. Despite the policy debates referred to in the last chapter, Peking has continued to use centralized policy instruments, such as redistributing investment resources from rich to poor regions, subsidizing the social expenditures of less-developed areas, controlling the interindustry and interregional structure of wages to mitigate income inequality in the industrial sector, and regulating the terms of trade between industry and agriculture so as to transfer sizable income to the poorer rural population. How has the application of these relatively centralized policy instruments affected the character of China's development, particularly as compared with other countries? More important, what is the relevance of China's experience for less-developed countries that are grappling with the interrelated problems of economic growth and income distribution?

The character of China's development

A fundamental characteristic of the Chinese approach to development is its preference for eschewing the use of markets when distributive outcomes are at stake. Rather than relying on a market-oriented growth path that is frequently accompanied by growing interpersonal income inequality and sometimes even declining real incomes for the poorest members of society, the Chinese have adopted the view that sustained economic development is not likely to occur unless the incomes of all members of society are raised simultaneously and that this goal can be achieved most effectively through a planned economic system. This basic philosophy motivates Chinese use of nonmarket mechanisms to limit income disparities between urban and rural areas, to minimize wage differentials in the industrial sector, and to alleviate interregional inequalities. The effectiveness of China's planning system in improving the distribution of personal income is suggested by a growing body of empirical data.

In less-developed countries, growing disparities between incomes received in the agricultural and industrial sectors are frequently a principal cause of increased income inequality (Weisskoff). Minimum-wage and other social welfare legislation; rapidly rising wages in the government sector; the influence of labor unions or high-wage-paying subsidiaries of multinational corporations; and tariffs, quantitative restrictions, and overvalued exchange rates (all of which artificially increase the profitability of domestic manufacturing) are among the hypotheses suggested to explain the rapid rise of wages in the modern sector, even in the face of high and growing rates of urban unemployment (Turnam, 73–80; Little, Scitovsky, and Scott). At the same time, agriculture is frequently neglected and the rate of growth of output barely keeps up with population. Consequently, agricultural incomes rise relatively slowly. In China, however, the central government has carefully regulated the disparities between agricultural and modern-sector incomes both through its control of wages in industry and services and through other policy instruments. Particularly since 1957, the growth of real wages has been far below the growth of industrial productivity. During the First Five-Year Plan period, output per industrial worker increased by over 50 percent, according to official data. But, as is shown in Table 5.1, the central government, through its control of the wage level, limited the increase in real wages to about 30 percent. Since the decentralization of the economic system, worker productivity has continued to grow rapidly. Although data on the growth of the industrial labor force are quite limited, a substantial portion of the quintupling of national industrial output between 1957 and 1975 appears to be due to the continued growth of labor productivity rather than increased industrial-sector employment. In Shanghai, for example, the growth of labor productivity appears to have accounted for almost half of the incremental growth of industrial output between 1957 and 1974.[1]

As shown in Table 5.1, however, the average wage in the state sector of the economy remains at virtually the same level as that of 1957 despite these productivity increases. This freeze on urban

Table 5.1. *Wages in the state sector, 1952-75 (yuan)*

Year	Nominal wages (current-year yuan)		Retail price index	Real wages — All workers		Real wages — Industrial workers	
	All workers	Industrial workers		1952 yuan	Index	1952 yuan	Index
1952	446[a]	525[c]	100[e]	446	100	525	100
1956	610[a]	664[c]	106.3[e]	574	129	625	119
1957	637[a]	–	108.6[e]	587	131	–	–
1971	650[b]	–	115.6[f]	562	126	–	–
1975	–	720[d]	115.1[g]	–	–	626	119

Sources: [a]State Statistical Bureau 1960, 216. [b]*Peking Review,* no. 40 (1971): 14. [c]Chao I-wen, 32-3. [d]New China News Agency, 1 December 1975 in British Broadcasting Corporation, *Summary of World Broadcasts, Far East Weekly Economic Reports,* W856, p. A/1. [e]State Statistical Bureau 1960. [f]Perkins 1975b, 153. [g]Retail prices were reported to have fallen 2.9 percent in the 1965-75 decade (*Far Eastern Economic Review,* 14 November 1975, p. 41). This is an additional decline of .5 percent beyond that reported for the 1965-70 period, which was used by Perkins to calculate the price index for 1971.

wages was undertaken in 1957 in response to quite unfavorable labor market conditions and the recognition that the average living standard was rising somewhat more rapidly in urban than in rural areas. The growth of urban wages had attracted a substantial migration from the agricultural sector, contributing to a rate of growth of urban population that was more than twice that for the country as a whole. The increase in employment in the modern sector during the First Five-Year Plan was not sufficient to absorb even the increase in the indigenous urban population so urban unemployment tended to rise despite a very rapid rate of growth of industrial output. One estimate, for example, places the rate of unemployment in Shanghai in 1957 at 21 percent of the labor force (Howe, 39). Although aggregate national data are not as reliable as those for the municipality of Shanghai, one estimate shows that the rate of unemployment, after declining between 1949 and 1952, increased every year during the First Five-Year Plan and stood at about 20 percent in 1957 (Hou Chi-ming, 369). The solution embodied in the rational low-wage policy was to freeze the growth of urban-sector wages and to place severe limits on rural-urban migration.

Although the Chinese government has restricted the long-term rate of growth of real wages in the industrial sector, it has simultaneously

pursued tax, price, and social expenditure policies that have raised
the rate of real incomes in the agricultural sector substantially above
that implied by the 2.5 percent average annual rate of expansion of
the value of agricultural output between 1957 and 1973.[2] The central
government has reduced the tax burden on agricultural output from
12 percent in 1952 to 5 percent in 1975 (Lardy 1976b, 4). This decline in the tax burden will apparently continue because historically
the absolute level of the agricultural tax has been adjusted upward
only infrequently. Some statements by the Chinese suggest that the
current policy objective is to stabilize the absolute size of agricultural tax revenues, which would probably allow the relative tax
burden to decline more rapidly than in the past two decades.

The government's control of the terms of trade between the agricultural and industrial sectors has been even more important than the
reduction of the tax burden as a portion of farm output. Recent studies
suggest that the ratio between the prices of the products that peasants
sell and the prices of the industrial goods they purchase is among the
most important variables influencing the intersectoral distribution of
income. This ratio is heavily influenced by government policy even in
countries with market-oriented systems. The tariff, foreign exchange,
and tax policies adopted by the Indian and Pakistani governments to
encourage domestic manufacturing, for example, have substantially
raised the price level for manufactured goods. Because farmers spend
a portion of their incomes on manufactured goods, the implicit additional tax imposed by these import-substitution policies depresses the
agricultural sector's terms of trade below what they otherwise would
have been, directly reducing the incomes of rural inhabitants (Little,
Scitovsky, and Scott). Partly as a result of these policies, there was no
improvement in the relative prices received by Indian farmers during
the first three five-year plans (1951–65).[3]

Even in Taiwan, when import substitution policies gave way to
economic liberalization (i.e., reduced tariff barriers, reform of mul-
tiple-exchange-rate and import-licensing systems, and devaluation of
the exchange rate) and rapid growth of exports, more direct policy
instruments continued to be used to control the relative prices between agricultural products and manufactured goods. Although economic liberalization in Taiwan began in the latter half of the 1950s
and continued through the 1960s (Little, Scitovsky, and Scott, 254–
8), until 1973 the government dominated crucial markets for both
agricultural output and inputs produced by the industrial sector. The

Table 5.2. *The terms of trade of agriculture*

Year	1. State purchase prices of farm products (1952 = 100)	2. Prices of industrial goods sold in rural areas (1952 = 100)	Terms of trade (1 ÷ 2)
1950	82.2	91.2	90.1
1951	98.3	100.5	97.8
1952	100.0	100.0	100
1953	110.1	98.5	111.8
1954	113.8	100.2	113.6
1955	113.2	101.4	111.6
1956	116.6	100.4	116.1
1957	122.4	101.6	120.5
1958	125.1	101.0	123.9
1963	154.7	114.3	135.3
1971	156.2	104.0	150.2
1974	164.4	100.3	163.9

Source: Lardy 1976b, 6.

barter ratio between chemical fertilizer, which was produced under a government monopoly, and rice, which was sold in a government-dominated market, was a major determinant of intersectoral income transfers. Despite the comparatively rapid growth of manufactured goods during the 1950–70 period, the agricultural sector's terms of trade improved only slightly over these years.[4] Because the physical quantity of food grains delivered by the peasants to the state at controlled prices rose sharply during this period, there was a continuous large net transfer of resources from agriculture to industry.[5]

The contrasting situation in China is shown in Table 5.2. Part of the increase in the prices of agricultural products through 1952 reflected free market forces. But even after initiating the system of compulsory procurement in 1953, the state continued to raise procurement prices during the First Five-Year Plan. At the same time the retail prices of industrial products (such as chemical fertilizer, machinery, and manufactured consumer goods) sold by the state in rural areas were relatively stable. Thus even during the First Five-Year Plan, when the industrial sector received the bulk of the investment resources allocated through the state budget, the improvement in agriculture's terms of trade appears to be a quite significant source of increased purchasing power in the agricultural sector. Official data, which take into account the increased earnings from sales of agricultural products to the state and the decrease in earnings that resulted from both marginal increases in the prices of manufactured goods purchased from the state as well as from marginal increases in prices of agricultural goods sold to food-deficit agricultural regions, show a net cumulative improvement in purchasing power of 10,600 million yuan during the 1953–7 period (TCKT Data Section 1957a, 5; State Statistical Bureau 1960, 163). The increase in the net value of agricultural output between 1952 and 1957 (measured in constant 1952 prices) was 9,877 million yuan, and the cumulative annual increments above the 1952 level of net output value sum to 23,900 million yuan (Ishikawa, 56).

Official data suggest that improvements in agriculture's terms of trade since 1957 continue to be a major source of increased farm purchasing power.[6] The retail prices of industrial products sold in rural areas rose almost 15 percent between 1958 and 1963 but by 1974 they had declined to the level of 1951–2. During this same 1957–74 period, agricultural procurement prices were raised another 34 percent. Consequently, the terms of trade have moved decisively in favor of agriculture. In the mid-1970s, farmers received almost two-thirds more industrial goods for each unit of agricultural product delivered to the state than they did on the eve of the First Plan in 1952. Thus in contrast to other less-developed countries, China's price policies have transferred purchasing power to rather than away from the agriculture sector, reducing the burden of industrialization on the agricultural sector.

Real welfare in the agricultural sector has also been improved by the growth of government expenditures for rural health, education, and welfare programs. Particularly since the Cultural Revolution, there has been a renewed emphasis on programs to improve rural health care and education. Not only have total national budgetary expenditures for health, education, and welfare programs doubled between 1957 and 1971,[7] but since the mid-1960s there has been a substantial shift in the distribution of these expenditures in favor of rural areas. Prior to the Cultural Revolution, two-thirds of budgetary funds for medical and health care were spent in urban areas. As a result of the policies introduced during the Cultural Revolution, this proportion was reduced to less than 40 percent by the mid-1970s.[8]

Cumulatively, these programs appear to have resulted in substantially less intersectoral income inequality than would have prevailed in a market system. During the First Five-Year Plan period, the growth of industrial-sector wages outstripped those in agriculture, leading to a widening of intersectoral income disparities. The ratio of urban to rural personal incomes widened from about 1.8:1 in 1952 to 2.1:1 in 1957, an increase of about 15 percent (Schran 1976, 19). Since 1957, however, a growing gap between industrial and agricultural worker productivity has been accompanied by a reduction in the income differential between industrial and farm workers. The rate of growth of agricultural output, 2.5 percent, is only marginally greater than the rate of rural population growth, indicating little increase in farm worker productivity. Despite this extremely slow growth of per capita farm output, tentative estimates place the increase in per capita rural personal incomes over this same period at 15 to 19 percent. On the other hand, the productivity of industrial workers may have almost doubled since 1957,[9] while real wages have been unchanged. Consequently, the ratio of urban to rural personal incomes has been diminished and now stands at roughly the level of 1952 (Schran 1976, 19).[10]

The central government has not only controlled the level of industrial wages to mitigate income disparities between the industrial and agricultural sectors, but its relatively egalitarian wage structure has also tended to make the distribution of income within the industrial sector somewhat more even than in many other rapidly growing, less-developed countries. The state has not attempted to eliminate wage disparities. The importance of wage differentials in providing worker incentives has always been acknowledged either explicitly or implicitly and the 3:1 differential between the highest- and lowest-paid workers in China appears to be approximately the same as in most other less-developed countries. It is primarily at the level of technical, engineering, and managerial manpower that Chinese wage policy appears to diverge most widely from that of other developing countries. The highest-paid managers and technical personnel in Chinese enterprises are usually paid only about five times the wage of unskilled workers, whereas in many less-developed countries in Africa and Asia, ratios of from 30:1 up to 50:1 are not unusual (Eckstein 1975, 348–9).

Not only is the initial distribution of wages relatively more egalitarian, but both the structure of prices and rationing of some consumer goods tend to equalize further real consumption among industrial workers. The most important consumer goods, such as food grains, edible oils, and cotton cloth, are rationed and sold at prices that reflect heavy budgetary subsidies. For example, although the government has doubled the price paid to farmers for food grains since 1950, retail prices in urban areas have remained stable. Procurement prices are now almost as high as retail prices, and in effect the state now absorbs the costs of transporting, storing, and distributing grain sold to urban workers. Housing is also heavily subsidized through the state budget–workers pay only a nominal 4 to 5 percent of their wages in rent. Medical care is available free to industrial workers and at subsidized rates to their dependents. On the other hand, nonnecessities, such as cigarettes and wine, carry much higher price tags. As a result, the structure of prices has a redistributive effect similar to a progressive income tax and makes the distribution of real consumption somewhat more equal than the distribution of wage income.

Finally, the state has used relatively centralized policy instruments within the agricultural sector to influence the distribution of income among rural residents. The most important determinant of rural income distribution is the pattern of land ownership. The Chinese elimination of concentrated land ownership and the redistribution of a comparatively high portion of cultivated area in the land reform program of the early 1950s led to a significant redistribution of income in favor of the rural poor. Land reform may have reduced the share of farm income accruing to the wealthiest 20 percent of the rural population by about one-fifth, while roughly doubling the income share of the poorest 20 percent (Perkins 1976). The redistributive effect of land reform was strengthened in the cooperativization campaign of the mid-1950s. That is, pooling land among larger groups of peasants and basing wage payments on labor contributions alone, rather than on both labor and land, further reduced inequities arising from interpersonal variations in the quality and size of landholdings within each cooperative (Perkins 1976).

Even after agricultural cooperativization had been carried out, substantial intraregional inequality remained. This arose not only because of differences in land quality but also because of variations in the number of able-bodied workers per household. This latter factor is an important consideration, for it means that a portion of inequality among rural households at any time simply reflects different stages of the family life cycle. Looking at these households over the longer term, a substantial portion of these inequalities would be evened out. This of course contrasts with many other less-developed societies, where income differences at any given point in time are likely to be sustained for long periods of time because they reflect differential holdings of land, access to credit, etc.

A major attempt to eliminate the contribution of differential land quality to the distribution of income within villages was made during the early stages of the commune movement of the Great Leap Forward. The extremely egalitarian principles of income distribution embodied in the commune system in the late 1950s were, however, abandoned almost immediately and since the early 1960s the lowest administrative level of the commune, the team, has served as the basic accounting unit. Periodic efforts to move the level of economic accounting from the team to the next larger area of rural administration, the brigade, which would substantially reduce income differentials within communes, have failed to take hold. As a result, average team incomes within some communes are reported to vary by as much as three to one or more.[11] The Chinese are sensitive to these inequalities, but have adopted the view that they can be reduced only gradually.[12]

Although the land reform substantially increased the income share of the poorest members of China's rural society, it is important to recognize that the land reform did nothing to alleviate interregional inequality. That is, while the land reform substantially reduced inequality in the distribution of land among peasants within each village (*hsiang*) it did nothing to reduce inequality between villages, which some studies have suggested was the major source of income inequality in the countryside after the completion of land reform.[13] Furthermore, there is some evidence that the concentration of modern industrial inputs in regions with the greatest potential growth of agricultural productivity may have exacerbated the inequalities inherited from the 1950s.[14]

Diminution of these regional inequalities would require a more extractive tax and procurement policy in richer regions or a redistributive state investment policy in the agricultural sector. As was discussed in Chapter 3, in 1958 the Chinese implemented highly differentiated tax rates in order to capture some of the differential rent in the agricultural sector. Although the overall tax burden on agriculture has been reduced since that time, interregional differentials appear to have been retained. Tax rates in regions such as Tibet and Sinkiang remain below the national average.[15]

Chinese economic planners have also manipulated the terms of trade between industry and agriculture in a manner that tends to favor less-developed agricultural regions. Between 1950 and 1956, the state raised purchase prices for agricultural products in inland provinces by 47.9 percent, while in coastal areas the increase was only 31.2 percent (TCKT Data Section 1957a, 6). Because prices of industrial goods sold in rural areas on the average rose by about 10 percent in both regions, the net improvement of the terms of trade for agriculture was roughly twice as great for inland as compared to coastal areas. The manipulation of the terms of trade on a regional basis is also reflected in the terms-of-trade data reported by individual provinces.[16] The improvement in the terms of trade of agriculture in Kansu, for example, was substantially above the national average.[17] In Kirin, on the other hand, an unusually large rise in agricultural purchase prices was partially offset by an above-average increase in the prices of industrial goods sold in rural areas.[18] This rise in the prices of industrial goods constituted an additional tax, essentially reinforcing the above-average direct tax already imposed on agriculture in Kirin. This policy of manipulating the terms of trade on a regional basis to benefit less-developed agricultural areas has continued since the 1950s. In Sinkiang and Tsinghai, for example, the terms of trade of agriculture since the mid-1950s have improved considerably more than the national average.[19]

Although the Chinese acknowledge that they are far from achieving equality in the distribution of rural income, on balance their efforts to mitigate the income differentials arising from the application of modern industrial inputs, such as chemical fertilizer and electricity for controlling irrigation water, compare quite favorably with other developing countries. India, the only other less-developed country comparable to China in terms of continental size, diversity of conditions of agricultural cultivation, and the portion of the labor force employed in the agricultural sector, has made no effort to capture differential rents that arise from varying natural conditions. The states, rather than the federal government, have the sole power to levy taxes on agricultural income and estate taxes on agricultural land, leading to widely divergent agricultural tax rates. Some states exempt all agricultural income from taxation, and in general agricultural tax rates are lower in the richest agricultural regions – the opposite of the tax structure in China.

Furthermore, China's commune system of agricultural organization has meant that labor-saving innovations have not led to widespread permanent unemployment. Labor released by the mechanization of food processing, for example, has made possible a further expansion of multiple-cropping and the development of a rural small-scale industrial sector that offers employment to a growing number of rural residents. Continued employment and income is assured for all, if not at the same absolute level in all regions. By contrast, in some regions of India widespread mechanization of large farms, encouraged by distorted prices and unequal access to credit, has displaced part of the rural labor force. The lack of alternative employment frequently means permanent loss of rural income, accelerating the flight of peasants to cities that are unable to provide productive jobs even to many of their existing residents.

Finally, China's pattern of regional development differs fundamentally from most less-developed countries. In many developing countries, the pattern of first increasing and then decreasing interregional inequality (discussed in the last chapter) tends to exacerbate parallel trends in the distribution of personal income. In the early stages of economic growth increasing income inequality is associated with the more rapid growth of incomes of those workers who find employment in high-productivity sectors – particularly industry. Comparatively rapid growth of some regions within a country usually reflects a relatively rapid transfer of labor from agriculture to industry. Because there usually is a positive relationship between the level of wages and level of regional development, growing interregional differences in per worker industrial output contribute directly to the trend of greater inequality in the size distribution of income. In short, the variation in per capita output in more- and less-developed regions within countries is due to both the differing sectoral allocation of labor and to regional differences in per worker output within the same sector. Thus to the extent that the transfer of labor to the industrial sector is concentrated in the high-productivity, high-wage regions, the distribution of personal income becomes more unequal. Because the structure of wages in China is controlled by the state, these productivity differences have only a marginal effect on the distribution of personal income. But in most other less-developed countries where wages are more closely linked to productivity, interregional variations in development have been found to contribute significantly to inequality in the distribution of personal income.

I must emphasize that in the absence of data on the personal distribution of income in China the above analysis is quite preliminary. The overall effect of the central government's manipulation of

both the terms of trade and the agricultural tax on a regional basis
has not yet been thoroughly investigated, and almost no research on
the regional burden of government grain procurements has been
completed. It is quite possible that more detailed data would show
that the improvements in the distribution of income have been less
profound than those suggested by my discussion above. It does
appear, however, that at least through the mid-1970s the Chinese
have made deliberate and sustained efforts to reduce intersectoral
and interregional income inequality. These policies alone have certainly resulted in a distribution of income that is more favorable
than that which would have prevailed under a more market-oriented system. In addition, the Chinese have also adopted policies
that tend to reduce income disparities within the industrial and
agricultural sectors. On balance, these policies appear to have had a
quite favorable effect on the distribution of income but in the absence of more detailed data the magnitudes involved cannot be
precisely measured.

Not only is this evidence preliminary but there is no assurance
that the Chinese will continue to pursue relatively redistributive
policies. My own sense, based on reading Chinese sources as well
as on comparisons with other countries, is that the policy of subsidizing the investment and social expenditures of backward regions
and the policy of placing ceilings on the real wages in the industrial
sector while transferring income to agricultural workers through
raising the procurement prices for agricultural products have both
been highly divisive. Although we know very little about the inner
workings of the decision-making process within the Chinese government, these redistributive policies obviously could not have
been sustained without strong political support at the highest level.
These policies certainly bear the stamp of Mao Tse-tung, particularly his concern for reducing interregional and urban-rural inequality (Mao Tse-tung, 1969, 377–8; Mao Tse-tung 1977, 12–13). But
from the present vantage point it is virtually impossible to judge
whether Mao's views enjoyed genuine widespread support at the
highest level or were imposed on a deeply divided leadership.

In addition, a sharp decline in industrial growth between 1974
and at least the first part of 1977, which is at least indirectly linked
to the absence of real wage increases, may erode whatever level of
support had previously existed for the low-wage policy followed
since 1957. It is evident that in 1974 during the political uncer-

tainty surrounding the campaign against the followers of Lin Piao (Mao's heir apparent who died while apparently attempting to escape to the Soviet Union) and again in 1976 during the events surrounding the change in political leadership following the deaths of both Mao Tse-tung and Chou En-lai, certain groups capitalized on growing worker unrest. Although wage policy did not create spontaneous opposition by workers, the lack of any improvement in real wages over two decades apparently contributed to an environment in which political factionalization led to labor strikes, work stoppages, and in some cases physical violence. It is now possible to document the quite sharp declines in industrial output during 1974 and 1976 in a number of provinces and municipalities in which disruption was particularly severe. For example, in Chekiang province, where the army was finally called in to restore order in many plants in mid-1975, the 1973 level of production was not reattained until 1977. In Kweichow, industrial output fell by 30 percent between the fall of 1975 and the spring of 1976. The previous peak level of output attained in September 1975 was not regained until May 1977.[20]

Partly in response to the widespread dissatisfaction of workers, the Chinese government formally announced in the spring of 1977 that it would convene a nationwide conference on employment and wages (Yü Ch'iu-li, 21). Although the outcome of the reexamination of wage policy is not yet apparent, one might postulate that, in the face of a sharp decline in worker incentives, support at the highest levels of the new leadership for reducing intersectoral income disparities will evaporate. The average level of real wages in industry might be raised significantly, perhaps over a period of years as in the First Five-Year Plan. Similarly, in a further effort to bolster the economy's sagging industrial performance the allocation of investment activity might be shifted somewhat in favor of more-developed regions where the rate of return on investment is probably still somewhat higher than elsewhere, at least in the short run. Clearly these shifts, if both sharp and sustained, would signal a profound shift in the character of China's development strategy in the post-Mao era.

However, at present this is pure speculation. Even as the nature of Chinese development strategy evolves, one must search for the sources of what to date has been China's distinct approach to the problems of growth and distribution and ask whether other countries can learn from the Chinese experience.

The relevance of the Chinese model

China's success in achieving a relatively rapid rate of growth of domestic product while simultaneously improving the distribution of income (or at a minimum avoiding the most palpable inequities of the type observed in India) raises the obvious question of whether other less-developed countries might benefit by borrowing from China's development experience. Broadly speaking, does the Chinese model or any particular element of it as it has evolved up to the mid-1970s offer developing countries a more effective means of dealing with the interrelated problems of growth and distribution?

Although the ultimate answer to this question can be provided only by the developing countries, I believe that there are several factors that considerably reduce the relevance of the Chinese model for other nations. This is not to say that China's experience may not provide unique evidence of the efficacy of alternative approaches to problems such as the delivery of medical services to the rural poor, controlling the rate of population growth, or expanding employment opportunities for rural residents through a small-scale industrialization program. Adoption of China's highly centralized approach to dealing with the problems of growth and distribution in other countries will, however, be limited by the absence of specific historical, cultural, and other elements that I believe provide the vital foundation for the Chinese model. These include not only the special nature of the revolution that brought the Communists to power in 1949 and the system of economic planning that has evolved in the ensuing decades, but also specific favorable historical and cultural factors that are usually absent in other less-developed countries.

The nature of the Chinese revolution

It is difficult to overestimate the influence that the nature of the Chinese revolution has had on the course of economic development over the last twenty-five years. The education, skills, and training the Chinese population had accumulated prior to 1949, the relative scarcity of land in China's resource endowment, and the sectoral and geographic distribution as well as the size of the inherited capital stock have all had an important effect on the course of economic and social development. It is perhaps fair to say, however, that none of these has been as profound as the character of the revolution in influencing how the benefits of rapid economic growth have been shared. In the words of Dwight Perkins, "much of what distinguishes Chinese economic development could only have occurred through a revolution that put the poor in command" (Perkins 1976, 29).

The agrarian basis of the Chinese revolution not only partially explains the nature of the land reform program in the early 1950s and much of the ensuing reorganization of the agricultural sector, but also many related policies discussed above. Specifically, the rural-based nature of the revolution appears to have imbued the leadership with an acute and sustained sensitivity to income differentials between the urban and rural sectors. This sensitivity underlies the policies of reducing the burden of the agricultural tax, manipulating the terms of trade between industry and agriculture for the benefit of the agricultural sector, and restricting the growth of real industrial wages. These policies alone make the Chinese growth path more equitable than that observed in many other developing countries.

The revolutionary heritage also elucidates much of China's regional investment policy. The revolution was fought not only primarily in rural areas, but also largely in the interior. Particularly after 1930, when the Chinese Communist Party abandoned its Comintern-oriented policy of urban-based revolution, the locus of the Party's activities was in regions far removed from the more-developed coastal areas. In the 1930s, Party activity centered first in rural Kiangsi and, following the Long March through Southwest China, in Yenan in the Northwest. Although Communist-controlled base areas later expanded rapidly, this formative decade of organization and struggle in relatively poor and remote interior rural areas left an indelible impression that profoundly influenced Chinese development policy after 1949.

The desire of the leadership to accelerate the growth of inland areas after 1949 was also partly conditioned by the nationalistic nature of the Communist revolution. The leadership believed that the concentration of industrial development in China's coastal cities in 1949 reflected a century of foreign expoitation that had begun with the Treaty Port System. Following China's defeat by the British in the Opium War in 1842, the rights of foreigners, and particularly foreign investors, were systematically expanded. By the end of the century, foreigners controlled the Chinese railroad system and dominated industries such as mining, shipbuilding, and public utilities. The Japanese occupation and development of Manchuria after 1931 was viewed as only the most blatant example of foreign exploitation. Although the net effect of this high degree of foreign participation in the Chinese economy is a matter of continuing dispute among Western social scientists, there is little doubt that the Communists viewed the development of the Northeast and the Treaty Port cities primarily as the result of a century of foreign domination rather than the result of a successful indigenous development effort. Consequently, the strategy of developing new centers of industry was, at least initially, probably far less contentious than it would have been under other circumstances.

Historic and cultural factors

Certain long-run historic and cultural factors seem also to have facilitated the distributive choices made, as well as the policy instruments utilized after 1949. Perhaps the most important of these is the legacy of China as a unified and relatively centralized nation-state that dates back over two millenia to the founding of the Ch'in dynasty (220 B.C.). Although the rise and fall of numerous dynasties since the Ch'in testifies to its fragility, the conception of a unified and centralized national state under the ultimate authority of a single emperor remained the ideal. In the years following unification, the bureaucratic-administrative means of achieving this ideal were increasingly refined. The Chinese evolved a sophisticated bureaucracy, which reached from the imperial capital through the provinces to the localities and served as an instrument of central control. Thus, the centralized political and economic system established after 1949 was founded on a long-established tradition.

The penetration of the imperial bureaucracy was, however, relatively superficial, and the survival of each dynasty depended crucially on the fiscal relations between the central authority and local governments. Because the ultimate source of revenues in China's traditional agrarian society was locally collected land taxes, the financial integrity of each dynasty depended on its ability to extract resources from the provincial governments. As early as the T'ang dynasty (618–907), the imperial government abandoned its attempt to require provincial and local governments to act exclusively as revenue-collection agents for the center and instead substituted a system of revenue sharing not dissimilar in form from that adopted by the Communists in the early 1950s.

Under the system of revenue sharing established by the "two tax system" (*liang-shui fa*) in 780, land taxes were divided between the center and the provinces.[21] The Imperial Finance Commission established a revenue quota for each province to remit to the center but allowed the provinces considerable freedom both in collecting taxes and in spending retained revenues. The taxes collected within each province were also divided between those retained by the prefecture and those remitted to the province. This system was designed to provide the central government with a sustained flow of revenues while decentralizing the actual administration of the land tax. Although the imperial government frequently lacked the ability to force provinces to remit their quotas, the system of decentralized tax collection and revenue sharing persisted as a central characteristic of fiscal relations between the central government and the provinces in subsequent dynasties.

The conception of a geographically balanced pattern of economic development also has a pre-1949 origin. As early as the Ming dynasty (1369–1643), the imperial government feared that regional imbalance would undermine the larger political unity and thus it sought to minimize interregional inequality, partly through the tax system.[22] The efforts of the government, however, were insufficient and later overwhelmed by the influence of foreign investment that began near the end of the Ch'ing dynasty.

Finally, China's cultural heritage facilitated the post-1949 policy of creating an economically more unified nation-state in which geographic imbalances tend to be diminished rather than accentuated. The almost complete domination of China's culture by the Han race has tended to reduce regional fractionalization based on ethnic and religious cleavages that has frequently frustated efforts to achieve balanced regional growth in other countries. Although China's population is 6 percent non-Han, this minority is divided both ethnically and geographically. There are about fifty minority groups and minority populations seldom constitute a majority, even in specially designated autonomous regions and special districts.

Cumulatively, the nature of the Chinese revolution, the legacy of a relatively unified state in which regional balance was an explicit if unattained goal, and the absence of divisive ethnic and religious forces, provides the foundation for a relatively centralized economic system in which distributive goals are unusually salient. This distinctiveness is particularly apparent when one contrasts the policy instruments used to mitigate interregional income inequality in China with those used in other systems where reducing severe interregional income inequality is an important policy goal.

India's federal system, for example, is far less effective in alleviating interregional income inequality than China's unified planning and fiscal system. Neither expenditure or tax programs in India have a significant redistributive effect and interregional income inequality appears to have increased in the three decades since independence. The central government's tax authority is significantly weaker than in China. The Indian federal system gives considerable tax autonomy to state governments, giving rise to considerable variation in tax effort. Thomas Eapen's calculations show not only that state tax collections per thousand rupees of state income in the state where the tax burden is most heavy are more than twice those collected by the state with the lowest tax effort, but that some more-developed states rank low in tax effort and vice versa (Eapen, 471). In short, the revenue system seems to be somewhat regressive, with proportionately higher tax burdens in low-income states. Presumably this pattern could be reversed by the pattern of central government transfers to the states. The available transfer mechanisms include tax sharing and grants-in-aid administered by the Finance Commission and special development grants administered by the Planning Commission. Because collectively these transfers are the source of almost 40 percent of the income of the Indian states, they are a potentially powerful redistributive policy instrument (Echols, 279). There is, however, little coordination between the Planning and Finance Commissions and the overall results have not been redistributive. The special development grants in particular have been distributed on a simple per capita basis or according to other nondistributive criteria rather than giving significant weight to the level of state development (Echols, 277). Finally, the degree of central control of state expenditures in India pales in comparison with China.

Yugoslavia offers an even more instructive comparison because the declining ability of the central government to achieve regional distributive goals can be directly related to the increasingly decentralized economic system initiated after the early 1950s (Lang). Up until the mid-1950s, the federal government was able to channel a disproportionately high share of investment funds to poor regions. But because investment was allocated to industries characterized by unusually high capital-output ratios and with limited income- and employment-generation effects, the growth of backward regions was comparatively slow, despite these favorable investment allocations. Economists from more-developed areas, as was pointed out in the introduction, increasingly objected to this investment policy on the ground that it was simply too costly in terms of growth foregone. This debate led to a significant decentralization of economic decision making. Conventional rate-of-return criteria, rather than the objective of regional balance, increasingly dominated investment decisions. As a result, the investment share of less-developed areas fell dramatically–from about 34 percent in the 1950–5 period to 24 percent in the 1955–9 period (Dubey, 206).

Because the locus of authority over investment allocations shifted first in favor of republican governments and subsequently in favor of industrial enterprises, the portion of investment funds controlled by the central government was markedly reduced compared with the early 1950s. Even the increasing importance of the banking system as a source of investment funds failed to increase the geographic mobility of funds, because the banks were organized primarily along regional lines. Beginning with the Social Development Plan for 1966–70, the "Fund for the Accelerated Development of Underdeveloped Regions" was established to provide the central government with a policy instrument for redistributing investment resources. However, the fund's resources are quite limited and the investment share of backward areas remains substantially below that of the 1950–5 period. Because of the inability of the central government to redistribute funds interregionally and the reluctance of republican governments and enterprises to invest their own funds in other republics, less-developed regions have grown relatively slowly. In marked contrast to China, the coefficient of variation of interregional income inequality actually rose significantly between 1952 and 1971 (Dubey, 194).

The absence of both centralized policy instruments and decentralized means for redistributing investment funds appears to be very much a product of Yugoslavia's fractionalized historical, cultural, and revolutionary heritage. In conspicuous contrast to China's long history as a comparatively unified nation-state, the territories that came together to form Yugoslavia in 1918 comprised seven distinct political, legal, and administrative units. Two had histories as independent nation-states, whereas others had formed part of the Austrian-Hungarian empire. This mixed political heritage was compounded by important cleavages along ethnic, religious, and linguistic lines.

The Yugoslav revolution was also marked by factional struggles. Although the Communist Party in 1946 explicitly recognized the pluralistic nature of Yugoslavia's history and culture by adopting a federal form of government, it initially pursued a relatively centralized economic system based on the Soviet model. Unlike China, however, where the centralized model was fully implemented in the 1950s, in Yugoslavia it never took hold. Because the underlying divisions along geographic, ethnic, cultural, and linguistic lines were not healed by the revolution, the centralized system was rapidly abandoned following the political break with the Soviets in 1948. By contrast, partially because of more favorable historic and cultural factors, the degree of centralization of China's system of economic planning was far less radically altered following its split with the Soviet Union in 1960.

Although development economists frequently argue that there is a trade-off between growth and equity goals, particularly in the early stages of economic growth, the Chinese have been relatively successful in simultaneously pursuing both goals. The long-run rate of growth of domestic output since 1952 has been about 6 percent–a rate attained by many less-developed countries for short periods since World War II but seldom sustained for over two decades. Per capita consumption has roughly doubled between 1952 and 1975 (Eckstein 1977, 305). Data on the distribution of personal income are not available, but all evidence supports the view that at a minimum the Chinese have placed a floor on the incomes of all members of society, eliminated the uncertainty that surrounded the lives of many members of China's pre-1949 society, and made strenuous efforts to alleviate urban-rural disparities and interregional inequalities that have been important sources of personal income inequality elsewhere. All this has been achieved with what by contemporary standards must be considered an extremely modest quantity of foreign financial assistance. Indeed, "China has depended on foreign financial aid on either concessionary or commercial terms to a lesser degree than any other less-developed country that has achieved a sustained period of economic growth" (Perkins 1976, 19).

The achievement of both growth and distributive goals in China is intimately related through the centralized planning system. That is, the ability of the leadership to largely defer increases in industrial wages since 1957 has not only led to some reduction of income disparities between urban and rural residents, but has also increased industrial profits, the major source of funds for increasing China's already high rate of investment. This high rate of investment, in turn, has been largely responsible for China's rapid rate of growth. Thus the centralized system of planning contributes to the achievement of both equity and growth goals.

More strikingly, even when there appears to be a conflict, at least in the short run, between growth and equity the Chinese have sometimes chosen to sacrifice some growth in the pursuit of equity goals. This seems clearly to have been the case in China's regional investment decisions. There is little doubt that the leadership was aware that by concentrating resources in areas of existing industrial capacity and deferring the industrialization of inland regions for a period of several decades they could have achieved higher rates of industrial growth. The conscious rejection of this strategy reflects the relatively high priority placed both on achieving an economically more integrated and less dualistic society and on reducing China's vulnerability to military attack. But actually reducing inequality in the distribution of production capacity in turn depended on the availability of centralized policy instruments. The record of other developing countries suggests almost certainly that a more market-oriented growth path would have been accompanied by growing interregional inequality leading to sharply rising personal income inequality.

It seems unlikely that China's use of a relatively centralized system of economic planning to deal with the problems of growth and distribution will be widely emulated by other less-developed countries. Although planning is widely adopted, nowhere is there evidence of power to allocate resources comparable to that exercised by central planners in China. Both in terms of the share of GNP allocated through the budget and the extent of central control of the magnitude and distribution of local expenditures, the Chinese system is without parallel in the developing world. Furthermore, other countries usually have neither the revolutionary nor historical heritage that provides the foundation for this highly centralized system of economic planning. Finally, because the linkages between growth and distribution are increasingly well understood, it is now apparent that less far-reaching policies can be used to improve the distribution of income within the framework of more market-oriented economic systems. These more modest policies appear to be more congruent with the strength of economic policy instruments in most less-developed economies.

Appendix A. Tables

Table A.1. *Gross value of industrial output by province, 1952, 1957, and 1974 (millions of yuan; 1952 constant prices)*

Province	1952	1957	1974
National	34,330	78,390	387,247
Northeast			
Liaoning	4,523	11,710	48,951
Kirin	1,102	2,378	10,296
Heilungkiang	1,889	3,930	17,038
North			
Hopei	1,342	2,805	25,220
Shantung	2,091	4,068	22,775
Honan	881	1,705	11,582
Shansi	643	1,832	6,976
Inner Mongolia	192	757	9,323
Peking	825	2,300	20,400
Tientsin	1,836	4,300	19,266
East			
Kiangsu	2,584	4,553	25,874
Anhui	628	1,501	6,808
Chekiang	1,099	2,374	8,664
Shanghai	6,510	12,969	60,066
Central			
Hupei	955	2,799	11,870
Hunan	770	1,819	9,222
Kiangsi	575	1,173	5,590
South			
Kwangtung	1,745	3,812	18,684
Kwangsi	343	798	5,044
Fukien	414	1,224	4,969
Southwest			
Szechuan	1,649	4,873	15,750
Kweichow	269	605	3,400
Yünnan	333	1,101	3,780
Northwest			
Shensi	381	1,263	7,259
Kansu	230	560	5,670
Tsinghai	37	101	874
Sinkiang	175	446	1,785
Ninghsia	10	25	390

Source: Field, Lardy, and Emerson.

Table A.2. *Gross value of agricultural output by province, 1952 and 1957 (millions of yuan)*

Province	1952	1957
National	48,390	60,350
Northeast		
Liaoning[a]	1,690	1,817
Kirin[b]	1,414	1,373
Heilungkiang[c]	1,959	2,300
North		
Hopei[d]	3,477	4,450
Shantung[e]	3,999	4,125
Honan[f]	3,028	4,298
Shansi[g]	936	1,455
Inner Mongolia[h]	1,062	1,225
Peking[i]	—	80
Tientsin[j]	—	64
East		
Kiangsu[k]	2,679	3,716
Anhui[l]	1,704	3,028
Chekiang[m]	1,934	2,424
Shanghai[n]	60	76
Central		
Hupei[o]	2,878	3,500
Hunan[p]	2,657	3,481
Kiangsi[q]	1,542	1,937
South		
Kwangtung[r]	2,690	3,620
Kwangsi[s]	1,299	1,754
Fukien[t]	870	1,160
Southwest		
Szechuan[u]	4,149	6,040
Kweichow[v]	1,075	1,608
Yünnan[w]	1,101	1,839
Northwest		
Shensi[x]	1,240	2,282
Kansu[y]	900	1,423
Tsinghai[z]	213	372
Sinkiang[aa]	560	901

Notes: The provincial data are subject to somewhat larger margins of error than the industrial data shown in Table A.1. This is because provincial reports on the value of agricultural output tend to be less complete than reporting on industry and because less work in the West has been completed on the agricultural data. Values are in 1952 yuan, except as noted below.

Sources: For national figures: State Statistical Bureau 1960, 16. [a] *Liaoning shih-nien* (Ten years of Liaoning) (Shenyang: Liaoning People's Publishing House, 1960). [b] *Chi-lin jih-pao*, 18 March 1959, 1 October 1959; *Jen-min jih-pao*, 9 March 1959. [c] *Hei-lung-kiang jih-pao*, 19 September 1958. [d] *Hopei jih-pao*, 10 January 1958. [e] *Ch'ingtao jih-pao*, 5 October 1959. [f] *Ho-nan jih-pao*, 1 January 1959, 1 October 1959. [g] *Shan-hsi jih-pao*, 5 September 1955, 10

Table A.2. (cont.)

October 1959. Value for 1957 is probably in 1957 prices. [h]Inner Mongolia Statistical Bureau, *Statistics on achievements in the economic and cultural construction in the Inner Mongolia Autonomous Region* (Huhohaot'e 1960), p. 39. These data are probably in 1957 prices. [i]*Peiching jih-pao*, 9 August 1956, gives the value of agricultural output in 1955 as 73.6 million yuan. I assumed that the total growth between 1955 and 1957 was 10 percent. [j]Based on the assumption that the value of per capita agricultural output is the same as Peking. [k]*Hsin-hua jih-pao*, 10 January 1958. [l]*Anhui jih-pao*, 12 February 1959. [m]*Chekiang kung-jen pao*, 3 January 1958, 22 January 1958. [n]*Chieh-fang jih-pao*, 30 August 1957, 20 January 1958, 30 August 1959. [o]*Ch'ang-chiang jih-pao*, 11 March 1958; *Hu-pei jih-pao*, 6 February 1957, 11 September 1959, 31 October 1959. Value for 1957 is probably in 1957 prices. [p]*Hsin Hunan pao*, 4 May 1958. [q]*Chiang-hsi jih-pao*, 3 July 1958. [r]*Hsin-hua pan-yüeh k'an*, no. 5, 1958. [s]*Kuang-hsi jih-pao*, 5 October 1955, 27 January 1960. [t]*Fu-chien jih-pao*, 30 September 1959. Value for 1957 is probably in 1957 prices. [u]*Ta-kung pao*, 21 August 1957. [v]*Kueichou jih-pao*, 8 April 1960. [w]*Yün-nan jih-pao*, 3 January 1958; Field, Lardy, and Emerson, 20. [x]*Shen-hsi jih-pao*, 4 February 1958. [y]*Kan-su jih-pao*, 26 September 1957. [z]*Ch'ing-hai jih-pao*, 4 July 1958, and the assumption that the growth of the value of agricultural output value was proportionate to the growth of grain output. Later data from *Provincial Agricultural Statistics for Communist China* (Ithaca, N.Y.: Social Science Research Council, 1969). Value for 1957, and implicitly for 1952, is probably in 1957 prices.

Table A.3. *Provincial social expenditures, 1953–9 (thousands of yuan)*

Province	1953	1954	1955	1956	1957	1958	1959
Northeast							
Liaoning[b]		155,160		175,570	177,240		
Kirin[c]			72,460	103,260	112,170	119,690	158,290
Heilungkiang[d]			79,370	113,000			
North							
Hopei[a,e]			169,879	281,676	290,773		339,000
Shantung[f]			137,189	185,301		237,935	
Honan[g]			132,416	172,890	193,893	202,780	
Shansi[h]			75,931	103,199	103,200		152,462
Inner Mongolia[i]	47,414	41,988	40,253	74,351	81,565	86,776	
Peking[j]			66,190	82,326	76,899		
East							
Kiangsu[k]			142,820	204,261	224,357	229,517	284,682
Anhui[l]			115,623	157,860	151,064	137,042	193,750
Chekiang[m]			66,435	102,051	104,550		
Shanghai[n]		71,290	67,590	104,650	137,016	171,000	208,000
Central							
Hupei[o]				127,840			
Hunan[p]				124,019	132,342	125,630	146,632
Kiangsi[q]	64,011	66,290	71,564	86,112	91,012	96,910	
South							
Kwangtung[r]	125,176	142,350	142,269	192,523		205,610	
Kwangsi[s]		55,768	57,196	92,984	108,132		
Fukien[t]		60,830					

Table A.3. (cont.)

Province	1953	1954	1955	1956	1957	1958	1959
Southwest							
Szechuan[u]			158,509	198,231		225,140	256,330
Kweichow[v]			32,715	51,832	54,350	57,440	75,560
Yünnan[w]			48,640	67,550		80,580	86,450
Northwest							
Shensi[x]			81,670	107,028			
Kansu[y]					69,939	74,033	102,906
Tsinghai[z]			14,529	28,577	29,313	39,910	
Sinkiang[aa]	38,580	44,590	53,376	77,790	66,113	79,500	82,309

Note: All numbers are based on final-account data except 1959 data for Kansu and Kiangsu, which are expenditure levels estimated by Chinese sources.

[a] Data for 1957 and 1959 include Tientsin municipality.

Sources: [b] Li T'ao; Huang Ta; Liaoning Provincial People's Council. [c] Wang Huan-ju 1956, 1957, 1958, 1959, 1960. [d] Ch'en Chien-Fei; Yang I-ch'en. [e] Hu K'ai-ming 1957, 1958; Chou Cheng-hsin; Sung Ching-i 1958. [f] Yüan Tzu-yang; Chang Chu-sheng; Li Yü-ang. [g] Li Yü-san; Chi Wen-chien 1957, 1959. [h] Wu Kuang-t'ang 1956, 1957, 1958, 1960. [i] Inner Mongolia Statistical Bureau, p. 46. [j] Chang Yu-yü 1956, 1957, 1958. [k] Ch'en Shu-t'ung 1957, 1958, 1959. [l] Chang Huo 1957, 1958; T'ien Lei. [m] Jen I-li; Li Wen-hao. [n] Sung Chi-wen; Ts'ao Ti-ch'iu 1956, 1957; Ma I-hsing 1958, 1959, 1960. [o] An Tung-t'ai. [p] Chang Po-shen 1957, 1958; Shang Tzu-chin 1959, 1960. [q] Liang Ta-shan 1955, 1956; Hsü Kuang-yüan 1957, 1958, 1959. [r] Ho Hsi-ming; Chang Yung-li; Chi Chin-chang 1956, 1957; Wei Chin-fei 1959. [s] Li Fa-nan; Liao Yüan; Tung Ching-chai; Kuo Ch'eng. [t] Fukien Province Finance Department. [u] Chang Hu-ch'en 1957, 1959, 1960. [v] Hsü Chien-shang 1957, 1958, 1960; Chang P'ing. [w] Wu Tso-min 1957, 1960; Liu Cho-fu. [x] Chao Po-p'ing; Chang I-ch'en. [y] Wang Kuo-jui; Kansu Finance Department, 199, 201–2. [z] Sun Chün-i 1957, 1958; Yüan Jen-yüan. [aa] Liu Tzu-mo 1956, 1957, 1959, 1960.

200

Appendix B. Government administrative structure

Chinese term	U.S. term or equivalent
chung-yang	central government
ta-hsing cheng-ch'ü	large administrative region (abolished 1954)
sheng	province
tzu-chih ch'ü	autonomous region (equivalent to province)
chih-hsia shih	municipality directly administered by the central government (equivalent to province)
chuan-ch'ü[a]	special district or prefecture
hsien	county
ch'ü	district
hsiang	administrative village
ts'un	natural village

Note: This is a highly simplified chart. It does not include a large number of different sub-provincial levels of government administration in use in some provinces. For a more complete listing see U.S. Central Intelligence Agency, 10.

[a]Since 1970 the name of this level of administration has been changed to *ti-ch'ü*. Since 1975 Peking has translated this as prefecture.

Notes

1. Economic growth and equity in a dualistic economy

1. A comprehensive examination of Chinese economic growth can be found in the papers of the Social Science Research Council Conference on Quantitative Measures of China's Economic Development, edited by Alexander Eckstein (forthcoming).

2. Recent surveys of the relationship between modern economic growth and income distribution include Ahluwalia, Cline, and Paukert.

3. For a lucid summary of this literature see Hurwicz 1973.

4. Chinese statistical treatment of animal husbandry makes cross-provincial comparisons of the value of agricultural output extremely difficult. The statistical methods used to value animal husbandry appear to result in a substantial upward bias in the value of agricultural output in sparsely populated regions where animal husbandry is the predominant form of agriculture. This appears to be a significant problem in Inner Mongolia, Shensi, Kansu, Tsinghai, and Sinkiang.

5. Simon Kuznets's data for twelve less-developed countries show that per worker output in the nonagricultural sector exceeded that in agriculture by 60 percent. See *Modern Economic Growth* (New Haven: Yale University Press, 1966), p. 402. Using a higher nonagriculture labor force estimate made by Liu Ta-chung and Yeh Kung-chia would somewhat reduce the disparity in per worker productivity in China from that shown in Table 1.2 (Liu Ta-chung and Yeh Kung-chia, 66, 69).

6. In a federal fiscal system the use of the terms national, provincial, and local is not a source of ambiguity. However, in a unified fiscal system, ambiguity frequently arises. For example, under a unified fiscal system, provincial expenditures include not only the outlays of the provincial government itself, but also those of its subordinate levels of budgetary administration. Thus the word "provincial" could refer to expenditures either inclusive or exclusive of subordinate units. To minimize these problems, I generally use the words "provincial" and "local" interchangeably to mean noncentral, that is, inclusive of all subnational units. Only in a few specific, clearly defined cases is "provincial" used to mean provincial exclusive of its subordinate units. When discussing levels of government below the provincial level, I use the term "subprovincial" or refer to some particular level such as the county (*hsien*) or township (*hsiang*) rather than using the term "local." See Appendix B for a chart of levels of government administration.

7. The value of output produced by state-managed enterprises under local control in 1952 was 3,920 million yuan (State Statistical Bureau 1960,

103). The total value of state-managed industry in 1952 can be calculated as 15,131 million yuan (State Statistical Bureau 1960, 16, 38), making the local share 25.9 percent.

8. See Table 2.6. The central-state share of all investment, including investment in the agricultural sector that did not flow through the budget, would be somewhat lower.

9. The most important of the missing documents is Chou En-lai's June 1956 speech to the National People's Congress. Only a New China News Agency summary is available (Chou En-lai 1956a). Ch'en Yun's speech to the Third Plenum of the Eighth Chinese Communist Party Central Committee in September-October 1957 also is not available. Reference to this speech is in Chinese Communist Party 1958.

10. TCKT Data Section 1957b. In 1956, less than 1 percent of total output of the following commodities was distributed outside the state system of unified distribution: pig iron, nonferrous metals, caustic soda, diesel engines, machine tools, and transformers. In the first two years of the First Five-Year Plan period, from 3 to 45 percent of these products was distributed through the market. For example, 16 and 16.8 percent of machine tools were so distributed in 1953 and 1954. In 1956, the percent distributed through the market had fallen to .1 percent.

11. See, for example, the lead editorial in *Chi-hua ching-chi*, no. 9, (1957): 1–4, which cites the relatively slow growth of agricultural production as a principal constraint on the overall growth of the economy.

12. For example, Abram Bergson estimates that per capita gross domestic product in the Soviet Union in 1955 was $920. See "The Comparison of National Income of the USSR and the US," in *International Comparisons of Prices and Output,* edited by D. J. Daly (New York: National Bureau of Economic Research, 1972), p. 149. For estimates of GNP in Eastern Europe in the mid-1960s, see Thad P. Alton, "Economic Structure and Growth in Eastern Europe," *Economic Developments in Countries of Eastern Europe* (Washington, D.C.: U.S. Government Printing Office, 1970), pp. 41–67.

13. A more vigorous price debate emerged after 1963 but it appears to have had little effect on Chinese price policy.

14. Of course this analogy with conventional balance of payments accounting is somewhat artificial both because the government enjoys a monopoly position in these short-term and long-term markets and because the long-term flows are interest free and are never repaid.

2. Centralization of economic and financial planning, 1949–1957

1. Rather than listing these three roughly equivalent types of administrative units, I use the term *province* to refer to all of them. During most of the years since 1949, China has been divided into twenty-one provinces, five autonomous regions, and three independent municipalities. Only twenty-eight of these units are listed in Table 1.1, because data on the absolute level of output in Tibet is not available. In subsequent tables, the number of units given varies both because complete data are frequently not available and because of changes over time in the number of provincial-level administrative units. For example, in April 1958, Tientsin lost its status as an inde-

pendent municipality and was incorporated into Hopei province. In 1965, Tientsin regained its former status.

2. See Appendix B for a chart of the administrative structure of the government.

3. Chou Ching (p. 11) reports that investment in the light-industrial sector during the 1950–70 period was equivalent to profits in light industry in 1970 alone. Thus, most of the profits from nineteen years of light industry have been reallocated to producer goods, agriculture, and other sectors.

4. The development of local budgetary administration is discussed below in this chapter.

5. Their primary revenue source was the agricultural surtax, which in 1950 was 15 percent of the regular agricultural tax (Government Administrative Council 1950b).

6. The rate of growth of state revenues during each year of the First Five-Year Plan period was as follows: 1953, 23.9 percent; 1954, 20.5 percent; 1955, 3.7 percent; 1956, 5.7 percent; 1957, 7.9 percent (State Statistical Bureau 1960, 21).

7. In 1954, the sum of the agricultural and industrial and commercial taxes was 46 percent of national government revenues (Table 2.2). In addition, local governments collected other minor taxes such as amusement, vehicle, and slaughter taxes that brought the total to over 50 percent.

3. The 1958 decentralization

1. Initially, the rates were fixed for three years (State Council 1957c), but in April 1958 the State Council decreed that in order to facilitate local planning for the Second Five-Year Plan (1958–62) the rates would be unchanged for five years (State Council 1958i).

2. See Table 2.2.

3. Author's estimate, based on urban population and municipal public utilities surtax revenues in Peking, Shansi, and Chungking (Chang Yü-yü 1958; Wu Kuang-t'ang 1958; Ch'en Ch'ou 1956).

4. One percent of industrial and commercial tax revenues in 1958 and 1959, respectively (Li Hsien-nien 1959, 22; 1960, 59).

5. Calculated on the basis of local budgetary expenditure data in Table 1.4.

6. An earlier brief statement (Lardy 1975b) of the argument and the empirical results set forth below has drawn comment from one of the most articulate advocates of the hypothesis of increased provincial autarky (Donnithorne 1976). I believe I have addressed her major concerns below. Readers interested in the full details will wish to read her comment and my reply (Lardy 1976a).

7. In the discussion below, the word *social* is used as an abbreviation for the expenditure category "culture, education, public health, and welfare." As discussed in Chapter 2, this category includes expenditures on a variety of related programs.

8. The provincial investment magnitude referred to here is inclusive of the following three categories: local investment financed through the provincial budget; direct central government investment undertaken within a province; and extrabudgetary investment.

9. The ratio between the provinces with the highest and lowest per capita social expenditures was 8.7 in 1955, 8.2 in 1956, 6.0 in 1957, 6.5 in 1958, and 6.0 in 1959.

10. In 1959, social expenditures in Kansu and Sinkiang (data for 1959 are not available for Tsinghai) were 35 percent greater than 1957. The average national increase was 26 percent (Li Hsien-nien 1959, 1960).

11. In a simple linear regression for a sample of nineteen provinces for which data are available, the level of provincial development as measured by industrial output alone or by net value added in industry and agriculture was not a significant variable in explaining changes in social expenditures. This result holds whether level of provincial development is measured in aggregate or per capita terms.

12. Based on the estimate of insurance funds given in Table 2.1 and social expenditure data given in the annual budget reports by Li Hsien-nien.

13. Based on the estimate given above that the extrabudgetary funds of local governments were 690–705 million yuan in 1958 and 705–20 million yuan in 1959 and the data on local government expenditures in Table 1.4.

14. Again, in a linear regression the level of provincial development was not a significant variable in explaining changes in provincial shares of national investment. This result also is not sensitive to the choice of aggregate or per capita measures of the level of provincial development.

15. Although some of these facilities were financed from the budget of the central government, and thus do not contribute to interprovincial expenditure differentials, most of these institutions were financed from provincial budgets.

16. Based on data in Tables 3.3 and 3.6.

17. Total budgetary expenditures for social programs in 1956 were 3,916 million yuan (Li Hsien-nien 1956, 6).

18. *Nan-fang jih-pao*, 6 December 1955. Cited in Vogel 1969, 131.

19. Calculated on the basis of data in Table 3.3.

20. The sum of local budgetary and extrabudgetary investment in Szechuan in 1958 and 1959 was 1,070 million yuan and 1,460 million yuan, respectively (*Szechuan jih-pao*, 24 June 1959; Chang Hu-ch'en 1960). This was 4.0 and 4.6 percent of total national investment in those years. Szechuan's share of national investment in 1957, including central government direct investment, was 4.0 percent (Table 3.5).

21. Michel Oksenberg, unpublished interview protocols, 28 September 1965.

22. These rates give the tax as the percent of the assessed "normal yield." The normal yield for an area is the harvest that should be expected in that area in a normal year based on the area's natural conditions and general economic situation.

23. Although final accounts are not available for Liaoning after 1957, it presumably also experienced a large increase in its remission rate because it had not shared in enterprise profits and adjustment revenues prior to 1959.

24. For eight provinces, both the planned first-quarter rate and the actual annual rate are available. For these eight, the average absolute difference between planned and actual rates was less than six percentage points.

25. Because the proportionate share of total expenditures undertaken by local governments increased from under a third to over half (Table 1.4) between 1957 and 1959, the percentages in Table 2.9 cannot be compared directly to those in Tables 3.11, 3.12, and 3.13. The comparison must be made in relative terms.

26. Available evidence suggests that only a few provinces actually issued local economic construction bonds in 1959. Only Anhui, Kirin, and Szechuan are known to have issued bonds (T'ien Lei; Wang Huan-ju 1960; Chang Hu-ch'en 1960). Local bond issues were planned but later withdrawn in Kiangsu, Kweichow, Kwangtung, and Peking (Ch'en Shu-t'ung 1959; Chang P'ing; Wei Chin-fei 1959; Ch'eng Hung-i).

4. Economic planning since the First Five-Year Plan

1. Chekiang Provincial Radio, 13 January 1969. Cited by Donnithorne 1972b, 616–17.

2. The provincial growth rates referred to here and elsewhere in this chapter are calculated from data in Field, Lardy, and Emerson. Because of a lack of adequate data on the level of industrial output in the 1950s, Tibet is excluded from this discussion of the pattern of provincial industrial growth.

3. This summary measure, and others cited below, was calculated based on the inclusion of the municipalities of Shanghai, Peking, and Tientsin within their adjacent provinces.

4. Note also that Hopei and Shantung grew so slowly during the First Plan that they moved from the category of above-average to that of below-average level of per capita output. Thus they are included in the lefthand column of Table 4.1 but the righthand column of Table 4.2. Conversely, rapid growth in Fukien and Inner.Mongolia moved them into the category of above-average level of development by 1957. This shift points out the fact that the analysis presented in the text, based on the simple two-way classification of above- and below-average level of development, is quite crude. I have used it because I believe it conveys the general relationship between the level of development and the rate of growth. Of course, using the coefficient of variation avoids this problem entirely by treating level of development as a continuous variable (Lardy 1977).

5. With the exception of Hsinhsiang (Honan), these comparisons are based on official data reported in the Chinese media. The provincial data are summarized in Field, Lardy, and Emerson. The municipal data were culled from a large number of Chinese media reports but have not yet been systematically compiled outside China. The assessment of Hsinhsiang (Honan) is in Dwight Perkins et al., pp. 219–20. This analysis of intraprovincial inequality is, of course, quite tentative. The sample of cities for which industrial output data are available is most restricted and municipal population data, which would enable comparisons of trends in per capita inequality within provinces, are not available.

6. "Shang-hai kung-yeh ti kai-ts'ao ho k'uang-chan," (The Transformation and expansion of Shanghai's industry) in *Hsin Chung-kuo erh-shih wu-nien* (Twenty-five years of New China) (Hong Kong, 1975), p. 203; British Broadcasting Corp., *Summary of World Broadcasts, Far East, Weekly Economic Report*, no. 874, p. A/2, hereafter abbreviated in the form BBC, *SWB/FE/W874/A/2*.

7. The gross domestic product (GDP) estimates by Field and Perkins are both calculated in 1957 constant prices, whereas the budgetary data are almost certainly in current-year prices. It is possible, although on current evidence unlikely, that the growth of GDP measured in current-year prices would be somewhat higher because of a rise in the overall price level. This could reduce (or perhaps even reverse the sign of) the difference between the growth of budgetary revenues and the growth of GDP. Although agricultural prices have risen since 1957, raising the rate of GDP growth measured in current-year prices, this has probably been largely offset by reductions in the prices of manufactured goods. A final assessment of this issue will be possible only after further research on China's price structure has been completed.

8. See Table 2.1.

9. Prior to 1958, budgetary allocations included enterprise outlays for the so-called four items expenditure – expenditures for the trial manufacture of new products, for technical and organizational improvements in production, technical security and labor protection, and purchase of miscellaneous fixed assets. Beginning in 1958, these items were no longer financed through the budget but were to be financed from enterprises' retained profits (State Council 1957a). In 1958, enterprise expenditures on these items were reported to have been 900 million yuan, almost one-third of their total retained profits (T'ao Sheng-yü and Tan Ya-sheng, 14).

10. A Ministry of Finance directive (1959b, 89) includes labor insurance funds in the category of "worker and staff welfare expenditures." In previous years, these expenditures were not included because they were extrabudgetary. There is some indication that the change actually may have been made in 1958 (Wei Li, 12–13).

11. Anhui Provincial Service, 22 August 1973, in British Broadcasting Corp., *SWB/FE/W740/A/1*. Hunan Provincial Service, 26 June 1972, in *SWB/FE/W680/A/2*. For Yünnan, New China News Agency (NCNA), 19 March 1973, in *SWB/FE/W717/A/2*. Kiangsi Provincial Service, 28 May 1976, in *SWB/FE/W881/A/1*. Shantung Provincial Service, 26 June 1975, in Foreign Broadcast Information Service, *Daily Report, People's Republic of China*, 2 July 1975, p. G8. For Kansu, NCNA 26 July 1976, in *SWB/FE/W889/A/1*.

12. *Cheng-chih ching-chi hsüeh chi-ch'u chih-shih* (Fundamentals of political economy), 2nd edition (Shanghai: Shanghai People's Publishing House, 1975), p. 400.

13. The output of commune- and brigade-level industry in Kwangtung in 1975 was reported as 1,500 million yuan (Kwangtung Provincial Service, 9 July 1976, in BBC, *SWB/FE/W887/A/2*). This is 7.5 percent of the estimated value of industrial output for the province as a whole (Field, Lardy, and Emerson, 11).

14. Kansu Radio, 31 January 1977, in Foreign Broadcast Information Service, *Daily Report, People's Republic of China*, 4 February 1977, p. M1, and estimate of Kansu provincial industrial output (Field, Lardy, and Emerson, 11).

15. On present evidence, it would appear, for example, that in Shanghai, by all accounts a stronghold of leftist strength in the latter half of the 1960s, industrial production was less disrupted than elsewhere. In contrast, between 1966 and 1968 industrial output fell considerably more sharply in Kirin and Hupei than in the country as a whole, and recovery to the pre-Cultural Revolution peak levels of production lagged a year behind the pace of recovery nationally. Unfortunately, data for the years 1966 through 1969 are particularly sparse, so it is impossible to undertake a systematic year-by-year analysis of provincial industrial performance for this period.

5. China's distributive policies in comparative perspective

1. Shanghai's industrial labor force tripled from 770,000 in 1957 (*Hsin-wen jih-pao*, 28 December 1957) to about 2,300,000 in 1975 (*Peking Review*, no. 27 (1975): 17). During the same period, the value of industrial output almost quintupled from 11,402 million yuan to 55,707 million yuan, in constant 1957 prices (Field, Lardy, and Emerson, 11).

2. *Cheng-chih ching-chi hsüeh chi-ch'u chih-shih* (Fundamentals of political economy), 2nd edition (Shanghai: Shanghai People's Publishing House, 1975), p. 406 and *Ten Great Years* (State Statistical Bureau 1960, 118).

3. John W. Mellor, "The Functions of Agricultural Prices in Economic Development," *Indian Journal of Agricultural Economics*, vol. 23, no. 1: (1968): 29.

4. T. H. Lee, *Intersectoral Capital Flows in the Economic Development of Taiwan, 1895–1960* (Ithaca, N.Y.: Cornell University Press, 1971), p. 91. Economic Planning Council, *Taiwan Statistical Data Book 1975* (Taipei, 1975), p. 161.

5. Lee, *Intersectoral Capital Flows*, p. 92.

6. The essential role of relative price changes in transferring resources to the agricultural sector is evident in official data for the Third Five-Year Plan period (1965–70). Improvements in the terms of trade during this period added more than 10,000 million yuan to farm purchasing power (New China News Agency (NCNA), 1 December 1975, in British Broadcasting Corp. (BBC), *SWB/FE/W856/A/1*). Value added in the agricultural sector is estimated to have been 49,100 million yuan in 1965 and 59,960 million yuan in 1970–a 10,800 million yuan increase (Perkins 1976, 9). Although Perkins has not estimated value added in agriculture for the intervening years 1966–9, based on data on the growth of food grain output (the major component of value added in agriculture), the cumulative annual increments above the 1965 level of value added are probably about 23,000 million yuan. Thus both in the 1952–7 and 1965–70 periods the value of increased farm purchasing power due to improvements in agriculture's terms of trade was almost half the cumulative annual increments to net output value.

It is important to note that although these changes in relative prices have increased the purchasing power of agriculture relative to what it otherwise would have been, this does not imply that there is no longer any net transfer of resources out of the agricultural sector. Perkins (1975a, 364), for example, argues that even after allowing for these relative price changes that agriculture products continue to be underpriced, in effect constituting an implicit tax burden on agriculture. A resolution of this issue of the real burden on agricultural depends on further research on the structure of Chinese prices and more detailed study of the real intersectoral resource flows that have occurred since the early 1950s.

7. NCNA, 25 September 1972, in *BBC/SWB/FE/W693/A/2*.

8. NCNA, 25 June 1976, in *BBC/SWB/FE/W885/A/3*.

9. Because the Chinese have released no data on the size of the national industrial labor force in the 1970s, this estimate is subject to a large margin of error. It is a crude estimate based on the belief that the 65 percent increase in output per worker that occurred in Shanghai between 1957 and 1975 (calculated from data in note 1, above) must be above the national average.

10. The procedure used by Schran to derive this estimate implicitly assumes that the rate of female labor force participation in urban areas has not changed significantly since 1957. In Shanghai, however, almost 20 percent of the growth of the industrial labor force during this period has been due to increased female participation. To the extent that this is a significant factor in the growth of the national industrial labor force, the average income of urban families must have continued to grow despite the constancy of the average wage per worker since 1957. This would mean that the differential between urban and rural areas would have been diminished by an amount smaller than that cited in the text.

11. William L. Parish, Jr., "Socialism and the Chinese Peasant Family," *Journal of Asian Studies,* vol. 34, no. 3 (1975): 628. Martin King Whyte, "Inequality and Stratification in China," *China Quarterly,* no. 64 (1975): 687–8.

12. "In the Communes – Ownership on Three Levels," *China Reconstructs,* vol. 23, no. 1 (1974): 38.

13. This theme has been advanced in an unpublished paper of Charles Roll.

14. Alva Lewis Erisman, "China: Agriculture in the 1970's," in *China: A Reassessment of the Economy,* a compendium of papers presented to the U.S. Congress Joint Economic Committee (Washington, D.C.: U.S. Government Printing Office, 1975), p. 330.

15. Both report tax rates of 4.5 percent, whereas the national average is 5 percent (*Peking Review,* no. 26 (1975): 19; NCNA, 27 September 1975, in BBC, *SWB/FE/W854/A/2;* NCNA, 23 September 1974, in *Survey of the People's Republic of China Press,* 7–11 October 1974, p. 21).

16. The rate of increase of purchase prices of various types of agricultural products varied from year to year. Price data disaggregated into the categories grain crops, commercial crops, animal husbandry, and native products have been published (TCKT Data Section 1957a, 5). The rate of increase in the average purchase price for each province presumably largely reflects the mix of the province's output among these categories.

17. *Kan-su jih-pao,* 6 October 1959, p. 8.

18. *Kirin jih-pao,* 23 September 1959, p. 4.

19. NCNA, 27 September 1975, in BBC, *SWB/FE/W854/A/3; Peking Review,* no. 19, (1975): 18.

20. Chekiang Provincial Radio, 16 August 1977, in BBC, *SWB/FE/W994/A/5.* Yünnan Provincial Radio, 28 June 1977, in BBC, *SWB/FE/W937/A/10.*

21. Denis C. Twitchett, *Financial Administration under the T'ang Dynasty,* 2d ed. (Cambridge: Cambridge University Press, 1970), pp. 39–42.

22. Ray Huang, *Taxation and Government Finance in Sixteenth-Century Ming China* (Cambridge: Cambridge University Press, 1974), pp. 1–2.

References

The following abbreviations are used in the References. Note that several of the abbreviation explanations refer the reader to a main entry in the References where the full citation for the abbreviated source is given.

CB   *Current Background*

CCYC   *Ching-chi yen-chiu*

CHCC   *Chi-hua ching-chi*

CYTCFKHP   *Chung-yang ts'ai-cheng fa-kuei hui-pien* (See Ministry of Finance 1955–9 for full citation.)

CYTCFLHP   *Chung-yang ts'ai-ching cheng-ts'e fa-ling hui-pien* (See Government Administrative Council, Financial and Economic Commission, for full citation.)

ECMM   *Extracts from China Mainland Magazines*

EPO   *Economic Planning and Organization in Mainland China* (See Chao Kuo-chün for full citation.)

FKHP   *Chung-hua jen-min kung-ho-kuo fa-kuei hui-pien* (See State Council, Bureau of Legal Affairs, for full citation.)

HCS   *Hsin chien-she*

HH   *Hsüeh-hsi*

HHPYK   *Hsin-hua pan-yüeh k'an*

HHTCFKHP   *Hsien-hsing ts'ai-cheng fa-kuei* (See Ministry of Finance 1951b for full citation.)

HHYP   *Hsin hua yüeh-pao*

JMJP   *Jen-min jih-pao*

JMST   *Jen-min shou-ts'e*

JMSW   *Jen-min shui-wu*

JPRS   Joint Publications Research Service

KMJP   *Kwang-ming jih-pao*

LLHH   *Li-lun hsüeh-hsi*

NCNA   New China News Agency

NFJP   *Nan-fang jih-pao*

PR   *Peking Review*

SCMP   *Survey of the China Mainland Press*

SSST   *Shih-shih shou-ts'e*

TC   *Ts'ai-cheng*

TCKT   *T'ung-chi kung-tso*

TCKTTH   *T'ung-chi kung-tso t'ung-hsün*

TCTLHP   *Shih-nien lai ts'ai-cheng tzu-liao hui-pien* (See Ministry of Finance 1959d for full citation.)

TCYC   *Ts'ai-ching yen-chiu*

214   *References*

TKP   *Ta kung pao*
TLCS   *Ti-li chih-shih*

The following Chinese periodicals are cited in the References:

Chiao-hsüeh yü yen-chiu (Education and Research)
Chi-hua ching chi (Economic Planning)
Ching-chi yen-chiu (Economic Research)
Hsin chien-she (New Construction)
Hsin-hua pan-yüeh k'an (New China Semimonthly)
Hsin-hua yüeh-pao (New China Monthly)
Hsin k'uai-chi (New Accounting)
Hsüeh-hsi (Study)
Jen-min shui-wu (People's Taxation)
Li-lun hsüeh-hsi (Theoretical Study)
Min-tsu t'uan-chieh (Nationalities Unity)
Peking Review
Shih-shih shou-ts'e (Current Affairs Handbook)
Ti-li chih-shih (Geographical Knowledge)
Ts'ai-cheng (Finance)
Ts'ai-ching yen-chiu (Finance and Economics Research)
T'ung-chi kung-tso (Statistical Work)
T'ung-chi kung-tso t'ung-hsün (Statistical Work Bulletin)

For directives, regulations, and primary source materials listed under Government Administrative Council, Ministry of Finance, and State Council, the year immediately following the source name refers to the original date of issue. When these materials are available in the West only in official compendiums of later years, this information occurs later in the entry.

Adelman, Irma, and Cynthia Taft Morris. 1973. *Economic Growth and Social Inequality in Developing Countries.* Stanford, Calif.: Stanford University Press.
Ahluwalia, Montek S. 1974. "Income Inequality: Some Dimensions of the Problem." In *Redistribution with Growth,* ed. by Hollis Chenery, et al., pp. 3–37. London: Oxford University Press.
Aird, John S. 1974. *Population Estimates for the Provinces of the People's Republic of China: 1953–1974.* International Population Reports, series P-95, no. 73. Washington, D.C.: U.S. Department of Commerce.
An Tung-t'ai. 1957. "Sheng ts'ai-cheng t'ing-chang An Tung-t'ai pao-kao pen-sheng ts'ai-cheng yü-chüeh-suan chih-chu" (The director of the Provincial Finance Department, An Tung-t'ai, reports on this province's financial budget and final account). *Ch'ang-chiang jih-pao,* 27 August.
Balassa, Bela. 1970. "The Economic Reform in Hungary." *Economica,* n.s. 37, no. 145: 1–22.
Bardhan, Pranab K. 1974. "Some Country Experience–India." In *Redistribution with Growth,* ed. by Hollis Chenery, et al., pp. 255–62. London: Oxford University Press.
Berger, Roland. 1975. "Economic Planning in the People's Republic of China." *World Development,* vol. 3, nos. 7 & 8: 551–64.

Bettelheim, Charles. 1974. *Cultural Revolution and Industrial Organization in China: Changes in Management and the Division of Labor.* New York: Monthly Review Press.

Cassou, Pierre-Henri. 1974. "The Chinese Monetary System." *China Quarterly,* no. 59: 559–66.

Chang Chu-sheng. 1958. "Kuan-yü Shan-tung 1957-nien ts'ai-cheng chüeh-suan ho 1958-nien ts'ai-cheng yü-suan ts'ao-an ti pao-kao (chai-yao)" [Report on Shantung Province's 1957 financial final accounts and 1958 draft financial budget (summary)]. *Ta-chung jih-pao,* 3 November.

Chang Feng-chi. 1956. "The relationship between coastal and inland industries." *LLHH,* no. 12. Trans. in *ECMM* 60: 24–6.

Chang Hsüan-san. 1956. "Lun kuo-min ching-chi chi-hua ling-t'ao chi-chung yü fen-san" (Centralization and decentralization in our national economic plan leadership). *TKP,* 25 November.

Chang Hu-ch'en. 1957. "Kuan-yü Szu-ch'uan sheng 1956-nien ts'ai-cheng chüeh-suan ho 1957-nien ts'ai-cheng yü-suan ts'ao-an ti pao-kao" (Report on Szechuan Province's 1956 financial final account and 1957 draft financial budget). *Szu-ch'uan jih-pao,* 24 August.

 1959. "Szu-ch'uan sheng 1958-nien ts'ai-cheng chüeh-suan ho 1959-nien ts'ai-cheng yü-suan ts'ao-an ti pao-kao" (Report on Szechuan Province's 1958 financial final account and draft financial budget). *Szu-ch'uan jih-pao,* 25 June.

 1960. "Szu-ch'uan sheng 1959-nien ts'ai-cheng chüeh-suan ho 1960-nien ts'ai-cheng yü-suan ts'ao-an ti pao-kao" (Report on Szechuan Province's 1959 financial final account and 1960 draft financial budget). *Szu-ch'uan jih-pao,* 27 May.

Chang Huo. 1957. "Kuan-yü An-hui sheng 1956-nien ts'ai-cheng chüeh-suan ho 1957-nien ts'ai-cheng yü-suan ts'ao-an ti pao-kao" (Report on Anhui Province's 1956 financial final account and 1957 draft financial budget). *An-hui jih-pao,* 24 September.

 1958. "Kuan-yü An-hui sheng 1957-nien ts'ai-cheng chüeh-suan ho 1958-nien ts'ai-cheng yü-suan ts'ao-an ti pao-kao" (Report on Anhui Province's 1957 financial account and 1958 draft financial budget). *An-hui jih-pao,* 10 November.

Chang I-ch'en. 1957. "Shan-hsi sheng 1956-nien chüeh-suan ho 1957-nien yü-suan (ts'ao-an) pao-kao" (Report on Shensi Province's 1956 final account and 1957 draft budget). *Shan-hsi jih-pao* (Hsian), 30 August.

Chang P'ing. 1959. "Kuan-yü Kuei-chou sheng 1958-nien ts'ai-cheng chüeh-suan ho 1959-nien ts'ai-cheng yü-suan ts'ao-an ti pao-kao" (Report on Kweichow Province's 1958 financial final account and 1959 draft financial budget). *Kuei-chou jih-pao,* 3 October.

Chang Po-shen. 1957. "Hu-nan sheng 1957-nien ts'ai-cheng yü-suan chih-hsing ch'ing-k'uang ho 1958-nien ts'ai-cheng yü-suan an-p'ai ti i-chien" (The conditions of implementation of Hunan Province's 1957 financial budget and opinions on the arrangement of the 1958 financial budget). *Hsin Hu-nan pao,* 22 December.

 1958 "Kuan-yü Hu-nan sheng 1957-nien ts'ai-cheng chüeh-suan ho 1958-nien ts'ai-cheng yü-suan chih-hsing ch'ing-k'uang ti pao-kao" (Report on Hunan Province's 1957 financial final account and the conditions of implementation of the 1958 financial budget). *Hsin Hu-nan pao,* 4 July.

Chang Ting-an. 1957. "Kuan-yü Pao-t'ou shih 1956-nien ts'ai-cheng chüeh-suan ho 1957-nien ts'ai-cheng yü-suan ts'ao-an ti pao-kao (chai-

216   *References*

yao)" [Report on Paot'ou Municipality's 1956 financial final account and 1957 draft financial budget (summary)]. *Pao-t'ou jih-pao*, 13 August.

Chang Yen-hsing. 1957. "An-chao chih-chien chien-kuo fang-chen an-p'ai ch'eng-shih chien-she kung-tso." (The arrangement of urban construction work must be according to the national policy of economy in construction). *CHCC*, no. 12: 4–9.

Chang Yu-yü. 1956. "Kuan-yü Pei-ching shih 1955-nien ts'ai-cheng shou-chih chüeh-suan ho 1956-nien ts'ai-cheng shou-chih yü-suan ti pao-kao (chai-yao)" [Report on Peking Municipality's 1955 financial income and expenditure final account and 1956 financial income and expenditure budget (summary)]. *Pei-ching jih-pao*, 9 August.

1957. "Kuan-yü 1956-nien ts'ai-cheng shou-chih chüeh-suan ho 1957-nien ts'ai-cheng shou-chih yü-suan ti pao-kao (chai-yao)" [Report on the 1956 financial income and expenditure final account and the 1957 financial income and expenditure budget (summary)]. *Pei-ching jih-pao*, 24 July.

1958. "Kuan-yü Pei-ching shih 1957-nien ts'ai-cheng shou-chih chüeh-suan ho 1958-nien ts'ai-cheng shou-chih yü-suan ti pao-kao" (Report on Peking Municipality's 1957 financial income and expenditure final account and 1958 financial income and expenditure budget). *Pei-ching jih-pao*, 23 August.

Chang Yün-shan. 1957. "Kuan-yü Ch'ing-tao shih 1956-nien-tu ts'ai-cheng chüeh-suan ho 1957-nien-tu ts'ai-cheng yü-suan ts'ao-an ti pao-kao (chai-yao)" [Report on Tsingtao Municipality's 1956 financial final account and 1957 draft financial budget (summary)]. *Ch'ing-tao jih-pao*, 12 September.

Chang Yung-li. 1955. "Kuan-yü i-chiu wu-szu nien Kuang-tung sheng chüeh-suan ho i-chiu-wu-wu nien Kuang-tung sheng yü-suan ti pao-kao" (Report on Kwangtung Province's 1954 final account and Kwangtung province's 1955 budget). *Nan-fang jih-pao*, 3 December.

Chao I-wen. 1957. *Hsin chung-kuo ti kung-yeh* (New China's industry). Peking: Statistical Publishing House.

Chao Kuo-chün. 1963. *Economic Planning and Organization in Mainland China: A Documentary Study, 1949–1957 (EPO)*. 2 vols. Cambridge, Mass: Harvard East Asian Research Center.

Chao Po-p'ing. 1956. "Kuan-yü Shan-hsi sheng 1955-nien chüeh-suan ho 1956-nien yü-suan ti pao-kao" (Report on Shensi Province's 1955 final account and 1956 budget). *Shan-hsi jih-pao* (Hsian), 2 November.

Chao Shou-shan. 1955. "Shensi provincial First Five-Year Plan." *Shan-hsi jih-pao* (Hsian), 9 October. Trans. in *Weekly Information Report on Communist China*, 21 September 1956.

Ch'en Chien-fei. 1957. "Kuan-yü Hei-lung-chiang sheng 1955-nien ts'ai-cheng chüeh-suan ho 1956-nien ts'ai-cheng yü-suan chih-hsing ch'ing-k'uang ti pao-kao" (Report on Heilungkiang Province's 1955 financial final account and the conditions of implementation of the 1956 financial budget). *Hei-lung-chiang jih-pao*, 13 January.

Ch'en Ch'ou. 1956. "Szu-ch'uan sheng Ch'ung-ch'ing shih jen-min wei-yüan hui kuan-yü 1955-nien ts'ai-cheng chüeh-suan ho 1956-nien ts'ai-cheng yü-suan ti pao-kao" (Report of the Szechuan Province Chungking Municipality People's Council concerning the 1955 financial final account and the 1956 financial budget). *Ch'ung-ch'ing jih-pao*, 27 December.

1957. "Szu-ch'uan sheng Ch'ung-ch'ing shih 1956-nien ts'ai-cheng chüeh-suan ho 1957-hien ts'ai-cheng yü-suan ti pao-kao" (Report on Szechuan Province Chungking Municipality's 1956 financial final account and 1957 financial budget). *Ch'ung-ch'ing jih-pao*, 9 August.

Ch'en Hsüeh. 1956. "Chin-i-pu chia-ch'iang ti-fang ts'ai-cheng kuan-li kung-tso ti chih-ch'üan" (Further strengthening the authority of local financial management). *TC*, no. 1: 11–13.

Ch'en Shu-t'ung. 1957. "Kuan-yü Chiang-su sheng 1956-nien chüeh-suan ho 1957-nien yü-suan ti pao-kao (chai-yao)" [Report on Kiangsu Province's 1956 final account and 1957 budget (summary)]. *Hsin-hua jih-pao*, 17 May.

1958. "Chiang-su sheng i-chiu wu-ch'i nien chüeh-suan ho i-chiu-wu-pa nien yü-suan ts'ao-an ti pao-kao (chai-yao)" [Report on Kiangsu Province's 1957 final account and 1958 draft budget (summary)]. *Hsin-hua jih-pao*, 16 October.

1959. "Chiang-su sheng i-chiu-wu-pa nien chüeh-suan ho i-chiu-wu-chiu nien yü-suan ts'ao-an ti pao-kao" (Report on Kiangsu Province's 1958 final account and 1959 draft budget). *Hsin-hua jih-pao*, 31 December.

Ch'en Ta-lun. 1958. "Wo-kuo kung-yeh kuan-li t'i-chih ti kai-ko" (The reform of our country's industrial management system), *CCYC*, no. 3: 29–38.

Ch'en Wei-kan. 1957. "Liao-ning sheng Shen-yang shih jen-min wei-yüan-hui kuan-yü i-chiu-wu-liu nien ti-fang chüeh-suan ho i-chiu-wu-ch'i nien ti-fang yü-suan ti pao-kao" (Report of Liaoning Province Shenyang Municipality People's Council concerning the 1956 local final account and the 1957 local budget). *Shen-yang jih-pao*, 21 July.

Ch'eng Chang. 1957. "Mu-chien ti-fang ts'ai-cheng kuan-li chung ts'un-tsai ti chi-ko wen-t'i" (Several currently existing problems in local financial management). *TC*, no. 7: 16–18.

Cheng Chien-jen and Li Chih-chih. 1957. "Chieh-shao 1958-nien kuo-chia yü-suan shou-chih k'o-mu" (Introducing the 1958 state budget revenue and expenditure categories). *TC*, no. 12: 14–15.

Ch'eng Fang. 1958. "Balance in the financial economic system and planning." *HCS*, no. 8: 33–6. Trans. in *ECMM* 146: 40–7.

Ch'eng Hung-i. 1959. "Kuan-yü Pei-ching shih 1958-nien ts'ai-cheng shou-chih chüeh-suan ho 1959-nien ts'ai-cheng shou-chih yü-suan ti pao-kao (chai-yao)" [Report on Peking Municipality's 1958 income and expenditure final account and 1959 income and expenditure budget (summary)]. *Pei-ching jih-pao*, 11 September.

Chi Chin-chang. 1955. "Pi-hsü chien-ch'üan hsien i-chi ts'ai-cheng" (We must have sound *hsien* finance). *NFJP*, 11 October.

1956 "Kuan-yü 1955-nien Kuang-tung sheng chüeh-suan ho 1956-nien Kuang-tung sheng yü-suan ti pao-kao" (Report on Kwangtung Province's 1955 final account and Kwangtung Province's 1956 budget). *Nan-fang jih-pao*, 5 August.

1957. "Kuan-yü 1956-nien Kuang-tung sheng chüeh-suan ho 1957-nien Kuang-tung sheng yü-suan ts'ao-an ti pao-kao" (Report on Kwangtung Province's 1956 final account and Kwangtung Province's 1957 draft budget). *Nan-fang jih-pao*, 27 July.

Ch'i Wen-chien. 1957. "Kuan-yü Ho-nan sheng 1956-nien ts'ai-cheng chüeh-suan ho 1957-nien ts'ai-cheng yü-suan ts'ao-an ti pao-kao" (Report on Honan Province's 1956 financial final account and 1957 draft financial budget). *Ho-nan jih-pao*, 25 August.

1959. "Kuan-yü Ho-nan sheng 1957-nien ts'ai-cheng chüeh-suan, 1958-nien ts'ai-cheng yü-suan chih-hsing ch'ing-k'uang ho 1959-nien ts'ai-cheng yü-suan ts'ao-an ti pao-kao" (Report on Honan province's 1957 financial final account, the conditions of implementation of the 1958 budget, and the 1959 draft financial budget). *Ho-nan jih-pao*, 1 January.

218   *References*

Chiao Lin-i. 1958. "Kuan-yü Kuang-chou shih 1957-nien chüeh-suan ho 1958-nien yü-suan ts'ao-an ti pao-kao" (Report on Canton Municipality's 1957 final account and 1958 draft budget). *Kuang-chou jih-pao,* 11 March.

Chin Ming. 1959. "Tsai she-hui chu-i ko-ming ho she-hui chu-i chien-she chung ti chung-kuo ts'ai-cheng" (China's finance in the socialist revolution and the socialist construction). In Ministry of Finance, *Chung-hua jen-min kung-ho-kuo shih-nien ts'ai-cheng ti wei-ta ch'eng-chiu* (Ten great years of financial accomplishments of the People's Republic of China), pp. 20–44. Peking: Finance Publishing House.

Chinese Communist Party. 1956. "Proposals of the Eighth National Congress of the Communist Party of China for the Second Five-Year Plan for Development of the National Economy (1958–1962)." In *Eighth National Congress of the Communist Party of China,* vol. I (documents), pp. 229–60. Peking: Foreign Languages Press.

1958. "Chung-kung chung-yang ti-san tzu ch'üan-t'i hui-i (k'uo-ta)" [Third Plenum of the Chinese Communist Party Central Committee (enlarged)]. *JMST,* p. 182. Peking: Ta-kung Publishers.

Chou Cheng-hsin. 1960. "Kuan-yü Ho-pei sheng 1958-nien, 1959-nien ts'ai-cheng chüeh-suan ho 1960-nien ts'ai-cheng yü-suan ts'ao-an ti pao-kao (chai-yao)" [Report on Hopei Province's 1958 and 1959 financial final account and 1960 draft financial budget (summary)]. *Ho-pei jih-pao,* 22 February.

Chou Ching. 1972. "Light industry develops apace." *PR,* no. 41: 11–13.

Chou Chung-fu. 1955. "Kuan-yü hsien chi-hua wei-yüan-hui ti jen-wu tsu-chih ho tso-yung" (The responsibility, organization, and work of *hsien* planning commissions). *CHCC,* no. 10: 19–21.

Chou En-lai. 1956a. "On government work at concluding session of National People's Congress." NCNA. 30 June. In *CB* 398: 9–10.

1956b. "Report on the proposals for the Second Five-Year Plan for Development of the national economy." In Chinese Communist Party, *Eighth National Congress of the Communist Party of China,* vol. 1 (documents), pp. 261–328. Peking: Foreign Languages Press.

Chu Jung-chi. 1956. "The full utilization of coastal industry." *CHCC,* No. 6. Trans. in *ECMM* 50: 20–3.

Chu Kuang. 1957. "Kuan-yü Kuang-chou shih 1956-nien chüeh-suan ho 1957-nien yü-suan ti pao-kao" (Report on Canton's 1956 final account and 1957 budget). *Kuang-chou jih-pao,* 26 April.

Cleaver, Thomas W. 1971. "Regional Income Differentials in Japanese Economic Growth." Unpublished Ph.D. dissertation, Harvard University.

Cline, William R. 1975. "Distribution and Development: A Survey of the Literature." *Journal of Development Economics,* vol. 1, no. 4: 359–400.

Davies, Robert W. 1958. *The Development of the Soviet Budgetary System.* Cambridge: Cambridge University Press.

Donnithorne, Audrey. 1966. "Central Economic Control in China." In *Contemporary China,* ed. by Ruth Adams, pp. 151–78. New York: Vintage Books.

1967. *China's Economic System.* New York: Praeger.

1972a. *The Budget and the Plan in China: Central-Local Economic Relations.* Canberra: Australian National University Press.

1972b. "China's Cellular Economy: Some Economic Trends Since the Cultural Revolution." *China Quarterly,* no. 52: 605–19.

1974a. "China's Anti-Inflationary Policy." *Three Banks Review*, no. 103: 3–25.

1974b. "Recent Economic Developments." *China Quarterly*, no. 60: 772–4.

1976. "Comment." *China Quarterly*, no. 66: 328–40.

Dubey, Vinod. 1975. *Yugoslavia: Development with Decentralization*. Baltimore: Johns Hopkins University Press.

Durand, François J. 1965. *Le financement du budget en Chine Populaire*. Paris: Editions Sirey.

Eapen, Thomas A. 1967. "Federal-State Fiscal Arrangements in India." In U.S. Congress, Joint Economic Committee, *Revenue Sharing and Its Alternatives: What Future for Fiscal Federalism?*, vol. I (*Lessons of Experience*), pp. 450–75. Washington, D.C.: U.S. Government Printing Office.

Echols, John M. 1975. "Politics, Budgets, and Regional Equality in Communist and Capitalist Systems." *Comparative Political Studies*, vol. 8, no. 3: 259–92.

Ecklund, George N. 1966. *Financing the Chinese Government Budget: Mainland China 1950–1959*. Chicago: Aldine.

Eckstein, Alexander. 1975. *China's Economic Development: The Interplay of Scarcity and Ideology*. Ann Arbor: University of Michigan Press.

1977. *China's Economic Revolution*. Cambridge: Cambridge University Press.

Eckstein, Alexander, Kang Chao, and John Chang. 1974. "The Economic Development of Manchuria: The Rise of a Frontier Economy." *Journal of Economic History*, vol. 34, no. 1: 239–64.

Editorial. 1951a. "Chin-i-pu cheng-li ch'eng-shih ti-fang ts'ai-cheng" (Further arrange municipal and local finance). *JMJP*, 6 April.

1951b. "Lun chung-yang yü ti-fang ts'ai-ching kung-tso chih-ch'üan ti hua-fen" (On the division of authority in economic and financial work between the center and localities). *JMJP*, 26 May.

1956. "Exploit the potentiality of coastal industry." *JMJP*, 8 July. Trans. in *SCMP* 1335: 5–8.

1957. "Kai-chin kung-yeh shang-yeh ho ts'ai-cheng ti kuan-li t'i-chih" (Reform the industrial, commercial, and financial management systems). *JMJP*, 18 November.

1958a. "An important measure to develop the production forces." *JMJP*, 25 June. *Trans.* in *SCMP* 1803: 3–6.

1958b. "Kuan-ch'e chih-hsing nung-yeh shui t'iao-li, nu-li wan-ch'eng nung-yeh shui chih-tu" (Thoroughly carry out the agricultural tax regulations, strive to complete the agricultural tax reform). *TC*, no. 7: 10–11.

1958c. "Why do we want to issue local economic construction bonds?" *JMJP*, 6 June. *Trans.* in *SCMP* 1791: 2–3.

Emerson, John Philip. 1965. *Nonagricultural Employment in Mainland China: 1949–1958*. International Population Statistics Reports, series P-90, no. 21. Washington, D.C.: U.S. Government Printing Office.

Etienne, Gilbert. 1974. *La voie chinoise: La longue marche de l'économie, 1949–1974*. Paris: Presses Universitaires de France.

Fang Ping-chu. 1963. "Tao-lun ti-ch'ü kuo-min shou-ju t'ung-chi ti tso-yung ho ti-ch'ü tsung-ho p'ing-heng ti i-hsieh wen-t'i" (A discussion of the use of regional national income statistics and of several problems in comprehensive regional balances). *CCYC*, no. 4: 1–15.

220   *References*

Fang Wei-t'ing and Wen Tzu-fang. 1958. "T'an-t'an shih-hsing hsin ts'ai-cheng t'i-chih hou ti-fang yü-suan tzu-chin yün-yung wen-t'i" (A discussion of the problems of utilizing local budgetary funds after the implementation of the new financial system). *TC*, no. 1: 5–6.

Feng Ch'i-hsi. 1957a. "1958-nien ti chung-yang chi tan-wei yü-suan piao-ko ti chieh-shao" (The introduction of the 1958 central level units budget tables). *TC*, no. 11: 19–20.

    1957b. "The growth of the national economy as viewed from the state budget." *TCKT*, no. 12: 28–33. Trans. in *ECMM* 96: 27–37.

Feng Ching-ch'uan. 1957. "Szu-ch'uan sheng Ch'eng-tu shih 1956-nien ts'ai-cheng chüeh-suan ho 1957-nien ts'ai-cheng yü-suan ts'ao-an ti pao-kao" (Report on Szechuan Province Ch'engtu Municipality's 1956 financial final account and 1957 financial draft budget). *Ch'eng-tu jih-pao*, 11 September.

    1958 "Szu-ch'uan sheng Ch'eng-tu shih 1957-nien ts'ai-cheng chüeh-suan ho 1958-nien ts'ai-cheng yü-suan ts'ao-an ti pao-kao (chai-yao)" [Report on Szechuan Province Ch'engtu Municipality's 1957 financial final account and 1958 draft financial budget (summary)]. *Ch'eng-tu jih-pao*, 20 May.

Feng Li-t'ien. 1956. "Ts'ai-cheng chi-hua." (Financial planning). *CHCC*, no. 8: 31–3.

Field, Robert Michael. 1976. "Real Capital Formation in the People's Republic of China: 1952–1973." Unpublished manuscript, July.

Field, Robert M., Nicholas R. Lardy, and John P. Emerson. 1976. *Provincial Industrial Output in the People's Republic of China, 1949–1975*. Foreign Economic Report, no. 12. Washington, D.C.: U.S. Department of Commerce.

Fishlow, Albert. 1972. "Brazilian Size Distribution of Income." *American Economic Review*, vol. 62, no. 2: 391–402.

Fukien Province Finance Department. 1955. "Fu-chien ts'ai-cheng t'ing-ch'ang pao-kao yü-suan" (Fukien Finance Department director reports on the budget). *Wen-hui pao* (Hong Kong), 16 February.

Government Administrative Council. 1950a. "Kuan-yü pien-tsao i-chiu-wu-i nien-tu ts'ai-cheng shou-chih yü-suan ti chih-piao" (Directive on compiling the 1951 financial revenue and expenditure budget). *TCTLHP* 2: 17–21.

    1950b. "Kuan-yü t'ung-i kuan-li i-chiu-wu-ling nien-tu ts'ai-cheng shou-chih ti chüeh-ting" (Decision on unified management of 1950 financial revenue and expenditures). *TCTLHP* 1: 35–40.

    1950c. "Notice concerning guaranteeing the unification of state financial and economic work." *CYTCFLHP* 1: 31–2. Trans. in *EPO* 1: 202–8.

    1950d. "Regulations on administration of national taxation." *CYTCFLHP*, August, pp. 181–4. Trans. in *EPO* 1: 223–7.

    1950e. "Regulations on the implementation of currency control." *CYTCFLHP* 2: 549–61. Trans. in *EPO* 1: 255–7.

    1950f. "Regulations on the national depository." *CYTCFLHP* 1: 243–4. Trans. in *EPO* 1: 240–2.

    1951a. "Kuan-yü chin-i pu cheng-li ch'eng-shih ti-fang ts'ai-cheng ti chüeh-ting" (Decision on improving the arrangement of municipal and local finance). *TCTLHP* 1: 136–8.

    1951b. "Kuan-yü hua-fen chung-yang yü ti-fang tsai ts'ai-cheng ching-chi kung-tso shang kuan-li chih-ch'üan ti chüeh-ting" (Decision on the division of management authority between the center and the localities in financial and economic work). *CYTCFLHP* 3: 81–3.

1951c. 'Kuan-yü i-chiu-wu-i nien-tu ts'ai-cheng shou-chih hsi-t'ung hua-fen ti chüeh-ting" (Decision concerning the division of revenue and expenditures in 1951). *TCTLHP* 1: 118–21.

1952. "Kuan-yü i-chiu-wu-san nien-tu ko-chi yü-suan ts'ao-an pien-chih pan-fa ti t'ung-chih" (Directive on the method of compiling the various levels' 1953 draft budgets). *TCTLHP* 2: 47–52.

1953. "Kuan-yü pien-tsao i-chiu-wu-szu nien yü-suan ts'ao-an ti chih-piao" (Directive on the compilation of the 1954 draft state budget). *TCTLHP* 2: 80–7.

Government Administrative Council, Financial and Economic Commission. 1950–2. *Chung-yang ts'ai-ching cheng-ts'e fa-ling hui-pien* (Collection of Laws and Regulations on Financial and Economic Policies of the Central Government) (CYTCFLHP). Vol. 1 (2 parts), 1950; vol. 2, 1951; vol. 3, 1952. Peking: New China Bookshop.

Government of the PRC (People's Republic of China). 1956a. *First Five-Year Plan for the Development of the National Economy of the People's Republic of China in 1953–1957.* Peking: Foreign Languages Press.

1956b. *Labor Laws and Regulations of the People's Republic of China.* Peking: Foreign Languages Press.

Green, Alan A. 1961. "Regional Inequality, Structural Change, and Economic Growth in Canada, 1890–1956." *Economic Development and Cultural Change,* vol. 17, no. 4: 567–83.

Hai Ch'ü-niao. 1957. "Chung-yang kung-yeh yao ho ti-fang kung-yeh hsiang chieh-ho" (Central industry must unite with local industry). *JMJP*, 16 November.

Harding, Henry, Jr. 1972. "China: The Fragmentation of Power." *Asian Survey,* vol. 12, no. 1: 1–15.

Harper, Paul. 1971. "Workers' Participation in Management in Communist China." *Studies in Comparative Communism,* vol. 4, nos. 3–4: 111–40.

Hayek, Friedrich A. von, ed. 1935. *Collectivist Economic Planning.* London: Routledge & Kegan Paul.

Heng K'ai. 1957. "Kuang-tung sheng 1956-nien ts'ai-cheng kung-tso ti chi-tien t'i-hui" (Several points of realization on Kwangtung Province's 1956 financial work). *TC*, no. 8: 8–9.

Hicks, John R. 1959. *Essays in World Economics.* Oxford: Clarendon Press.

Hirschman, Albert O. 1958. *The Strategy of Economic Development.* New Haven, Conn.: Yale University Press.

Ho Hsi-ming. 1954. "I-chiu-wu-szu nien Kuang-tung sheng yü-suan pao-kao" (Report on Kwangtung Province's 1954 budget). *Nan-fang jih-pao,* 17 August.

Hou Chi-ming. 1968. "Manpower, Employment, and Unemployment." In *Economic Trends in Communist China,* ed. by Alexander Eckstein, Walter Galenson, and Ta-chung Liu, pp. 329–96. Chicago: Aldine.

Howe, Christopher. 1971. *Employment and Economic Growth in Urban China 1949–1957.* Cambridge: Cambridge University Press.

Hsiao, Katherine Huang. 1971. *Money and Monetary Policy in Communist China.* New York: Columbia University Press.

Hsü Chien-sheng. 1957. "Kuan-yü Kuei-chou sheng 1956-nien ts'ai-cheng chüeh-suan ho 1957-nien ts'ai-cheng yü-suan ts'ao-an ti pao-kao" (Report on Kweichow Province's 1956 final financial account and 1957 draft financial budget). *Kuei-chou jih-pao,* 15 August.

1958. "Kuan-yü Kuei-chou sheng 1957-nien ts'ai-cheng chüeh-suan ho

1958-nien ts'ai-cheng yü-suan ts'ao-an ti pao-kao" (Report on Kweichow Province's 1957 financial final account and 1958 draft financial budget). *Kuei-chou jih-pao,* 25 September.

1960. "Kuan-yü Kuei-chou sheng 1959-nien ts'ai-cheng chüeh-suan ho 1960-nien ts'ai-cheng yü-suan ts'ao-an ti pao-kao" (Report on Kweichow Province's 1959 financial final accounts and 1959 draft financial budget). *Kuei-chou jih-pao,* 13 December.

Hsü Fei-ch'ing. 1957. "Wo tui kai-chin ts'ai-cheng kuan-li t'i-chih ti chi-tien jen-shih" (Several points of opinion with regard to the reform of the financial management system). *TC,* no. 12: 3–5.

1959. "T'ung-i ling-tao fen-chi kuan-li shih kuo-chia yü-suan kuan-li kung-tso ti cheng-chüeh fang-chen" (Unified leadership and multi-level administration is the correct policy for state budgetary management). *TC,* no. 19: 11–15.

Hsü Kuang-yüan. 1957. "Chiang-hsi sheng 1956-nien chüeh-suan ho 1957-nien yü-suan ti pao-kao" (Report on Kiangsi Province's 1956 final account and 1957 budget). *Chiang-hsi jih-pao,* 1 April.

1958. "Kuan-yü Chiang-hsi sheng 1957-nien chüeh-suan ho 1958-nien yü-suan ti pao-kao" (Report on Kiangsi Province's 1957 final account and 1958 budget). *Chiang-hsi jih-pao,* 5 July.

1959. "Kuan-yü Chiang-hsi sheng 1958-nien ts'ai-cheng chüeh-suan ho 1959-nien ts'ai-cheng yü-suan ts'ao-an ti pao-kao" (Report on Kiangsi Province's 1958 final financial account and 1959 draft financial budget). *Chiang-hsi jih-pao,* 2 July.

Hsüeh Mu-ch'iao. 1957. "Tui hsien-hsing chi-hua kuan-li chih-tu ti ch'u-pu i-chien" (Preliminary opinions on the current system of plan management). *CHCC,* no. 9: 20–4.

Hu K'ai-ming. 1957. "Kuan-yü Ho-pei sheng i-chiu-wu-liu nien ts'ai-cheng chüeh-suan ho i-chiu-wu-ch'i nien ts'ai-cheng yü-suan ti pao-kao" (Report on Hopei Province's 1956 financial final account and 1957 financial budget). *Ho-pei jih-pao,* 24 August.

1958 "Kuan-yü Ho-pei sheng i-chiu wu-ch'i nien ts'ai-cheng chüeh-suan ho i-chiu wu-pa nien ts'ai-cheng yü-suan ti pao-kao" (Report on Hopei Province's 1957 financial final account and 1958 budget). *Ho-pei jih-pao,* 17 April.

Hu Tzu-ming. 1957. "Kuan-yü ti-fang yü-suan chung chi-ko wen-t'i ti shang-ch'üeh" (Consultation on several local budget problems). *TC,* no. 8: 10.

Huan Wen. 1958. "Shih-hsing hsin ts'ai-cheng t'i-chih hou ti-fang yü-suan kuan-li-shang ti chi-ko wen-t'i" (Several problems in local budgetary management after putting the new financial system into effect). *TC,* no. 1: 7–8.

Huang Ta. 1957. "Kuan-yü Liao-ning sheng i-chiu-wu-liu nien ts'ai-cheng chüeh-suan ho i-chiu-wu-ch'i nien ts'ai-cheng yü-suan ti pao-kao" (Report on Liaoning Province's 1956 financial final account and 1957 financial budget). *Liao-ning jih-pao,* 15 May.

Hupei Economic Studies Association National Economic Planning Group. 1962. "T'ao-lun ti-ch'ü tsung-ho p'ing-heng wen-t'i" (A discussion of the problems of local comprehensive balancing). *TKP,* 29 August.

Hurwicz, Leonid. 1960. "Conditions for Economic Efficiency of Centralized and Decentralized Structures." In *Value and Plan,* ed. by Gregory Grossman, pp. 162–83. Berkeley: University of California Press.

1971. "Centralization and Decentralization in Economic Processes." In *Comparison of Economic Systems: Theoretical and Methodological Ap-*

proaches, ed. by Alexander Eckstein, pp. 79–102. Berkeley: University of California Press.

1973. "The Design of Mechanisms for Resource Allocation." *American Economic Review,* vol. 63, no. 2: 1–30.

Inner Mongolia Statistical Bureau. 1960. *Hui-huang ti shih-erh-nien: Nei-meng-ku tzu-chih ch'ü ching-chi ho wen-hua chien-she ch'eng-chiu ti t'ung-chi* (The glorious twelve years: Statistics on achievements in economic and cultural construction in the Inner Mongolia Autonomous Region). Huhohaot'e: Inner Mongolia People's Publishing House.

Institute of the Study of Chinese Communist Problems. 1967. *I-chiu-liu-ch'i nien fei-ching nien-pao* (1967 Yearbook on Chinese Communism). Taipei: Institute for the Study of Chinese Communist Problems.

Ishikawa, Shigeru. 1965. *National Income and Capital Formation: An Examination of Official Statistics.* Tokyo: Institute of Asian Economic Affairs.

Jen I-li. 1958. "Che-chiang sheng 1956-nien ts'ai-cheng chüeh-suan ti shu-mien pao-kao" (A written report on the 1956 final financial account of Chekiang province). *Che-chiang jih-pao,* 23 January.

Jung Tzu-ho. 1957. "The question of equilibrium for the state budget, for state credit, and the supply and demand of commodities." *TC,* no. 6. Trans. in *ECMM* 90: 11–16.

1958. "Several problems on the reform of the financial management system." *TC,* no. 1: 1–4. Trans. in *ECMM* 126: 48–57.

1959. "Ten years of our country's finance." *TC,* no. 18: 14–22. Trans. in *ECMM* 202: 18–28.

Kansu Finance Department. 1959. "Kan-su ts'ai-cheng ti wei-ta shih-nien" (Ten great years of finance in Kansu). *TCTLHP,* pp. 199–218.

Kao Yün-fan. 1956. "Ha-erh-pin shih 1955-nien ts'ai-cheng shou-chih chüeh-suan ho 1956-nien ts'ai-cheng shou-chih yü-suan pao-kao" (Report on Harbin Municipality's 1955 financial revenue and expenditure final account and 1956 financial revenue and expenditure budget). *Ha-erh-pin jih-pao,* 19 December.

1958. "Kuan-yü Ha-erh-pin shih 1956-nien ts'ai-cheng shou-chih chüeh-suan ho 1957-nien ts'ai-cheng shou-chih yü-suan ts'ao-an ti pao-kao" (Report on Harbin Municipality's 1956 financial revenue and expenditure final account and 1957 financial revenue and expenditure draft budget). *Ha-erh-pin jih-pao,* 3 August.

Ko Chih-ta. 1956a. "Jen-chih kuan-ch'e shih-hsing 't'ung-i ling-tao, fen-chi kuan li' ti ts'ai-cheng fang-chen" (Take seriously the thorough implementation of the financial policy of "unified leadership and multilevel administration"). *TKP,* 12 July.

1956b. "Wo kuo kuo-chia yü-suan ti pen-chih ho t'a tsai kuo-tu shih-ch'i ti tso-yung" (The nature of the state budget in our country and its function in the transition period). *CCYC,* no. 3: 67–80.

1957a. "Kai-chin ts'ai-cheng kuan-li chih-tu ti hao-ch'u" (The advantages of the reform of the financial management system). *TKP,* 28 November.

1957b. *Kuo-tu shih-ch'i ti chung-kuo yü-suan* (China's Budget in the Transition Period). Peking: Finance Publishing House.

Ko Ling. 1959. "Tu Li Hsien-nien fu tsung-li kuan-yü 1958-nien kuo-chia chüeh-suan ho 1959-nien kuo-chia yü-suan ts'ao-an ti pao-kao" (Study Vice-Premier Li Hsien-nien's report on the state's 1958 final accounts and the 1959 draft state budget). *TC,* no. 9: 19–20.

224   *References*

Koopmans, Tjalling C. and John Michael Montias. 1971. "On the Description and Comparison of Economic Systems." In *Comparisons of Economic Systems: Theoretical and Methodological Approaches,* ed. by Alexander Eckstein, pp. 27–78. Berkeley: University of California Press.

Kuo Ch'eng. 1958. "Kuan-yü Kuang-hsi sheng 1957-nien ts'ai-cheng yü-suan chih-hsing ch'ing-k'uang ho Kuang-hsi-chuang tzu-chih ch'ü 1958-nien ts'ai-cheng yü-suan ts'ao-an ti pao-kao" (Report on the conditions of implementation of Kwangsi Province's 1957 budget and Kwangsi Chuang Autonomous Region's 1958 draft financial budget). *Kuang-hsi jih-pao,* 15 March.

Kuo Tzu-ch'eng. 1955. "Yün-shu chi-hua" (Transport Planning). *CHCC* no. 8: 30–3.

Lang, Nicholas R. 1975. "The Dialectics of Decentralization: Economic Reform and Regional Inequality in Yugoslavia." *World Politics,* vol. 25, no. 3: 309–35.

Lange, Oscar. 1938. "On the Economic Theory of Socialism." In *On the Economic Theory of Socialism,* ed. by Benjamin E. Lippincott, pp. 55–143. Minneapolis: University of Minnesota Press.

Lardy, Nicholas R. 1975a. "Central Control and Redistribution in China: Central-Provincial Fiscal Relations Since 1949." Ph.D. dissertation, University of Michigan.

  1975b. "Centralization and Decentralization in China's Fiscal Management." *China Quarterly,* no. 61: 25–60.

  1975c. "Economic Planning in China: Central-Provincial Fiscal Relations." In *China: A Reassessment of the Economy,* a compendium of papers submitted to the U.S. Congress Joint Economic Committee, pp. 94–115. Washington, D.C.: U.S. Government Printing Office.

  1976a. "Centralization and Decentralization in China's Fiscal Management, Reply." *China Quarterly,* no. 66: 340–54.

  1976b. Economic Planning and Income Distribution in China." *Current Scene,* vol. 14, no. 11: 1–12.

  1977. "Regional Growth and Income Distribution: The Chinese Experience." Unpublished manuscript.

Li Cha. 1969. *Chung-kung shui-wu chih-tu* (The Chinese Communist Tax System). Hong Kong: Union Research Institute.

Li Ch'eng-jui. 1957. "Hsin ti ts'ai-cheng t'i-chih yu na-hsieh hao-ch'u" (The new financial system has many advantages). *TC,* no. 12: 6–9.

  1959. *Chung-hua jen-min kung-ho-kuo nung-yeh shui shih-kao* (A draft history of the agricultural tax of the People's Republic of China). Peking: Finance Publishing House.

  1964. "Shih-lun ti-ch'ü ching-chi ti tsung-ho p'ing-heng" (An examination of local economic comprehensive balancing). *KMJP,* 16 November, p. 4.

Li Chin. 1958. "T'an-t'an fa-hsing ti-fang ching-chi chien-she kung-chai wen-t'i" (A discussion of the problems in issuing local economic construction bonds). *TC,* no. 7: 19–20.

Li Choh-ming. 1964. "China's Industrial Development, 1958–1963." In *Industrial Development in Communist China.* New York: Praeger.

Li Fa-nan. 1955. "Kuan-yü Kuang-hsi sheng i-chiu-wu-szu nien ti-fang chüeh-suan ho i-chiu-wu-wu nien ti-fang yü-suan pao-kao (chai-yao)" [Report on Kwangsi Province's 1954 local final account and 1955 local budget (summary)]. *Kuang-hsi jih-pao,* 6 October.

Li Fu-ch'un. 1955. "Report on the First Five-Year Plan for Development of the National Economy." *People's China,* 16 August.

Li Hsien-nien. 1955. "Report on the state's 1954 final accounts and the state's 1955 budget." *HHYP*, no. 8: 23–32. Trans. in *CB* 336: 1–25.
1956. "Report on the state's 1955 final account and the state's 1956 budget." *HHPYK*, no. 14: 1–9. Trans. in *CB* 392: 1–18.
1957. "Report on the state's 1956 final account and the 1957 draft state budget." *HHPYK*, no. 14: 16–28. Trans. in *CB* 464: 1–31.
1958. "Report on conditions of implementation of the 1957 state budget and the 1958 draft state budget." *HHPYK*, no. 5: 3–12. Trans. in *CB* 493: 1–22.
1959. "Report on the state's 1958 final account and the 1959 draft state budget." *HHPYK*, no. 9: 20–3. Trans. in *PR*, no. 17: 25–30.
1960. "Report on the state's 1959 final account and the state's 1960 draft budget." In *Second Session of the Second National People's Congress of the People's Republic of China (Documents)*, pp. 49–73. Peking: Foreign Languages Press.
Li Min-li. 1958. "Kai-chin ts'ai-cheng kuan-li t'i-chih ti ch'ung-ta i-i" (The main significance of the reformed system of financial management). *TCYC*, no. 1: 42–5.
Li Shu-te. 1957. "The Peasants' Burden in 1956: Conditions and Problems." *TC*, no. 8: 3–5. Trans. in *ECMM* 100: 16–22.
Li T'ao. 1955. "Liaoning Province's 1954 final account and 1955 budget." *Liao-ning jih-pao*, 21 October. Trans. in *Weekly Information Report on Communist China*, 29 February 1956, pp. 7–16.
Li Tung-ch'ao. 1956. "Kuan-yü Liao-ning sheng Lü-ta shih 1955 nien-tu ts'ai-cheng chüeh-suan ho 1956 nien-tu ts'ai-cheng yü-suan ti pao-kao" (Report on Liaoning Province Lüta Municipality's 1955 final account and 1956 budget). *Lü-ta jih-pao*, 7 August.
Li Wen-hao. 1958. "Kuan-yü Che-chiang sheng 1957-nien ts'ai-cheng chüeh-suan ho 1958-nien ts'ai-cheng yü-suan ts'ao-an ti pao-kao" (Report on Chekiang Province's 1957 financial final account and 1958 draft financial budget). *Che-chiang jih-pao*, 9 November.
Li Yü-ang. 1959. "Kuan-yü Shan-tung sheng 1958-nien ts'ai-cheng chüeh-suan ho 1959-nien ts'ai-cheng yü-suan (ts'ao-an) ti pao-kao (chai-yao)" [Report on Shantung Province's 1958 financial final account and 1959 (draft) financial budget (summary)]. *Ta-chung jih-pao*, 24 May.
Li Yu-san. 1956. "Kuan-yü Ho-nan sheng 1955-nien ts'ai-cheng chüeh-suan, 1956-nien ts'ai-cheng yü-suan ho chih-hsing ch'ing-k'uang i-chi 1957-nien ts'ai-cheng yü-suan ti ch'u-pu i-chien ti pao-kao" (Report on Honan Province's 1955 final financial account, 1956 financial budget and conditions of its implementation and preliminary opinions on the 1957 financial budget). *Ho-nan jih-pao*, 29 November.
Liang Ta-shan. 1955. "Chiang-hsi sheng i-chiu-wu-szu nien chüeh-suan ho i-chiu-wu-wu nien yü-suan ti pao-kao" (Report on Kiangsi Province's 1954 final account and 1955 budget). *Chiang-hsi jih-pao*, 28 August.
1956. "Chiang-hsi sheng 1955-nien chüeh-suan ho 1956-nien yü-suan ti pao-kao" (Report on Kiangsi Province's 1955 final account and 1956 budget). *Chiang-hsi jih-pao*, 2 November.
Liao Chi-li. 1958a. "Kuan-yü chi-hua kuan-li chih-tu kai-chin wen-t'i" (Problems in the reform of the plan management system). *TKP*, 26 January.
1958b. "T'an-t'an shuang-kuei chih" (A discussion of the double track system). *CHCC*, no. 8: 19 ff.
Liao Yüan. 1956. "Kuan-yü Kuang-hsi sheng 1955-nien ti-fang chüeh-suan ho 1956-nien ti-fang yü-suan ti pao-kao" (Report concerning Kwangsi Prov-

ince's 1955 local final account and local 1956 budget). *Kuang-hsi jih-pao,* 23 August.

Liaoning Provincial People's Council. 1958. "Kuan-yü Liao-ning sheng 1957-nien ts'ai-cheng chüeh-suan ho 1958-nien ts'ai-cheng yü-suan ti pao-kao" (Report on Liaoning Province's 1957 financial final account and 1958 financial budget). *Liao-ning jih-pao,* 3 December.

Lin Yün. 1958. "Lun wo-kuo 1958-nien ts'ai-cheng kuan-li t'i-chih ti kai-chin" (On the reform of our country's financial management system in 1958). *CCYC,* no. 10: 35–47 and no. 11: 41–53.

Little, Ian, Tibor Scitovsky, and Maurice Scott. 1970. *Industry and Trade in Some Developing Countries: A Comparative Study.* London: Oxford University Press.

Liu Chih-ch'eng. 1958. "Kuan-yü Shang-hai kung-yeh ti ch'ing-k'uang ho jo-ch'ien wen-t'i" (On the situation in Shanghai's industry and several problems). *TCYC,* no. 1: 60–4.

Liu Cho-fu. 1959. "Yün-nan sheng 1958-nien ts'ai-cheng chüeh-suan ho 1959-nien ts'ai-cheng yü-suan ti pao-kao" (Report on Yünnan Province's 1958 financial final account and 1959 financial budget). *Yün-nan jih-pao,* 18 July.

Liu Hsi-shu. 1951. "Yü-suan chüeh-suan chan-hsing t'iao-li shu-p'ing" (A discussion and evaluation of the temporary budget and final account regulations). *Hsin k'uai-chi,* no. 9: 6–15.

____ 1952. "Chieh-shao i-chiu-wu-erh nien ko chi ts'ai-cheng sui-ju sui-chih t'ung-i yü-suan k'o-mu" (Introduction to each level's 1952 financial income and expenditure budgetary categories). *Hsin k'uai-chi,* no. 1: 14–20 and no. 2: 28–37.

Liu Keng. 1957. "Kuan-yü Hsi-an shih 1956-nien ts'ai-cheng shou-chih chüeh-suan ho 1957-nien ts'ai-cheng shou-chih yü-suan chien-i shu-tzu ti pao-kao" (Report on Hsian Municipality's 1956 financial revenue and expenditure final account and suggested numbers for the 1957 financial revenue and expenditure budget). *Hsi-an-jih-pao,* 25 June.

Liu Shao-ch'i. 1956. "Political report of the Central Committee of the Communist Party." In Chinese Communist Party, *Eighth National Party Congress of the Chinese Communist Party,* vol. I (documents), pp. 13–111. Peking: Foreign Languages Press.

Liu Ta-chung and Yeh Kung-chia. 1965. *The Economy of the Chinese Mainland: National Income and Economic Development 1933–1959.* Princeton, N.J.: Princeton University Press.

Liu Tsai-hsing. 1956. "The rational distribution of industry during socialist construction." *HCS,* no. 11: 14–20. Trans. in *ECMM* 64: 11–20.

Liu Tsai-hsing and Chang Hsüeh-ch'in. 1959. "The great change in China's industrial map for the past decade." *TLCS,* no. 11. Trans. in *ECMM* 202: 10–17.

Liu Tzu-mo. 1956. "Kuan-yü Hsin-chiang wei-wu-erh tzu-chih ch'ü i-chiu-wu-wu nien ts'ai-cheng chüeh-suan ho i-chiu-wu-liu nien ts'ai-cheng yü-suan ti pao-kao" (Report on the Sinkiang-Uighur Autonomous Region's 1955 financial final account and 1956 financial budget). *Hsin-chiang jih-pao,* 3 August.

____ 1957. "Kuan-yü Hsin-chiang wei-wu-erh tzu-chih ch'ü 1956-nien ts'ai-cheng chüeh-suan ho 1957-nien ts'ai-cheng yü-suan ti pao-kao" (Report on the Sinkiang-Uighur Autonomous Region's 1956 financial final account and 1957 financial budget). *Hsin-chiang jih-pao,* 18 April.

1959. "Kuan-yü Hsin-chiang wei-wu-erh tzu-chih ch'ü 1957-nien ts'ai-cheng chüeh-suan, 1958-nien ts'ai-cheng yü-suan chih-hsing ch'ing-k'uang ho 1959-nien ts'ai-cheng yü-suan ti pao-kao" (Report on Sinkiang-Uighur Autonomous Region's 1957 financial final account, the conditions of implementation of the 1958 budget and the 1959 financial budget). *Hsin-chiang jih-pao*, 1 February.

1960. "Kuan-yü Hsin-chiang wei-wu-erh tzu-chih ch'ü 1959-nien ts'ai-cheng chüeh-suan ho 1960-nien ts'ai-cheng yü-suan ts'ao-an ti pao-kao" (Report on Sinkiang-Uighur Autonomous Region's 1959 financial final account and 1960 draft financial budget). *Hsin-chiang jih-pao*, 30 May.

Lo Keng-mo. 1959. "Kuan-yü tsung she-hui chu-i hsing kung-chang chu-i kuo-tu ti wen-t'i" (The problem of transition from socialism to communism). *HCS*, no. 8: 17.

Lü Chün-chieh. 1957. "An-p'ai ti-fang kung-yeh ti-erh ko wu-nien chi-hua ti chi-tien t'i-hui" (Several suggestions for the arrangement of local industry during the Second Five-Year Plan). *CHCC*, no. 6: 16–17.

Ma I-hsing. 1958. "Kuan-yü Shang-hai shih i-chiu-wu-ch'i nien chüeh-suan ho i-chiu-wu-pa nien yü-suan ts'ao-an ti pao kao" (Report on Shanghai Municipality's 1957 final account and 1958 draft budget). *Chieh-fang jih-pao*, 7 November.

1959. "Kuan-yü Shang-hai shih 1958-nien chüeh-suan ho 1959-nien yü-suan ts'ao-an ti pao-kao" (Report on Shanghai Municipality's 1958 final account and 1959 draft budget). *Chieh-fang jih-pao*, 14 June.

1960. "Kuan-yü Shang-hai i-chiu-wu-chiu nien chüeh-suan ho i-chiu-liu-ling nien yü-suan ts'ao-an ti pao-kao" (Report on Shanghai's 1959 final account and 1960 draft budget). *Chieh-fang jih-pao*, 18 May.

Ma Yin-ch'u. 1958. *Wo-ti ching-chi li-lun che-hsüeh szu-hsiang ho cheng-chih li-ch'ang* (My economic theory, philosophical thoughts, and political standpoint). Peking: Finance Publishing House.

MacFarquhar, Roderick. 1974. *The Origins of the Cultural Revolution: Contradictions Among the People 1956–1957*. New York: Columbia University Press.

Mao Tse-tung. 1969. "Reading notes on the Soviet Union's *Political Economy*." Written in 1961–2. In *Mao Tse-tung, Szu-hsiang wan-sui* (Long live Mao Tse-tung's thought), pp. 319–99.

1977. "On the ten major relationships." Speech of 25 April 1956. *Peking Review*, no. 1: 156–66.

Marschak, Thomas. 1959. "Centralization and Decentralization in Economic Organization." *Econometrica*, vol. 27, no. 3: 399–430.

Mellor, John. 1976. *The New Economics of Growth: A Strategy for India and the Developing World*. Ithaca, N.Y.: Cornell University Press.

Men Tso-min. 1957. "Hsi-ch'u 1956-nien wu-tzu kung-ying kung-tso chung ti chiao-hsün" (Learn the lessons of commodity supply work of 1956). *CHCC*, no. 2: 8–11.

Milenkovitch, Deborah D. 1971. *Plan and Market in Yugoslav Economic Thought*. New Haven, Conn.: Yale University Press.

Ministry of Finance. 1950a. "Ch'üan kuo ko-chi shui-wu chi-kuan chan-hsing tsu-chih kuei-ch'eng" (Provisional regulations on the organization of tax bureaus at various levels in the whole nation). *CYTCFLHP* 1: 217–22.

1950b. "I-chiu-wu-ling nien-tu ts'ai-cheng shou-chih yü-suan k'o-mu" (The financial revenue and expenditure categories for 1950). *HHTSFKHP*, vol. 1; part 1; 48–54.

1950c. "Chung-hua jen-min kung-ho-kuo i-chiu-wu-i nien-tu chan-hsing ts'ai-cheng shou-chih yü-suan k'o-mu" (People's Republic of China temporary financial revenue and expenditure categories for 1951). *HHTSFKHP*, vol. 1, part 1: 94–113.

1951a. "Kuan-yü pien-tsao i-chiu-wu-erh nien-tu yü-suan ti chih-piao" (Directive on compiling the 1952 budget). *TCTLHP* 2: 32–7.

1951b. *Hsien-hsing ts'ai-cheng fa-kuei hui-pien* (A collection of current financial laws and regulations). Peking: Hsin-ch'ao shu-tien.

1952. Main Tax Bureau. *Chung-yang shui-wu fa-ling hui-chi* (Compendium of tax laws of the central government). Peking: Finance Publishing House.

1954. "I-chiu-wu-wu nien ko-chi ts'ai-cheng shou-chih yü-suan k'o-mu chi kuo-chia tsung yü-suan hui-pien k'o-mu" (Each level's financial income and expenditure budgetary categories and the state's total budget compilation categories for 1955). *CYTCFKHP*, 1955, pp. 45–81.

1955a. "Kuo-ying ch'i-yeh 1954-nien ch'ao chi-hua li-jun fen-ch'eng ho shih-yung pan-fa" (The method of dividing and utilizing state enterprise profits that are in excess of the 1954 plan). *FKHP* 2: 523–4.

1955b. "I-chiu-wu-liu nien ko-chi ts'ai-cheng shou-chih yü-suan k'o-mu" (Each level's financial income and expenditure 1956 budgetary categories). *CYTCFKHP*, 1956, pp. 42–69.

1955–9. *Chung-yang ts'ai-cheng fa-kuei hui-pien* (Collection of the financial laws and regulations of the central government) (CYTCFKHP). 1955 (1 vol.), 1956 (1 vol.), 1957 (2 vols.), 1958 (1 vol.), 1959 (1 vol.). Peking: Finance Publishing House.

1957a. "Kuan-yü pien-tsao i-chiu-wu-pa nien chung-yang yü-suan ts'ao-an ti pu-ch'ung kuei-ting" (Supplementary rules on compiling the central government's 1958 draft budget). *CYTCFKHP*, 1957, 2: 14–15.

1957b. "Kuan-yü 1958-nien-tu ti-fang ts'ai-cheng hua-fen shou-ju ti chi-hsiang kuei-ting ti t'ung-chih" (Notice concerning several regulations concerning the division of revenue in local finance). *CYTCFKHP*, 1957, 2: 17–20.

1958a. "Chan-ting 1959-nien ti-i chi-tu ti-fang yü-suan shang-chieh chung-yang yü-suan ti tsung-o shang-chieh pi-li ti t'ing-chih" (Notice on the total amount proportionate remission rates of the local budget to the central government budget for the first quarter of 1959). *CYTCFKHP*, 1958, 2: 61.

1958b. "Kuan-yü pien-tsao i-chiu-wu-chiu nien kuo-chia yü-suan ts'ao-an ti t'ung-chih" (Notification on the compilation of the 1959 draft state budget). *FKHP* 8: 145–9.

1959a. "Kuan-yü kuo-chia yü-suan shou-chih k'o-mu ti chi-tien shuo-ming" (Several explanations concerning state budgetary revenue and expenditure classifications). *CYTCFKHP*, 1958, 2: 63–5.

1959b. "Kuo-chia yü-suan shou-chih k'o-mu" (State budgetary revenue and expenditure classifications). *CYTCFKHP*, 1958, 2: 65–90.

1959c. *Chung-hua jen-min kung-ho-kuo shih-nien ts'ai-cheng ti wei-ta ch'eng-chiu* (Ten great years of financial accomplishments of the People's Republic of China). Peking: Finance Publishing House.

1959d. Research Institute of Public Finance. *Shih nien lai ts'ai-cheng tzu-liao hui-pien* (Collection of materials on finance during the last ten years) (TCTLHP). 2 vols. Peking: Finance Publishing House.

Ministry of Trade. 1950. "Provisional regulations on currency control." *CYTCFLHP* 1: 238–42. Trans. in *EPO* 1: 250–5.

Mises, Ludwig von. 1974. "Economic Calculation in Socialism." In *Compar-*

ative Economic Systems: Models and Cases, ed. by Morris Bornstein, pp. 120–6. Homewood, Ill.: Irwin.

Montias, John Michael. 1977. "The Aggregation of Controls and the Autonomy of Subordinates." *Journal of Economic Theory,* vol. 15, no. 1: 123–34.

Myrdal, Gunnar. 1957. *Economic Theory and Underdeveloped Regions.* London: Duckworth.

National People's Congress Standing Committee. 1958. "Regulations governing the issuance of regional economic construction bonds of the People's Republic of China." Trans. in *SCMP* 1791: 1–2.

New China News Agency. 1958. "Chung-yang ch'i-yeh 80% hsia-fang ti-fang kuan-li" (80% of central government enterprises are already transferred down to local management). *HHPYK,* no. 13: 63.

Ni, Ernest. 1960. *Distribution of the Urban and Rural Population of Mainland China: 1953 and 1958.* International Population Reports, series P-95, no. 56. Washington, D.C.: U.S. Bureau of the Census.

Niu Chung-huang. 1959. *Wo-kuo ti-i-ko wu-nien chi-hua shih-chi ti sheng-chan ho hsiao-fei ti kuan-hsi* (The relation between production and consumption during the First Five-Year Plan in China). Peking: Finance and Economics Publishing House.

Obolenskiy, N. 1961a. "Distribution of Financial Accumulations of State Enterprises in China." *Finansy SSR,* no. 4: 70–6. JPRS trans. no. 4,721: 1–9.

1961b. "Organization of Revolving Funds in State Enterprises in the Chinese People's Republic." *Dengi i Kredit,* no. 7: 43–52. JPRS trans. no. 10,396: 1–12.

Oksenberg, Michel. 1974. "Political changes and their causes in China." *Political Quarterly,* vol. 45, no. 1: 95–114.

P'an Hsüeh-min. 1959. "Shang-hai kung-yeh ti fa-chan" (The development of industry in Shanghai). *TLCS,* no. 7: 302–5.

Paukert, Felix. 1973. "Income Distribution at Different Levels of Development: A Survey of Evidence." *International Labour Review,* vol. 108, nos. 2–3: 97–125.

Perkins, Dwight. 1966. *Market Control and Planning in Communist China.* Cambridge, Mass.: Harvard University Press.

1967. "Government as an Obstacle to Industrialization: The Case of Nineteenth-Century China." *Journal of Economic History,* vol. 27, no. 4: 478–92.

1968. "Industrial Planning and Management." In *Economic Trends in Communist China,* ed. by Alexander Eckstein, et al., pp. 597–635. Chicago: Aldine.

1975a. "Constraints Influencing China's Agricultural Performance." In *China: A Reassessment of the Economy,* a compendium of papers submitted to the U.S. Congress Joint Economic Committee, pp. 350–65. Washington, D.C.: U.S. Government Printing Office.

1975b. "Growth and Changing Structure of China's Twentieth Century Economy." In *China's Modern Economy in Historical Perspective,* ed. by Dwight Perkins, pp. 115–65. Stanford, Calif.: Stanford University Press.

1976. "The Central Features of China's Economic Development." Unpublished manuscript.

Perkins, Dwight, et al. 1977. *Rural Small-Scale Industry in the People's Republic of China.* Berkeley: University of California Press.

Po I-po. 1957. "Principles for 1958 Economic Plan Outlined by Po I-po." NCNA, Tientsin, 10 August. Trans. in *SCMP* 1602: 1–6.

Rawski, Thomas. 1975a. "China's Industrial System." In *China: A Reassessment of the Economy*, a compendium of papers submitted to the U.S. Congress Joint Economic Committee, pp. 175–98. Washington, D.C.: U.S. Government Printing Office.

1975b. "Measuring China's Industrial Performance, 1949–1973." Unpublished manuscript.

1975c. "Notes on China's Industrialization, 1911–1937." Unpublished manuscript.

Reynolds, Bruce L. 1975. "Central Planning in China: The Significance of Material Allocation Conferences." *Association for Comparative Economic Studies Bulletin*, vol. 17, no. 1: 3–14.

Richman, Barry. 1969. *Industrial Society in Communist China: A Firsthand Study of Chinese Economic Management and Development*. New York: Random House.

Robinson, Joan. 1974. "For Use, Not for Profit: A Report on a Recent Visit to China." *Eastern Horizon*, vol. 11, no. 4: 6–15. Reprinted in *People's China*, ed. by David Milton, Nancy Milton, and Franz Schurmann, pp. 47–58. New York: Vintage Books.

1975. *Economic Management in China*. Modern China series no. 4. London: Anglo-Chinese Educational Institute.

Schran, Peter. 1969. *The Development of Chinese Agriculture, 1950–1959*. Urbana: University of Illinois Press.

1976. "China's Price Stability: Its Meaning and Distributive Consequences." Unpublished manuscript.

Schurmann, Franz. 1966. *Ideology and Organization in Communist China*. Berkeley: University of California Press.

Shabad, Theodore. 1972. *China's Changing Map: National and Regional Development, 1949–1971*. Rev. ed. New York: Praeger.

Shang Tzu-chin. 1959. "Kuan-yü Hu-nan sheng 1958-nien ts'ai-cheng chüeh-suan ho 1959-nien ts'ai-cheng yü-suan ti pao-kao (chai-yao)" [Report on Hunan Province's 1958 financial final account and 1959 financial budget (summary)]. *Hsin Hu-nan pao*, 16 December.

1960. "Kuan-yü Hu-nan sheng i-chiu-wu-chiu nien ts'ai-cheng chüeh-suan ho i-chiu-liu-ling nien ts'ai-cheng yü-suan ti pao-kao (chai-yao)" [Report on Hunan Province's 1959 financial final account and 1960 financial budget (summary)]. *Hsin Hu-nan pao*, 23 December.

Shantung People's Congress. 1956. "Sheng jen-min tai-piao ta-hui ti-szu tz'u hui-i k'ai-mu t'ing-ch'ü Shan-tung sheng 1955-nien chüeh-suan ho 1956-nien yü-suan pao-kao" (The opening of the Fourth Session of the Provincial People's Congress hears the report on Shantung Province's 1955 final account and 1956 budget). *Ta-chung jih-pao*, 16 August.

She I-san. 1958. "T'an-t'an wu-tzu fen-p'ei t'i-chih ti kai-ko" (A discussion of the reform of the commodity distribution system). *CHCC*, no. 10: 34–6.

Shih Neng-hao. 1958. "Kuan-yü Hsia-men shih 1957-nien ts'ai-cheng chüeh-suan ho 1958-nien ts'ai-cheng yü-suan" (Amoy Municipality's 1957 financial final account and 1958 financial budget). *Hsia-men jih-pao*, 1 June.

Sigurdson, Jon. 1973. "Rural Industry and the Internal Transfer of Technology." In *Authority, Participation and Cultural Change in China*, ed. by Stuart R. Schram, pp. 199–232. Cambridge: Cambridge University Press.

SSST Editor. 1955. "Why should we change the goegraphical distribution of our industrial areas?" *SSST*, no. 17. Trans. in *ECMM*, 18: 36–7.

State Council. 1956a. "Ko ti-ch'ü shih-yung kung-tzu piao chun chung-lei ho sheng-huo fei pu-tieh piao" (Salary standard scales and cost of living differentials to be applied in each district). *CYTCFKHP*, 1956, pp. 239–46.

1956b. "Kuan-yü pan-fa kuo-chia chi-kuan kung-tso jen-yuan kung-tzu fang-an ti t'ung-chih" (Notice on the promulgation of a wage plan for workers and staff in state organs). *CYTCFKHP*, 1956, pp. 226–38.

1956c. "Kuan-yü pien-tsao i-chiu-wu-ch'i nien kuo-chia yü-suan ts'ao-an ti chih-piao" (Directive on compiling the 1957 draft state budget). *TCTLHP* 2: 206–11.

1956d. "Kuo-wu-yuan p'i-chuan ts'ai-cheng-pu kuan-yü 1956-nien nung-yeh shui-shou kung-tso chung chi-ko wen-t'i ti ch'ing-shih" (The State Council responds to the petition of the Ministry of Finance concerning several problems in 1956 agricultural tax work). *CYTCFKHP*, 1956, pp. 313–14.

1957a. "Kuan-yü kai-chin kung-yeh kuan-li t'i-chih ti kuei-ting" (Regulations on the reform of the industrial management system). *HHPYK*, no. 24, (1957): 57–9.

1957b. "Kuan-yü kai-chin shang-yeh kuan-li t'i-chih ti kuei-ting" (Regulations on the reform of the commercial management system). *HHPYK*, no. 24, (1957): 59–60.

1957c. "Kuan-yü kai-chin ts'ai-cheng kuan-li t'i-chih ti kuei-ting" (Regulations on the reform of the financial management system). *HHPYK*, no. 24, (1957): 60.

1957d. "Kuan-yü pien-tsao 1958-nien kuo-chia yü-suan ts'ao-an ti chih-piao" (Directive on the compilation of the 1958 draft state budget). *CYTCFKHP*, 1957, 2: 11–14.

1957e. "Kuan-yü t'iao-cheng hui-li chiao-ta ti ching-chi tso-wu ti nung-yeh shui fu-chia pi-li ti kuei-ting" (Regulations on adjustment of the agriculture tax surcharge rate for commercial crops for which profits are comparatively large). *HHPYK*, no. 2: (1958): 112.

1958a. "Chung hua jen-min kung-ho-kuo nung-yeh shui t'iao-li" (Agriculture tax regulations of the People's Republic of China). *HHPYK*, no. 12 (1958): 82–3.

1958b. "Ko sheng, tzu-chih-ch'ü, chih-hsia shih nung-yeh shui p'ing-chün shui-lü ti kuei-ting" (Regulations on the agricultural tax average rates for each province, autonomous region, and directly administered municipality). In Li Ch'eng-jui, *Chung-hua jen-min kung-ho-kuo nung-yeh shui shih-kao* (A draft history of the agricultural tax of the People's Republic of China), p. 325. Peking: Finance Publishing House.

1958c. "Kuan-yü kai-chin chi-hua kuan-li t'i-chih ti kuei-ting" (Regulations concerning the reform of the plan management system). *FKHP* 8: 96–9.

1958d. "Kuan-yü kai-chin liang-shih kuan-li t'i-chih ti chi-hsiang kuei-ting" (Several regulations concerning the reform of the grain management system). *FKHP* 7: 281–3.

1958e. "Kuan-yü kai-chin shui-shou kuan-li t'i-chih ti kuei-ting" (Notice on the reform of the tax management system). *FKHP* 7: 265–9.

1958f. "Kuan-yü kai-chin wu-tzu fen-p'ei chih-tu ti chi-hsiang kuei-ting" (Several regulations concerning the reform of the commodity distribution system). *FKHP* 8: 100–1.

1958g. "Kuan-yü kung-yeh ch'i-yeh hsia-fang ti chi-hsiang chüeh-ting" (Several decisions concerning the transfer of industrial enterprises to local control). *FKHP* 7: 331–2.

1958h. "Kuan-yü wu-chia kuan-li ch'üan-hsien ho yu kuan shang-yeh kuan-li t'i-chih ti chi-hsiang kuei-ting" (Several regulations concerning the authority over price control and the commercial management system). *FKHP* 7: 315–18.

1958i. "Kuan-yü ti-fang ts'ai-cheng ti shou-chih fan-wei, shou-ju hsiang-mu ho fen-ch'eng pi-li kai-wei chi-pen-shang ku-ting wu-nien pu-pien ti t'ung-chih" (Directive concerning that the scope of local financial revenue and expenditure, revenue items, and the sharing rates to be changed to be basically fixed for five years). *FKHP* 7: 234.

1958j. "Kuan-yü ts'ung 1959-nien ch'i t'ing-chih cheng-shou ts'un-k'uan li-hsi so-te shui ti p'i-fu" (The State Council gives an official reply concerning the ending of the collection of the interest income tax beginning in 1959). *CYTCFKHP*, 1959, 1: 115.

1958k. "Kung-shang t'ung-i shui t'iao-li" (Unified industrial and commercial tax regulations). *CYTCFKHP* 2: 173–5.

1958l. "Min-tsu tzu-chih ti-fang ts'ai-cheng kuan-li chan-hsing pan-fa" (Temporary methods of financial management in national autonomous regions). *FKHP* 7: 269–73.

State Council, Bureau of Legal Affairs. 1955–61. *Chung-hua jen-min kung-ho kuo fa-kuei hui-pien* (Compendium of laws and regulations of the People's Republic of China) (FKHP). 12 vols. Peking: Legal Publishing House.

State Council, General Office Theoretical Group. 1977. "In Commemoration of the First Anniversary of the Passing of Our Esteemed and Beloved Premier Chou En-Lai." *Peking Review*, no. 3: 8–21.

State Planning Commission. 1958. "Certain problems in the preliminary studies of the Second Five-Year Plan." *CHCC*, no. 4: 10–12. Trans. in Chao, *EPO* 1: 29–35.

State Statistical Bureau. 1956. *Report on National Economic Development and the Fulfillment of the State Plan in 1954*. Peking: Foreign Languages Press.

1960. *Ten Great Years: Statistics of the Economic and Cultural Achievements of the People's Republic of China*. Peking: Foreign Languages Press.

Sun Chün-i. 1957. "Ch'ing-hai sheng 1956-nien chüeh-suan ho 1957-nien yü-suan ti pao-kao" (Report on Tsinghai Province's 1956 final account and 1957 budget). *Ch'ing-hai jih-pao*, 14 August.

1958. "Kuan-yü Ch'ing-hai 1957-nien chüeh-suan ho 1958–nien yü-suan ti pao-kao" (Report on Tsinghai's 1957 final account and 1958 budget). *Ch'ing-hai jih-pao*, 6 July.

Sun Kang. 1959. "Kuan-yü 1958-nien ts'ai-cheng chüeh-suan ho 1959-nien ts'ai-cheng yü-suan ts'ao-an ti pao-kao" (Report on the 1958 financial final account and the 1958 draft financial budget). *Ch'ing-tao jih-pao*, 31 July.

Sun Yeh-fang. 1957. "Tsung 'tsung-ch'an-chih' t'an-ch'i" (A discussion starting with "gross value of output"). *TCKT*, no. 19: 8–14.

Sung Chi-wen. 1955. "Shang-hai shih jen-min wei-yüan hui kuan-yü pen-shih i-chiu-wu-szu nien chüeh-suan ho i-chiu wu-wu nien yü-suan ts'ao-an ti pao-kao" (Report of the Shanghai Municipal People's Council concerning this municipality's 1954 final accounts and 1955 draft budget). *Chieh-fang jih-pao*, 26 December.

Sung Ching-i. 1958. "Kuan-yü T'ien-chin shih 1957-nien ts'ai-cheng yü-suan chih-hsing ch'ing-k'uang ho 1958-nien ts'ai-cheng yü-suan ti pao-kao" (Report on the conditions of implementation of Tientsin Municipality's 1957 financial budget and on the 1958 financial budget). *T'ien-chin jih-pao*, 21 March.

——— 1959. "Kuan-yü T'ien-chin shih i-chiu-wu-pa nien ts'ai-cheng chüeh-suan ho i-chiu-wu-chiu nien ts'ai-cheng yü-suan ts'ao-an ti pao-kao (chai-yao)" [Report on Tientsin Municipality's 1958 financial final account and 1959 draft financial budget (summary)]. *T'ien-chin jih-pao*, 10 July.

——— 1960. "Kuan-yü T'ien-chin shih 1959-nien ts'ai-cheng chüeh-suan ho 1960-nien ts'ai-cheng yü-suan ts'ao-an ti pao-kao" (Report on Tientsin Municipality's 1959 financial final account and 1960 draft financial budget). *T'ien-chin jih-pao*, 27 May.

T'ao Chu. 1955. "Report on Kuangtung Province's First Five-Year Plan." *NFJP*, 24 September. Trans. in *SCMP* supplement 1237: 1–34.

T'ao Sheng-yü. 1956. "Kuan-yü kuo-ying ch'i-yeh t'i-ch'ü ch'i-yeh chiang-li chi-chin wen-t'i ti yen-chiu" (Research concerning problems of state-managed enterprises retaining enterprise bonus funds). *TC*, no. 3: 9–12.

T'ao Sheng-yü and Tan Ya-sheng. 1959. "Tui ch'i-yeh li-jun liu-ch'eng chih-tu ti hsiu-kai i-chien" (Revised opinions about the system of enterprises retaining profits). *TC*, no. 15: 13–14.

TCKT Data Section. 1957a. "Chieh-fang hou ch'uan-kuo kung-nung-yeh shang-p'in chia-ko chien-tao-ch'a pien-hua ch'ing-k'uang" (The changing situation of the scissors price differential between industrial and agricultural products in the nation since liberation). *TCKT*, no. 17: 4–7.

——— 1957b. "Description of the state distribution of commodities during the past year." *TCKT*, no. 13: 29–31. Trans. in *ECMM* 97: 21–7.

TCKTTH Data Section. 1956. "Several Problems in the Socialist Industrialization of Our Country." *TCKTTH*, no. 21: 3–7. Trans. in ECMM 69: 29–35.

Teiwes, Frederick C. 1971. "Provincial Politics in China: Themes and Variations." In *China: Management of a Revolutionary Society*, by John M. Lindbeck, pp. 116–89. Seattle: University of Washington Press.

T'ien Lei. 1960. "Kuan-yü An-hui sheng i-chiu wu-chiu nien ts'ai-cheng chüeh-suan ho i-chiu-liu-ling nien ts'ai-cheng yü-suan ts'ao-an ti pao-kao" (Report on Anhui Province's 1959 financial final account and 1960 draft financial budget). *An-hui jih-pao*, 13 May.

T'ien Yao-ch'i. 1957. "Kuan-yü Lo-yang shih 1956-nien ts'ai-cheng chüeh-suan ho 1957-nien ts'ai-cheng yü-suan (ts'ao-an) ti pao-kao" (Report on Loyang Municipality's 1956 financial final account and 1957 draft financial budget). *Lo-yang jih-pao*, 24 September.

Ts'ao Ti-ch'iu. 1956. "Kuan-yü pen shih 1955-nien chüeh-suan ho 1956-nien yü-suan ti pao-kao" (Report on this municipality's 1955 final account and 1956 budget). *Hsin-wen jih-pao*, 9 August.

——— 1957. "Kuan-yü Shang-hai shih 1956-nien chüeh-suan ho 1957-nien yü-suan ti pao-kao" (Report on Shanghai Municipality's 1956 final account and 1957 budget). *Wen-hui pao* (Shanghai), 28 August.

Tuan Ta-ming. 1959. "Szu-ch'uan sheng Ch'ung-ch'ing shih jen-min wei-yüan hui kuan-yü pen shih 1958-nien ts'ai-cheng chüeh-suan ho 1959-nien ts'ai-cheng shou-chih ch'u-pu an-p'ai i-chien ti pao-kao" (Report of Szechuan Province Chungking Municipal People's Council concerning this municipality's 1958 financial final account and opinions on the preliminary arrangements for the 1959 financial income and expenditures). *Ch'ung-ch'ing jih-pao*, 12 April.

1960. "Szu-ch'uan sheng Ch'ung-ch'ing shih i-chiu-wu-chiu nien ts'ai-cheng chüeh-suan ho i-chiu-liu-ling nien ts'ai-cheng yü-suan ts'ao-an ti pao-kao" (Report on Szechuan Province Chungking Municipality's 1959 financial final account and 1960 draft financial budget). *Ch'ung-ch'ing jih-pao*, 2 August.

Tung Ching-chai. 1957. "Kuan-yü Kuang-hsi sheng 1956-nien ts'ai-cheng chüeh-suan ho 1957-nien ts'ai-cheng yü-suan ts'ao-an ti pao-kao" (Report on Kwangsi Province's 1956 financial final account and 1957 draft financial budget). *Kuang-hsi jih-pao*, 25 August.

Turnam, David. 1971. *The Employment Problem in Less Developed Countries: A Review of Evidence*. Development Center Series. Paris: Organization for Economic Cooperation and Development.

Ullman, Morris B. 1961. *Cities of Mainland China: 1953 and 1958*. International Population Reports, series P-95, no. 59. Washington, D.C.: U.S. Department of Commerce.

Union Research Institute. 1957. *Communist China in 1956*. Hong Kong: Union Research Institute.

U.S. Central Intelligence Agency. 1959. *China: A Provisional Atlas of Communist Administrative Units*. Washington, D.C.: Central Intelligence Agency.

Vogel, Ezra. 1969. *Canton Under Communism: Programs and Policies in a Provincial Capital, 1949–1968*. Cambridge, Mass.: Harvard University Press.

n.d. "Notes on the Finance Ministry." Unpublished manuscript.

Wan Li. 1960. "Kuan-yü Pei-ching shih 1960-nien kuo-min ching-chi chi-hua, 1959-nien ts'ai-cheng shou-chih chüeh-suan ho 1960-nien ts'ai-cheng shou-chih yü-suan ts'ao-an ti pao-kao (chai-yao)" [Report on Peking Municipality's 1960 national economic plan, 1959 final revenue and expenditure account, and 1960 draft financial revenue and expenditure accounts (summary)]. *Pei-ching jih-pao*, 1 July.

Wang Ching-Chih. 1956. *Wo-kuo kuo-chia yü-suan* (China's state budget). Peking: Popular Reading Publishing House.

Wang Hu-sheng. 1962. "Ti-ch'ü ching-chi tsung-ho p'ing-heng ti jo-ch'ien wen-t'i" (Several problems in local economic comprehensive balancing). *CCYC*, no. 1: 22–36.

Wang Huan-ju. 1956. "Chi-lin sheng jen-min wei-yüan-hui kuan-yü 1955-nien ts'ai-cheng chüeh-suan ho 1956-nien ts'ai-cheng yü-suan ti pao-kao" (Report of the Kirin Provincial People's Council concerning the 1955 financial final account and the 1956 financial budget). *Chi-lin jih-pao*, 7 December.

1957. "Kuan-yü Chi-lin sheng 1956-nien ts'ai-cheng chüeh-suan ho 1957-nien ts'ai-cheng yü-suan ts'ao-an ti pao-kao" (Report on Kirin Province's 1956 financial final account and 1957 draft financial budget). *Chi-lin jih-pao*, 29 July.

1958. "Kuan-yü Chi-lin sheng 1957-nien ts'ai-cheng chüeh-suan ho 1958-nien ts'ai-cheng yü-suan ts'ao-an ti pao-kao" (Report on Kirin Province's 1957 financial final account and 1958 draft financial budget). *Chi-lin jih-pao*, 20 July.

1959. "Chi-lin sheng i-chiu-wu-pa nien ts'ai-cheng chüeh-suan ho i-chiu wu-chiu nien ts'ai-cheng yü-suan ts'ao-an ti pao-kao" (Report on Kirin

Province's 1958 financial final account and 1959 draft financial budget). *Chi-lin jih-pao*, 11 June.

1960. "Kuan-yü Chi-lin sheng i-chiu-wu-chiu nien ts'ai-cheng chüeh-suan ho i-chiu liu-ling nien ts'ai-cheng yü-suan ts'ao-an ti pao-kao" (Report on Kirin Province's 1959 financial final account and 1960 draft financial budget). *Chi-lin jih-pao*, 27 May.

Wang I-hsin. 1958. "Kuan-yü Liao-ning sheng An-shan shih 1957-nien ts'ai-cheng chüeh-suan ho 1958-nien ts'ai-cheng yü-suan ts'ao-an ti pao-kao (chai-yao)" [Report on Liaoning Province Anshan Municipality 1957 financial final account and 1958 draft financial budget (summary)]. *An-shan jih-pao*, 29 June.

Wang I-lun. 1957. "Kuan-yü Nei-meng-ku tzu-chih ch'ü 1956-nien chüeh-suan ho 1957-nien yü-suan ti pao-kao" (Report on the Inner Mongolia Autonomous Region's 1956 final account and 1957 budget). *Nei-meng-ku jih-pao*, 27 April.

Wang Kuei-wu. 1958. "Nien-tu chi-hua pien-chih fang-fa ti chung-ta kai-ko" (A major reform in the method of compiling annual economic plans). *CHCC*, no. 9: 13–15.

Wang Kuo-jui. 1959. "Sheng ts'ai-cheng t'ing t'ing-chang Wang Kuo-jui tai-piao sheng jen-min wei-yüan hui hsing-sheng erh-chieh jen ta erh-ts'u hui-i tso Kan-su sheng 1959-nien ts'ai-cheng yü-suan chih-hsing ch'ing-k'uang ho 1960-nien ts'ai-cheng yü-suan ts'ao-an ti pao-kao" (Director of the Provincial Finance Department, *Wang Kuo-jui*, representing the Provincial People's Council gives a report on the conditions of implementation of the 1959 budget and the 1960 financial draft budget at the Second Session of the Second Provincial People's Congress). *Kan-su jih-pao*, 21 December.

Wang Tsai-tien. 1958. "Nei-meng-ku tzu-chih ch'ü 1957-nien chüeh-suan ho 1958-nien yü-suan ti pao-kao" (Report on the Inner Mongolia Autonomous Region's 1957 final account and 1958 budget). *Nei-meng-ku jih-pao*, 28 June.

Wang Tzu-ying. 1957. "1956-nien kuo-chia yü-suan pien-tsao ho chih-hsing chung yu hsieh shen-ma ching-yen chiao-hsün" (Some experience and lessons from compiling and implementing the state's 1956 budget). *TC*, no. 1: 3–7.

Wang Wen-ching. 1953. *T'an-t'an wo-men ti kuo-chia yü-suan* (On Our National Budgeting). Peking: China Youth Press.

Wang Yung-k'uei. 1960. "Report on the Tibet Autonomous Region's 1959 final account and 1960 draft budget." *Hsi-ts'ang jih-pao*, 3 May. Trans. in JPRS trans. no. 5,689: 1–13.

Wei Chin-fei. 1954. "Kuang-chou shih jen-min cheng-fu kuan-yü i-chiu-wu-san nien-tu yü-suan chih-hsing ch'ing-k'uang ho i-chiu-wu-szu nien yü-suan ts'ao-an ti pao-kao" (Canton Municipality government report on conditions of implementation of the 1953 budget and the 1954 draft budget). *Kuang-chou jih-pao*, 7 August.

1959. "Kuan-yü i-chiu-wu-pa nien Kuang-tung sheng chüeh-suan ho i-chiu-wu-chiu nien Kuang-tung sheng yü-suan ti pao-kao" (Report on Kwangtung Province's 1958 final account and Kwangtung Province's 1959 budget). *Nan-fang jih-pao*, 13 October.

Wei Li. 1959. "Fu-chai kung-tzu ying-kai ta kai-ko" (The supplementary wage system should be greatly reformed). *CHCC*, 5: 12–13.

Wei Min. 1975. "China's Tax Policy." *Peking Review*, no. 37: 23–5.

236   *References*

Weisskoff, Richard. 1970. "Income Distribution and Economic Growth in Puerto Rico, Argentina, and Mexico." *Review of Income and Wealth,* series 16, no. 4: 303–32.

Wen Cheng-i. 1958a. "Min-tsu cheng-ts'e tsai ts'ai-cheng t'i-chih shang ti chin i pu kuan-ch'e" (Further advancing nationalities policy in the financial system). *TC,* no. 7: 18–19.

1958b. "Wo kuo min-tsu tzu-chih ti-fang ts'ai-cheng chung kuan-li t'i-chih ti chung-ta kai-ko" (An important reform in our national minorities financial management system). *Min-tsu t'uan-chieh,* no. 7: 9.

Wilczynski, J. 1972. *The Economics of Socialism.* Chicago: Aldine.

Wiles, P. J. D. 1964. *The Political Economy of Communism.* Cambridge, Mass.: Harvard University Press.

Williamson, Jeffery G. 1965. "Regional Inequality and the Process of National Development: A Description of the Patterns." *Economic Development and Cultural Change,* vol. 13, no. 4, part 2.

World Bank. 1974. *Land Reform.* Rural Development Series. Washington, D.C.: World Bank.

Wu Chun-yang. 1955. "The problem of geographical distribution of our country's industrial construction projects." *HH,* no. 2. Trans. in *ECMM,* 13: 29–36.

Wu Kuang-t'ang. 1956. "Shan-hsi sheng 1955-nien ts'ai-cheng chüeh-suan ho 1956-nien ts'ai-cheng yü-suan ti pao-kao (chai-yao)" [Shansi Province 1955 final financial account and 1956 financial budget (summary)]. *Shan-hsi jih-pao,* 9 December.

1957. "Kuan-yü Shan-hsi sheng 1956-nien ts'ai-cheng chüeh-suan ho 1957-nien ts'ai-cheng yü-suan ti pao-kao" (Report on Shansi Province's 1956 financial final accounts and 1957 financial budget). *Shan-hsi jih-pao,* 27 August.

1958. "Shan-hsi sheng 1957 nien ts'ai-cheng chüeh-suan ho 1958 nien ts'ai-cheng yü-suan ti an-p'ai chi yü-suan chih-hsing ch'ing-k'uang ti pao-kao" (Report on Shansi Province's 1957 financial final accounts and the arrangements for and the situation with regard to the implementation of the 1958 financial budget). *Shan-hsi jih-pao,* 8 December.

1960. "Kuan-yü Shan-hsi sheng i-chiu-wu-chiu nien ts'ai-cheng chüeh-suan ho i-chiu liu-ling nien ts'ai-cheng yü-suan ts'ao-an ti pao-kao (chai-yao)" [Report on Shansi Province's 1959 financial final accounts and the 1960 draft financial budget (summary)]. *Shan-hsi jih-pao,* 25 May.

Wu Neng-kuang. 1958. "Hu-pei sheng Wu-han shih jen-min wei-yüan-hui kuan-yü 1957-nien shih ts'ai-cheng chüeh-suan ho 1958 nien shih ts'ai-cheng yü-suan ts'ao-an ti pao-kao (chai-yao)" [Hupei Province Wu-han Municipal People's Council report on the municipality's financial final account and the municipality's 1958 draft financial budget (summary)]. *Ch'ang-chiang jih-pao,* 1 March.

Wu Po. 1958a. "Explanation of the draft agricultural tax regulations of the People's Republic of China." *JMJP,* 5 June. Trans. in *SCMP* 1792: 6–14.

1958b. "Explanation of the draft regulations of the People's Republic of China governing the consolidated industrial and commerical tax." *JMSW,* no. 18: 11–13. Trans. in *CB* 527: 19–24.

Wu Tso-min. 1957. "Yün-nan sheng 1956-nien ti-fang chüeh-suan yü 1957-nien ti-fang yü-suan ti pao-kao" (Report on Yünnan Province's 1956 local final account and 1957 local budget). *Yün-nan jih-pao,* 17 August.

1960. "Yün-nan sheng 1959-nien ts'ai-cheng chüeh-suan ho 1960-nien ts'ai-cheng yü-suan ts'ao-an ti pao-kao" (Report on Yünnan Province's 1959 financial final account and 1960 draft financial budget). *Yün-nan jih-pao*, 9 June.

Wuhan Municipal People's Congress. 1956. "Kuan-yü Wu-han shih 1955-nien ts'ai-cheng chüeh-suan ho 1956-nien ts'ai-cheng yü-suan ti pao-kao (chai-yao)" [Report on Wuhan Municipality's 1955 financial final account and 1956 financial budget (summary)]. *Ch'ang-chiang jih-pao*, 7 September.

Yang Hsiao-ch'u. 1956. "Shan-hsi sheng Hsi-an shih jen-min wei-yüan hui kuan-yü Shan-hsi sheng Hsi-an shih 1955-nien ts'ai-cheng shou-chih chüeh-suan ho 1956-nien ts'ai-cheng shou-chih yü-suan ti pao-kao" (Report of Shensi Province Hsian Municipal People's Council on Shensi Province Hsian Municipality's 1955 financial income and expenditure final account and 1956 financial income and expenditure budget). *Hsi-an jih-pao*, 27 December.

——— 1958. "Shen-hsi sheng Hsi-an shih jen-min wei-yüan hui kuan-yü Hsi-an 1957-nien ts'ai-cheng shou-chih chüeh-suan ho 1958-nien ts'ai-cheng shou-chih yü-suan ts'ao-an ti pao-kao" (Report of the Shensi Province Hsian Municipal People's Council on Hsian's 1957 financial revenue and expenditure final account and 1958 financial revenue and expenditure draft budget). *Hsi-an jih-pao*, 5 June.

Yang I-ch'en. 1957. "Hei-lung-chiang sheng jen-min wei-yüan hui kung-tso pao-kao" (Work report of the Heilungkiang Provincial People's Council). *Hei-lung-chiang jih-pao*, 25 September.

Yang Ju-p'eng. 1958. "Ch'ang-sha shih 1957-nien ts'ai-cheng chüeh-suan ho 1958-nien ts'ai-cheng yü-suan an-p'ai ti i-chien" (Report on Ch'angsha Municipality's 1957 financial final account and opinions on arrangements of the 1958 financial budget). *Ch'ang-sha jih-pao*, 7 February.

Yeh Kung-chia. 1968. "Capital Formation." In *Economic Trends in Communist China*, ed. by Alexander Eckstein, Walter Galenson, and Ta-chung Liu, pp. 509–47. Chicago: Aldine.

Yü Ch'iu-li. 1977. "Report on the National Conference on Learning from Taching in Industry on May 4, 1977." *Peking Review*, vol. 20, no. 22: 5–23.

Yü Mei-ch'ing. 1956. "Kuan-yü Kuang-chou shih 1955-nien chüeh-suan ho 1956-nien yü-suan chi-ch'i chih-hsing ch'ing-k'uang ti pao-kao" (Report on Canton Municipality's 1955 final accounts and 1956 budget and the conditions of its implementation). *Kuang-chou jih-pao*, 23 November.

Yü Wei-hsin. 1957. "Ti-fang yü-suan ho kuo-min ching-chi chi-hua ti kuan-hsi wen-t'i" (Problems in the relationship between local budgets and the national economic plan). *TC*, no. 3: 14.

Yüan Jen-yüan. 1959. "Kuan-yü wo sheng i-chiu-wu-pa nien kung-tso ch'ing-k'uang ho i-chiu-wu-chiu nien kung-tso an-p'ai i chien ti pao-kao" (Report on our province's 1958 work situation and opinions on arranging work for 1959). *Ch'ing-hai jih-pao*, 21 May.

Yüan Tzu-yang. 1957. "Kuan-yü Shan-tung sheng 1956-nien chüeh-suan ho 1957-nien yü-suan ts'ao-an ti pao-kao" (Report on Shantung Province's 1956 final accounts and 1957 draft budget). *Ta-chung jih-pao*, 17 August.

Yün Chung. 1956. *Wo-kuo ti chi-pen chien-she* (Basic construction in China). Peking: Workers' Publishing House.

Index

Adelman, Irma, 2
Administrative decentralization, *see* Decentralized command
Afghanistan, role of budget in, compared to China, 40
Agricultural cooperativization, and income distribution, 180
Agricultural tax: burden as a share of output, 167, 176, 187; controlled by central government, 57; in India, 182; 1958 reform of, 125–7; progressive rates of, 127, 181; in Shanghai, 68; sharing of, 62, 67, 97; as a source of budgetary revenues, 61; surtax, 51, 53, 65, 92, 98, 117, 118
Agriculture: central planning of, 6; in Chinese development strategy, 17, 31–2, 168; growth of, 10–11, 24; procurement policy, 181, 184; *see also* Commune
All-China Federation of Trade Unions, *see* Trade unions
Anhui Province: expenditures subsidized by central government, 130; industrial development in, 156; price and wage levels in, 113, 116; social expenditures in, 111, 116; urbanization in, 116
Animal tax, 57
Anshan iron and steel works, dual subordination of, 146
Autarky hypothesis, 36–7, 92–3, 99–103, 105, 108, 132, 135–6, 139, 155, 157; *see also* Ministerial autarky; Territorial subordinate autarky
Autonomous regions, central government policy toward, 98, 163

Balanced budget principle, 55–6
Banking system: and central planning, 14–15, 45, 47–8, 52, 58, 63, 125; and geographic resource transfers, 44–5, 102
Boat and vehicle license fees, 57, 65
Brazil, pattern of regional growth in, compared to China, 159
Budget: accounts, 58, 70–1, 82–6, 95–6; circulating funds, 59; credit funds, 63;

expenditures by level of government, 37–8, 71–5; reserves, 59; revenue collection by level of government, 38, 99, 161–2; share of gross domestic product allocated through, 40–2, 164, 168, 193; surpluses, 62–3, 64, 67, 68, 92, 169; unitary nature of, 41–2, 49, 50; *see also* Extrabudgetary funds; Fiscal system; Revenue sharing; Taxation, unified system of
Budgetary and planning process, stability of, 124–5, 169–72, 184–5
Burma, role of budget in, compared to China, 40

Canada, pattern of regional growth in, compared to China, 159
Canton, Kwangtung, 79, 120
Capital investment, *see* Investment
Centralization–decentralization, 3–4, 5, 6, 8–9, 19–36, 49; *see also* Decentralization; Decentralized command; Market decentralization
Central planning, *see* Planning
Changchou, Honan, 78, 119
Ch'angchou, Kiangsu, 160
Ch'angch'un, Kirin, 119
Chekiang Province: central government investment in, 154; industrial development in, 78, 154, 185; price and wage levels in, 113, 116; regionalism in, during Cultural Revolution, 151; remission of revenue to central government, 78, 132; social expenditures in, 116
Ch'eng Hung-i, 145
Ch'engtu, Szechuan, 119
Chiang Hua, 151
Ch'ich'ihaerh, Heilungkiang, 119
Chi-hua ching-chi (Economic Planning), 20, 120
China, as a model of development, 186–93
Ch'in dynasty, 188
Chinese Communist Party, 71, 151, 187; Eighth Congress of, 30, 32, 143
Chinese history and culture, effect on development policy, 188–90

Foreign economic assistance, role in Chinese development, 192
Foreign loans, as a revenue source, 61
Fourth Five-Year Plan, 151
France, pattern of regional growth in, compared to China, 159
Fukien Province: expenditures subsidized by central government, 130, 132; industrial development in, 154; price and wage levels in, 113; share of national investment in, 108, 122

Government administrative expenditures, 19, 71, 73, 75, 108
Great Leap Forward: economic planning during, 124; effect on income distribution, 181; effect on industrial growth, 170
Gross domestic product per capita: in China, compared to Soviet Union and Eastern Europe, 27; growth of since 1952, 192; pre-1949 growth of, 159

Harbin, Heilungkiang, 119
Hayek, Friedrich August von, 7, 9
Heilungkiang Province: agricultural development in, 11; agricultural tax in, 127; industrial development in, 78; price and wage levels in, 113; remission of revenue to central government, 78, 129, 132; share of national investment in, 108, 122
Hicks, Sir John, 158, 159
Hirschman, Albert, 158, 159
Honan Province: central government investment in, 78; industrial development in, 156; price and wage levels in, 113, 114; remission of revenue to central government, 78; social expenditures in, 111, 114; urbanization in, 111, 114
Hopei Province: price and wage levels in, 113; share of national investment in, 123, 157; social expenditures in, 111; urbanization in, 111
Horizontal coordination, see Planning: horizontal-territorial versus vertical-sectoral principles of
House tax, 57
Housing, government subsidy of, 180
Hsian, Shensi, 78, 79, 119
Hsiang, see Township
Hsiangt'an, Hunan, 160
Hsien, see County
Hsinhsiang, Honan, 160
Hunan Province: industrial development in, 13, 156; price and wage levels in, 113; social expenditures in, 111; urbanization in, 111
Hunchiang, Kirin, 160
Hungary, economic reform in, compared to China, 27
Hung-ch'i (Red Flag), 151

Hupeh Province: industrial development in, 156; price and wage levels in, 113
Hurwicz, Leonid, 8, 35

Imperial Finance Commission, 189
Import substitution, influence on agriculture's terms of trade, 176
Income distribution, 183–4; and economic growth, 1–3, 39, 173–4, 192–3; and price structure, 2, 179–80; and tax structure, 2; and wage structure, 4, 174–6, 179; see also Equity; Inequality; Land reform
India: agricultural terms of trade in, 176; income distribution in, 1, 183, 186; role of government budget in, 42; tax system in, 182, 190
Industrial and commercial tax: controlled by central government, 57; in Shanghai, 68; sharing of, 61–2, 67, 91, 97; surtax, 65, 92, 98
Industrial capacity utilization, effect on regional investment, 120–1
Industrial growth: provincial pattern of, 37, 100, 138, 152–7, 159–60, 183; see also Inequality: regional
Industrial output: central government versus local share of, 17, 139, 143; central government versus local share of, compared with Soviet Union, 149–50
Inequality: regional, 4, 10–13, 137, 174, 181; sectoral, 4, 11, 13, 174, 178; see also Equity, as a policy goal in China; Income distribution; Industrial growth, provincial pattern of
Inflation, 14, 53, 58, 108, 178
Information, see Decentralization and information; Planning and information
Inner Mongolia Autonomous Region: agricultural development in, 11; expenditures subsidized by central government, 130, 132, 163; industrial development in, 153; social expenditures in, 111; urbanization in, 111
Interest income tax, 57, 127
Inverted U-shaped pattern of development, 157–60
Investment: capital intensity, 24–5, 31–2; central and local, 17, 72–3, 94; coastal and inland, 88, 118–23, 154–5, 160, 187–8; high cost of inland, 120, 122, 157, 185; provincial distribution of, 101–3, 108–9, 119, 185; rate of, in China, 10, 23, 87–8, 122; and regional policy in Yugoslavia, 3, 190–2; sectoral allocation of, 10, 17, 42, 87, 93, 157, 177
Italy, pattern of regional growth in, compared to China, 159

Japan, pattern of regional growth in, compared to China, 159

Jung Tzu-ho, 19, 25, 125

Kansu: agricultural terms of trade in, 182; commune industry in, 168; expenditures subsidized by central government, 78, 103, 130; industrial development in, 78, 155
Key-point cities, 119
Kiangsi Province: Chinese Communist Party in, 187; expenditures subsidized by central government, 130; local expenditures in, 75; price and wage levels in, 113
Kiangsu: central government investment in, 154; industrial development in, 78, 153, 154, 156; price and wage levels in, 113; remission of revenue to central government, 132, 163; share of national investment in, 122
Kirin Province: agricultural terms of trade in, 182; industrial development in, 154, 156; price and wage levels in, 113; share of national investment in, 122; social expenditures in, 111; urbanization in, 111
Kwangsi Chuang Autonomous Region: expenditures subsidized by central government, 130, 163; industrial development in, 156; price and wage levels in, 113
Kwangtung Province: central government investment in, 154; commune industry in, 168; industrial development in, 78, 154, 156; local expenditures in, 75; remission of revenues to central government, 78, 132; revenue sharing with municipalities in, 89; share of national investment in, 122
Kweichow Province: expenditures subsidized by central government, 130; industrial development in, 11, 156, 185; price and wage levels in, 113, 114; share of national investment in, 108, 123; social expenditures in, 111, 114; urbanization in, 111
Kweilin, Kwangsi, 160
Kweiyang, Kweichow, 161

Labor: geographic redistribution of, 140, 154, 164; insurance funds, 51, 53, 93, 166; planning, 17, 22–3, 139–40; sectoral pattern of employment, 13
Labor productivity: growth of, 87, 174, 179; interprovincial variation in, 13–14; in the Soviet Union, 26–7
Lanchou, Kansu, 119, 161
Land reform, 2, 180–1, 187
Lange, Oscar, 7, 8, 9, 34–5
Large administrative region (ta-hsing cheng-ch'ü), as a level of financial administration, 59, 60, 64, 66

Liaoning Province: devolution of central government enterprises in, 144; industrial development in, 156; price and wage levels in, 113; remission of revenues to central government, 129; share of national investment in, 108, 122, 123; sharing of profits of central government enterprises in, 97; social expenditures in, 111; urbanization in, 111
Li Ch'eng-jui, 150
Li Hsien-nien, 86, 125
Lin Piao, 185
Liu Shao-ch'i, 30
Loyang, Honan, 78, 119
Luxury goods taxes, 57

Manchuria, see Northeast China
Mao Tse-tung: commitment to equity, 10, 184; views on coastal development, 120; views on decentralization, 21–2, 25–6, 28–9, 32, 89, 172
Market decentralization, 25–6, 27, 28
Marschak, Thomas, 8
Material-allocation conferences, 147–8
Material supply planning, 15, 17, 19, 21, 23, 33–4, 141, 146
Materials Allocation Bureau, 23
Military power, as an object of development policy, 10; see also Defense
Ming Dynasty, 189
Ministerial autarky, 149
Ministerial system: role of in China, 17, 20, 30, 33, 73, 146; role in China, compared to Soviet Union, 35, 143, 148–50
Ministry of Agriculture, 18
Ministry of Commerce, 125
Ministry of Finance: and budget administration, 43, 87, 88, 89, 124, 166; publications of, 47; Research Institute of Public Finance, 47; stability of, 125
Ministry of Food, 125
Ministry of Foreign Trade, 125
Ministry of Higher Education, 18
Ministry of Labor, 140; see also Labor: planning
Mises, Ludwig von, 3, 9
Mi-yün reservoir, 145
Morris, Cynthia, 2
Municipal public utilities surtax, 92, 98
Municipality, as a level of financial administration, 50, 60
Myrdal, Gunnar, 158, 159

National People's Congress, 89; Third Session of First, 29
New China News Agency, 28, 73
Ninghsia Hui Autonomous Region: expenditures subsidized by central government, 163; industrial development in, 155